Moved by the Dead

NOVENA " AS ALMAS AFLITAS "

Esta novena é rezada somente as " segundas-feiras "
Toda vez que a Igreja, "levar 09 (nove) cópias desta Novena, uma vela ", oferecendo as AMAS AFLITAS.

Antes de terminar a novena, já terás alcançado a graça.

PAI ETERNO, EU VOS OFEREÇO O SANGUE DE NOSSO SENHOR JESUS CRISTO, PARA ALÍVIO DAS ALMAS SOFREDORAS QUE AINDA PADECEM NO PURGATÓRIO. SUPLICO A VÓS, MEU JESUS CRISTO, O SALVADOR DO MUNDO, QUE LHE DELVOVAIS A LUZ PERDIDA, E VÓS ALMAS SANTAS E BENDITAS, QUE SOIS TÃO PODEROSAS. EU VOS SUPLICO, INTERCEDEI JUNTO AO NOSSO PODEROSO SENHOR JESUS CRISTO, REDENTOR DO MUNDO, PELOS VIVENTES SOFREDORES DA TERRA, ENTRE OS QUAIS EU TAMBÉM ME ENCONTRO. ROGO-VOS BENDITAS ALMAS QUE ACEITES A MINHA PRECE. DAI LHES SENHOR, O DESCANSO ETERNO E A LUZ PERPÉTUA AS ILUMINE. DESCANSEM EM PAZ, AMÉM (Fazer os Pedidos)

Rezar. 01 - Pai Nosso - 02 - Ave Maria - 03 - Gloria ao Pai Quem não tiver

fé, ficará comovido com o que acontecer.

É tão comovente que já na 3° Segunda-feira, verá seu pedido atendido
Boa Sorte!!!

NOVENA " THE AFFLICTED SOULS "

This novena is prayed only on " Mondays "
Every time the Church, " bring 09 (nine) copies of this Novena, one candle ", offering to the AFFLICTED SOUS.

After finishing the novena, you already will have received the grace.

ETERNAL FATHER, I OFFER YOU THE BLOOD OF OUR LORD JESUS CHRIST, FOR THE RELIEF OF THE SUFFERING SOULS THAT STILL ENDURE IN PURGATORY. I BEG YOU, MY JESUS CHRIST, THE SAVIOR OF THE WORLD, THAT YOU RETURN THEM THE LOST LIGHT, AND YOU HOLY AND BLESSED SOULS, WHO ARE SO POWERFUL. I BEG YOU, INTERCEDE TOGETHER WITH OUR POWERFUL LORD JESUS CHRIST, REDEEMER OF THE WORLD, FOR THE LIVING SUFFERERS ON EARTH, AMONG WHOM I ALSO FIND MYSELF. I BESEECH YOU, BLESSED SOULS, TO ACCEPT MY PRAYER. GIVE THEM, LORD, ETERNAL REST AND ILLUMINATE THEM IN PERPETUAL LIGHT. REST IN PEACE, AMEN. (MAKE THE PETITIONS)

Pray: 01 – Our Father – 02 – Hail Mary – 03 – Glory Be to the Father Who does not have

faith will be moved by what will happen.

It is so moving that by the third Monday, you will see your petition answered.
Good Luck!!!

WHERE RELIGION LIVES

Kristy Nabhan-Warren, editor

Where Religion Lives publishes ethnographies of religious life. The series features the methods of religious studies along with anthropological approaches to lived religion. The religious studies perspective encompasses attention to historical contingency, theory, religious doctrine and texts, and religious practitioners' intimate, personal narratives. The series also highlights the critical realities of migration and transnationalism.

A complete list of books published in Where Religion Lives is available at https://uncpress.org/series/where-religion-lives.

Moved by the Dead
*Haunting and Devotion
in São Paulo, Brazil*

Michael Amoruso

The University of North Carolina Press CHAPEL HILL

© 2025 The University of North Carolina Press
All rights reserved
Set in Merope Basic by Westchester Publishing Services
Manufactured in the United States of America

Library of Congress Cataloging-in-Publication Data
Names: Amoruso, Michael, author.
Title: Moved by the dead : haunting and devotion in São Paulo, Brazil / Michael Amoruso.
Other titles: Where religion lives.
Description: Chapel Hill : University of North Carolina Press, [2025] | Series: Where religion lives | Includes bibliographical references and index.
Identifiers: LCCN 2024044995 | ISBN 9781469685168 (cloth) | ISBN 9781469685175 (paperback) | ISBN 9781469685182 (epub) | ISBN 9781469687490 (pdf)
Subjects: LCSH: Catholic Church—Brazil—São Paulo—Customs and practices. | Prayers for the dead. | Religion and culture—Political aspects—Brazil—São Paulo. | Collective memory—Brazil—São Paulo. | Black people—Violence against—Brazil—History. | São Paulo (Brazil)—Religious life and customs. | BISAC: SOCIAL SCIENCE / Sociology of Religion | SOCIAL SCIENCE / Anthropology / Cultural & Social
Classification: LCC BX2170.D5 A55 2025 | DDC 248.3/2—dc23/eng/20241104
LC record available at https://lccn.loc.gov/2024044995

Cover art: Photograph by Michael Amoruso.

Frontspiece figures: Novena to the Afflicted Souls; original and translation (by author). Formatting and spelling errors preserved in translation.

For product safety concerns under the European Union's General Product Safety Regulation (EU GPSR), please contact gpsr@mare-nostrum.co.uk or write to the University of North Carolina Press and Mare Nostrum Group B.V., Mauritskade 21D, 1091 GC Amsterdam, The Netherlands.

For Gi and Chico

Contents

List of Illustrations xi
Acknowledgments xiii

Introduction 1
The Afflicted City

PART I | *Orientations*

    1 The Day of the Souls 23

    2 The Souls of São Paulo 44

PART II | *Trajectories*

    3 Religious Transit 69

    4 Sympathy for the Dead 86

    5 The Politics of Mnemonic Repair 102

Postscript 127
The Afflictions of Memory

Notes 139
Bibliography 163
Index 177

Illustrations

FIGURES

1.1 Edifício Joelma 5
1.2 The Church of the Holy Cross of the Souls of the Hanged 8
1.3 The Cross of the Thirteen Souls 12
2.1 The Chapel of Our Lady of the Afflicted 46
2.2 The Door of Chaguinhas 48
2.3 Rua Galvão Bueno 49
2.4 Historical map of São Paulo, 1800–1874 (detail) 53
5.1 *Ex-voto* for Chaguinhas 115
5.2 New image of Chaguinhas 118
5.3 The cortege for Chaguinhas 121

MAP

2.1 Liberdade 52

TABLE

1.1 Types of souls mentioned in written requests 33

Acknowledgments

This book details some of the ways in which suffering sustains the relationship between the living and the dead. But suffering, help, and human solidarity are not only linked in religious devotion. They are part of the human experience. When we suffer or struggle, we reach out to others. Every writer is familiar with the terror of the blank page. Without mentors and partners, it would be maddening work. So here I would like to thank the souls that led me to and through the abyss.

First, thank you to all the devotees, activists, and employees at the Chapel of the Afflicted and the Church of the Hanged. This project is about them as much as it is about those places. Early in my research, the insight, experience, and friendship of the church employees I pseudonymously call Rodrigo and Renata were especially helpful. Of the many activists working with groups like Union of the Friends of the Chapel of the Afflicted (UNAMCA) and the Movement of the Afflicted, I want to give special thanks to Abilio Ferreira, Aloysio Letra, and Eliz Alves. Eliz has unfailingly responded to my many questions with patience, care, and honesty. Abilio Ferreira and Aloysio Letra generously reviewed chapter 5, which details a funeral cortege of which they were a part. Their perspective has been essential to my own understanding of space, race, and memory in São Paulo.

Others in Brazil were also important to this project. Marcio Goldman at the Museu Nacional at Universidade Federal do Rio de Janeiro and José Guillerme Cantor Magnani at Universidade de São Paulo both agreed to be institutional affiliates for my Fulbright IIE Fellowship, and both provided mentorship and research contacts. The members of the Grupo de Estudos da Religião na Metrópole introduced me to new literature on urban anthropology and religion and helped me appreciate the complexity of Brazilian religion. Caroline Freitas alerted me to scholarship on religious transit and offered incisive anthropological insights at different stages of this project.

I was lucky to receive funding for different stages of research and writing. The bulk of my fieldwork was supported by a Fulbright IIE Fellowship, as well as by a Tinker Summer Travel Fellowship and a Billy Bob Draeger Summer Research Fellowship in the Humanities through the University of Texas at Austin. My dissertation writing was supported by a Charlotte W. Newcombe Doctoral Dissertation Fellowship, which offered the time to write free of the usual burdens of graduate study. An H. H. Powers Travel Grant from Oberlin College supported research in early 2018, and Amherst College generously funded a brief trip in September 2018, without which chapter 5 would not have been possible. At Occidental College, a MacArthur International Grant supported this book's final stages of research and writing.

This project never would have happened were it not for a Summer Foreign Language Area Studies (FLAS) grant to study in São Paulo in the summer of 2012. My thanks, then, to the FLAS program and Tulane University for providing and administering funding and to Christopher Dunn and Jeffrey Lesser for building such a special program. It was Jeff Lesser who first introduced me and other students to the Church of the Hanged, and his work on twentieth-century immigration to Brazil has deeply informed my understanding of São Paulo and the church's neighborhood, Liberdade. More than that, whether through his group dinners or his eagerness to engage young scholars' work in progress, Jeff has been an important mentor for a generation of young Brazilianists.

There are too many people to thank at the University of Texas at Austin. Ever since I started doctoral studies at UT Austin, Tom Tweed was a dedicated adviser. Even after he left for Notre Dame, Tom's dedication to his students never waned. Beyond giving valuable guidance on my dissertation at every step of the way, he helped me navigate a difficult job market. Virginia Garrard was an equally generous adviser and provided extensive feedback and guidance on the dissertation stage of this project. More than that, Ginny offered personal and professional advice with grace and humor. Jennifer Graber continually pushed me to write for a broad audience. Matthew Butler was a close and careful reader and is also to thank for my early interest in Kardecist Spiritism. Chad Seales provided years of guidance and encouragement and was a compassionate listener in darker moments. And the faculty and graduate students in the Religion in the Americas colloquium continually helped me refine my arguments.

Other scholars and colleagues also deserve thanks. Nate Millington's work on urbanism and repair, as well as his friendship and support, has deeply shaped my own thinking about São Paulo. Andrew Britt's work on Liberdade pushed me to reframe the dissertation and more closely attend to São Paulo's history of urban infrastructure. Justin Doran, Josh Urich, and Jorgen Harris have all read drafts of various chapters and, even more importantly, been good friends when I've needed them. So have Brian Bush, Aleksandar

Radosavljevic, Vera Mazarra, and Brad King, especially in the dark days of writing. I continue to be inspired by the late John Burdick's studies of religion in Brazil, and his comments during my dissertation defense shaped my subsequent revisions. The Religion Studies Department at Lehigh University, my undergraduate alma mater, sparked my interest in religion, and I thank (and sometimes curse) Norman Girardot for encouraging me to pursue a graduate career.

At Amherst College, Lloyd Barba, Andrew Dole, and Maria Heim gave helpful feedback on the material that found its way into chapter 5 and this book's introduction. Mona Oraby (Howard University) pushed me to sharpen the book's theoretical apparatus and consider the different audience(s) of each chapter. After I submitted the book proposal and sample chapters to the University of North Carolina Press years ago, Elaine Maisner and the manuscript's early anonymous reviewers helped me sharpen the book's argument and theoretical apparatus. After Elaine's retirement, I benefitted from the steady guidance of Mark Simpson-Vos. Lorraine Leu (University of Texas at Austin) and Kelly Hayes (Indiana University–Purdue University Indianapolis) read an early version of chapter 5 and offered important theoretical suggestions that sharpened that chapter. My colleagues Kristi Upson-Saia and Amy Holmes-Tagchungdarpa at Occidental College have been wonderful mentors and friends. Whether through reading drafts of grant and book proposals, offering sage advice, shepherding me through institutional bureaucracy, or commemorating achievements, they've both shown me boundless care.

My family has been a constant source of support. My parents, Janet and Donald, were committed to providing my siblings and me with a college education even when it was financially difficult. There were times in my undergraduate career when they each worked multiple jobs so we could stay in school. They may not have always been thrilled with my decisions—I still remember the fateful call during which I let my parents know I'd be switching my major from computer engineering to religious studies—but they always supported and trusted in me.

In September 2022, around the time that I hoped to be finishing this book, my wife and I welcomed our son, Chico, into the world. He has brought me joy in ways that still surprise me. The challenge of raising a child also showed us how much we needed the kind of care that only family can give. For six months, my mother- and father-in-law, Cecilia and Sydney, generously welcomed us to their home in São Paulo. Without their help, I'm not sure when (or if) I would have finished this book.

Most of all, I thank my wife, Giovana. A talented journalist and astute writer, Giovana reviewed multiple drafts of every chapter of this book from the dissertation stage onward. Her editing helped improve the manuscript both in terms of form and content. But more than that, she shepherded me through the darker periods of writing and the academic job search with love, wisdom, and patience. She helped me find confidence whenever I was lost in self-doubt. Obrigado por tudo, meu amoré.

Finally, quero agradeçer as almas, todos que vieram antes. Depois de fazer tanta reza como pratica etnográfica, e mesmo sendo ateu, me peguei orando nos momentos de desespero: na escrita, na ansiedade antes de Chico nascer, ou simplesmente quando eu fiquei perdido. As Eliz would say, "The souls always guide us." Agradeço.

Moved by the Dead

Introduction
The Afflicted City

On the morning of February 1, 1974, Edifício Joelma burned. A high-rise office tower in São Paulo, Brazil, the building caught fire due to a malfunctioning air-conditioning unit on the twelfth floor. When the blaze started at around 8:00 a.m., about seven hundred people, all employees of Crefisul Bank, were working in the building's upper floors. The fire spread quickly, first to the building's only stairwell and then to the upper floors. With the stairwell cut off, the building's two elevators were the only way out. Elevator operators managed to get some three hundred people out before fire reached the elevator shaft. The rest of the building's occupants were trapped inside. By 10:00 a.m., over a hundred fifty people gathered on the building's roof, where they hoped to be rescued by helicopter. But Joelma lacked a heliport, and the smoke and heat made approach impossible. Rather than be burned alive, some began to jump.[1]

Television crews arrived quickly, broadcasting the tragedy live across the country. Viewers watched as people climbed out onto the building's ledges to escape the fire and smoke and police stood on their cars with megaphones, trying to calm onlookers and those trapped inside. But there was little hope. Low water pressure rendered firehoses useless, and firefighters' ladders could only reach the building's fifteenth floor. One intrepid firefighter managed to run ropes from a nearby building to Joelma, but he could only rescue about twenty people before the rope burned. Helicopters tried to approach the building to no avail. People kept jumping. The crowd below held up signs to those inside reading, "Stay calm" and "Don't jump, help is near."

At around noon, a helicopter got close enough to rescue about eighty people on the building's roof, most of whom survived by shielding themselves behind roof tiles. Firefighters were finally able to enter the building at 1:00 p.m., when there was little left to burn. A newspaper reported that when rescue teams entered, they "encountered charred bodies, clothes and shoes strewn about, stuck fire sprinklers, paper, twisted steel."[2] Even after the fire was under control, dozens of those stranded on the building's ledges leaped to their deaths. A camera crew followed a priest in a black frock as he walked around the building to bless the dead, revealing their disfigured corpses as he pulled back the cloths that covered the dead.[3] By the end of the day, the fire claimed around two hundred lives and injured some three hundred more, making it one of the deadliest events in the city's recent history.[4]

TWO DAYS AFTER THE JOELMA FIRE, the journalist José Neumanne Pinto reflected on the tragedy in *Folha de São Paulo*, the city's newspaper of record: "São Paulo always seemed a city fated to die by drowning: the dirty, stagnant waters of the Tamanduatei, Tietê and Pinheiros rivers flood lowlands, knock over houses, provoke social dramas, and the dams around them are a constant invitation to suicide. But suddenly, the trauma of fire has spread through the heart of the city and, for two years, has come to dominate the everyday neurosis of the Paulistano [resident of São Paulo], already so accustomed to the city's insanity and incoherence."[5]

With over fifty-six inches of average annual rainfall, São Paulo is known as the *terra da garoa*, or "land of the drizzle." By some counts, over three hundred rivers, streams, and tributaries cross the city. One such waterway, the Anhangabaú, begins at the confluence of three streams just underneath Edifício Joelma. Folk etymology holds that the river's Tupí-Guaraní name means something like "evil river" (a Jesuit mistranslation), and city officials long saw its stagnant, unpotable waters as a source of disease and vice.[6] In 1796, for instance, members of the city council voiced concerns that "black people, *carijós* [Indigenous or mixed-race Indigenous and white people], and bastards gathered to play various games" on the Anhangabaú's banks, which "frequently resulted in thefts and deaths."[7] A century later, a public health movement influenced by neo-Lamarckian scientific racism would crystallize these associations, promoting drastic interventions in the built and natural landscape in an attempt to increase the New Republic's (1889–1930) productive capacity and "improve the race."

Like most of São Paulo's other waterways, the Anhangabaú was eventually canalized underground. Its burial in 1906 and the transformation of the surrounding valley into parkland in 1910 allowed for the development of the city center at a time of rapid population growth. But the river continued to haunt the city. In 1948, a house near its headwaters was the site of the infamous "Crime of the Well," in which a young assistant professor of chemistry murdered his mother and sisters and buried their bodies in the family's backyard well. When the police came to search the professor's yard, he excused himself to the bathroom and shot himself in the chest. Some say the

Joelma fire was the tragic consequence of an accumulated karmic debt, one that stretched back even further, when the site was home to the stockades or an old Tupí burial ground.[8]

Neumanne Pinto blamed the fire on more quotidian problems. Though investigators had not yet learned its cause, the journalist reminded readers that just two years earlier, Edifício Andraus, another office building in the city center, caught fire. Though far less deadly, that fire "revealed the dangerous infrastructure of the immense skeleton of reinforced concrete and cement that sustains and practically feeds the reason for being of a metropolis centered on its own enormity," he wrote.[9] But nothing changed. Building codes remained weak, and the fire department was underresourced and understaffed. In 1974, São Paulo had just thirteen fire stations for a population of six million; Chicago, by comparison, had over three hundred.[10] The city was buckling under the weight of nearly a century of explosive growth. Now, wrote Pinto, São Paulo had "lost its rhythm and its compass, as if the fire attacked a vital point in the living and complex organism that is the city."[11]

FOR DECADES, Paulistanos had celebrated what Neumanne Pinto called the city's "insanity and incoherence." "In 1935 the people of São Paulo liked to boast that their city was expanding at the rate of a house every hour," wrote the French anthropologist Claude Lévi-Strauss in *Tristes Tropiques*.[12] "São Paulo is growing so fast that you can't buy a map of it; there'd have to be a new edition every week." Slogans like "São Paulo Must Not Stop" and "São Paulo—the Fastest Growing City in the World" justified progress at all costs.[13] When Lévi-Strauss visited in 1935, the city's first skyscraper— Edifício Martinelli, a twenty-seven-story building in the city center—was the tallest in Latin America. By the time of the Joelma fire, highways and high rises dominated the urban landscape. As the "concrete expressions of modern technology and commerce," these structures signaled São Paulo's industrial might to the world.[14] They also remade urban life. Beginning in the 1940s, a combination of rising rents and demolitions to make way for "urban improvements" accelerated the displacement of poor and often Black communities from the city center, exacerbating patterns of de facto racial segregation along a new center-periphery model that has persisted (with some modification) until well into the twenty-first century.[15]

By the time of the Joelma fire, enthusiasm had given way to anxiety. Neumanne Pinto likened the city's agglomeration of one million poorly built structures to a "giant encampment" and lamented the sorry state of modern life. Now, he wrote, "the neurotic man, who already cannot leave home with the certainty he will return, who fears everything and everyone on the street, cannot even rest when he lays his head on his pillow, knowing he sleeps in a gigantic furnace in waiting."[16] One Joelma survivor told *Folha* that the fire's victims "paid with their lives the price of living in a city under a dominion of almost unhuman fear and insecurity."[17] The costs of the city's relentless pursuit of progress were laid bare.

On February 6, five days after the fire, the city of São Paulo held a public funeral for seven of the fire's victims whose bodies were burned beyond recognition. With its fleet of Volkswagen buses, the municipal funerary service led a cortege from the city morgue to Cemitério Vila Alpina, a new public cemetery in the city's Eastern Zone.[18] The newspaper *Folha de São Paulo* reported that over five hundred people braved the February sun and eighty-plus-degree weather to attend the service. Emotions ran high. *Folha* wrote that at the burial, one woman, though unrelated to any of the victims, had a "nervous crisis when she saw the first shovel full of earth fall over the coffin. She cried and hugged a friend, screaming, 'Oh, my God, have pity on these poor ones.'" Another attendee described Joelma as a grim consequence of modern life. "Thank God, I live in a house and I'm free of the drama of families that live in apartment buildings in the center of the city," she told *Folha*. "Here in Cemitério Vila Alpina, we have a crematorium with ovens to burn cadavers. These buildings are ovens that burn the living."[19]

On March 1, the city laid to rest six more unidentified victims alongside the initial seven. Though less badly burned, no friends or family had come forward to identify their remains, and when a month had passed since the fire, the city gave up hope. Normally, unidentified bodies would be buried as indigents in a potter's field. But in this case the city made an exception. "It isn't known whose body is whose," the funerary service's technical director told *Folha*, "but the loved ones of the unidentified will have a place to pay homage, knowing that the mortal remains of their deceased relatives can be encountered there."[20]

Forty years later, Edifício Joelma is unremarkable in appearance. Renamed Edifício Praça de Bandeirantes in 1978, the building's owners have renovated its interior and tried to erase its past. No memorial marks the fire, and security guards are forbidden from discussing it or permitting curious visitors to enter. But as Brian Ladd observes, memories tend to "cleave to the physical settings of events."[21] The building's proprietors still have difficulty renting the space, even at below-market rates. On the fortieth anniversary of the fire, the newspaper *O Estado de São Paulo* reported that Edifício Joelma continued

FIGURE I.1 Edifício Joelma. Taken during a walking tour of haunted sites in São Paulo with O que te assombra? (What Haunts You?), March 2023. Photograph by author.

to "inspire ghost stories" (fig. I.1). People report hearing screams from the building's dark corners, and some employees claim to have seen cars driving themselves.[22]

Like the Joelma building itself, the tombs of its thirteen unidentified victims are said to be haunted. They have also become a shrine. On Monday, "the day of the souls" in Brazil, dozens of devotees visit to pray to these thirteen blessed, wise, and knowing souls (*treze almas benditas, sabidas, e entendidas*). They light candles because "souls need light," as many told me. And knowing how the victims died, some pour water over each of the tombs in offering the souls relief. But they also pray because the souls of the dead—especially those who suffered in life—have a reputation as especially powerful in their ability to help the living.

In São Paulo, most of the thirteen souls' devotees understand them to be the thirteen anonymous victims of the Joelma fire. But as early as 1970, devotees in cities throughout the Brazilian southeast began publishing the Prayer to the Thirteen Souls as *ex-votos*, or votive offerings for graces received:

Prayer to The Thirteen Souls

Oh! My 13 blessed, wise, and knowing souls, I ask you, for the love of God, that my request be answered. My 13 blessed, wise, and knowing souls, I ask you, by the blood that Jesus shed, that my request be answered.

My 13 blessed, wise, and knowing souls, I ask you by the tears that Jesus left on his Sacred Body, may my request be answered. My Lord Jesus Christ, that your protection surrounds me, your arms keep me in your heart and that you protect me with your eyes.

Oh! God of kindness, you are my defender in life and death; I ask you that my request be answered, that you free me of evils and give me luck in life. Follow my enemies, that the eyes of evil do not see me, cut down the forces of my enemies. My 13 blessed, wise, and knowing Souls, if you would deliver this grace (make your request), I remain devoted to you and publish this prayer, as well requesting a mass be prayed. Pray 13 Our Fathers, 13 Hail Marys, for 13 days.

[Oração Das 13 Almas

OH! minhas 13 almas benditas, sabidas, entendidas, a vós peço, pelo amor de Deus, atenda o meu pedido. Minhas 13 almas benditas, sabidas, e entendidas, a vós peço, pelo sangue que Jesus derramou, atendei o meu pedido.

Minhas 13 almas benditas, sabidas e entendidas, peço-vos pelas lagrimas de Jesus Cristo derramou do seu Sagrado Corpo, atendei o meu pedido. Meu Senhor Jesus Cristo que a vossa proteção me cubra, que vossos braços me guardem no vosso coração e me proteja com os vossos olhos.

Oh! Deus de bondade, vós sois meu advogado na vida e na morte; peço-vos que ante os meus pedidos, e me livrai dos males e dai-me sorte na vida. Segui meus inimigos que olhos do mal não me vejam, cortai as forças dos meus inimigos. Minhas 13 Almas benditas, sabidas, e entendidas, se me fizerem alcançar esta graça (pede-se as graças), ficarei devota de vos e mandarei publicar esta oração mandando também rezar uma missa. Reza-se 13 Padres Nossos e 13 Ave Marias 13 dias.][23]

This prayer is nearly identical to what devotees use today. While its origins are obscure, some scholars have suggested it is a "very old popular devotion," perhaps with roots in the mysterious Book of St. Cyprian.[24] In 1977, the Franciscan monk Bernardino Leers called the devotion to the thirteen souls the "newest product of popular Catholic vitality."[25] But it is not clear whether the thirteen souls of Joelma precipitated the prayer's popularity or followed from it. Whatever the case, in São Paulo and elsewhere, the cult of the souls furnished a ritual grammar for transforming trauma into devotion.[26]

In *History and Presence*, the religious studies scholar Robert Orsi writes, "The broken world is lived through and survived, but the brokenness is not forgotten. This suggests that religion is less about the making of meaning than about the creation of scar tissue." Orsi describes a cancer survivor named Lizzie who sleeps with a bag of holy Chimayo dirt under her pillow. The dirt is not an amulet but a mnemonic aid. She keeps it close "because 'it has the whole history' of her illness and survival. The dirt holds her memories," he writes. Practices like this are not ways of escaping or explaining tragedy but rather are ways of reentering the world, Orsi suggests. The relief they bring is always partial, pregnant with the memory of pain that came before.[27]

In July 2019, I met a sixty-seven-year-old devotee named Leia at the tombs of the thirteen souls. She told me she came for nine consecutive Mondays, praying a novena and asking the souls for help. It worked. "I came for nine Mondays. I prayed thirteen Our Fathers, thirteen," she said, trailing off. "I came here even though I'm Evangelical . . . so I don't light candles or any of that. But I know the thirteen souls because I *saw* their suffering," Leia explained. She was a young professional when Joelma caught fire, and some of her friends worked in the building. "Imagine," she paused, shaking her head, "human beings throwing themselves off that [building]. Dreadful." Like the others I spoke with, Leia's practice did little to make sense of the Joelma fire. Rather, it was a way of living with its senselessness.[28]

The Devotion to Souls

Two years before I learned about the thirteen souls, I was on a walking tour of central São Paulo led by a historian friend. As we passed through Liberdade, he brought us to the Church of the Holy Cross of the Souls of the Hanged (fig. I.2). I was struck by its peculiar name and rich lore, both of which spoke to its place near the former site of the city gallows. Its contemporary setting was also strange: located in the middle of São Paulo's "Japanese neighborhood," the plain beige church contrasted with the rich red of the area's stereotypically "Oriental" facades. On that July evening, two

FIGURE I.2 The Church of the Holy Cross of the Souls of the Hanged, July 2023. Photograph by author.

mães-de-santo, or Candomblé priestesses, were sitting outside its front gates, casting cowrie shell divinations for paying clients.[29] A large religious supply store next to the church sold Catholic images from one half and Afro-Brazilian and esoteric ritual goods from the other. Inside the church, signs prohibiting colored candles were meant to dissuade ritual practices associated with Afro-Brazilian traditions.[30] As I looked around, Elizabeth McAlister's "The Madonna of 115th Street Revisited" came to mind. Perhaps even more so than the Church of Our Lady of Mt. Carmel in East Harlem, it seemed that the Church of the Hanged was a sort of "religious borderland," where visitors practiced a religiosity that scholars have alternately called syncretic, creole, or hybrid.[31]

Intrigued, I returned to the church in January 2014 to start fieldwork. At the start of my research, I visited the Church of the Hanged on different days and at different times, waiting for something to happen. It seemed like nothing ever would. The church was almost always empty. Sitting in the pews in the sweltering February heat, I took notes on the few congregants:

> *Thursday, January 16, 10:42 a.m.*: six visitors, one of whom was almost aggressively praying before a statue of Our Lady of Aparecida.
>
> *Wednesday, January 29, 6:00 p.m.*: mass, twelve congregants.
>
> *Sunday, February 2, 11:47 a.m.*: twenty-three congregants, with a steady flow of two to three people in the lower candle room. Nothing remarkable. The church seemed like it might be a dead end, and I began spending more time at other potential field sites.

But then, on a Monday morning in early February, I found the church transformed. Five women had set up tables and large umbrellas on the sidewalk in front of the church, some casting cowries and others offering Tarot card readings. Inside, the church's pews were nearly full even though it was 10:00 a.m. on a weekday. While some congregants participated in mass, others circulated the nave, praying at each of the icons that lined its walls. Down in the larger of the church's two candle rooms, hundreds of candles were burning, many in clusters of seven, eight, or thirteen. Eighteen devotees were quietly speaking their prayers, watching over their candles, and bearing the intense summer heat. Spotting a black and a purple candle burning, one of the church's caretakers shook his head and grabbed it, extinguishing it in water before throwing it into a bag of collected wax. Wedged in a corner, another candle—half black and half white, likely lit for the *pretos velhos* (lit. "old Blacks"), a line of "highly-evolved" spirit entities associated with the Afro-Brazilian religion Umbanda—had escaped his notice. A white and yellow candle was floating in the shallow water that surrounded the candles. In the space designated for "seven-day" votive candles, there were several cups of water and a bag full of *pão francês,* or small loaves of "French" bread.

Back in the nave, congregants' agony was palpable. Two middle-aged women and a young girl were sitting in one of the back pews, hunched over and crying. One of the older women put her hand on the young girl's back, rubbing it to console her, both of their shoulders shuddering with sobs. I began to feel a welling of emotions from all this, thinking about love and loved ones lost. What was happening here?, I asked an employee. "It's the day of the souls," he said, matter-of-factly. "It's always busy on Mondays." He pointed to a large mass schedule hanging high on the wall. There were three masses daily except for Mondays, when there were nine. Why Mondays? I asked a few people, but no one knew. "It's a tradition of the people," one suggested.

Up in the church's nave, I was waiting for noon mass when an employee suggested I chat with Rodrigo. Rodrigo worked security at the church and had done some research on its history. "People come on Mondays to pray for people who died," he told me. Gray metal fans mounted along the nave's walls whirred, offering little relief from the summer heat. Rodrigo's brow shimmered. As we talked, he occasionally glanced at the front entrance to size up visitors. He explained that the church had been named for the victims of the city gallows. Turning, he pointed toward a wooden cross behind the altar. That cross, he said, is two centuries old. It came from a popular devotion to Chaguinhas, a rebel soldier hanged in 1821. When he was hanged, the rope broke on the first few tries, and people thought it was a miracle. After he was executed, people started lighting candles for him and the souls of the hanged. And if you go downstairs, he said, you'll see people lighting thirteen candles. "It's for thirteen people who died in an elevator in a building on Av. 9 de Julho, in the city center," he said.

I left the church confused and curious. On the one hand, I knew enough about Brazil's mediumship religions that I was not surprised to see people ritually engaging the dead. On the other hand, this practice did not look like mediumship. Practitioners were not incorporating the dead; nor did they seem to be conjuring them. Rather, they treated the souls like saints, using candles, prayers, and novenas to petition their help. Still, despite having been raised Catholic in the northeastern United States, I had never seen a practice like this. Why were so many people praying to suffering souls? What power did these pitiable dead have to help the living? Why was the "day of the souls" on Monday, which is typically thought of as profane? And why were people praying to the victims of a fire there, at the Church of the Hanged?

This tradition, which following vernacular and academic usage I call the devotion to souls (*devoção às almas*) or cult of the souls (*culto das almas*), is widespread in Brazil. In São Paulo, thousands of devotees visit cemeteries and Catholic churches on Mondays to pray to, light candles for, and petition the help of the souls of the dead. Like the Church of the Hanged, most of the city's popular sites for the devotion evoke the memory of death and violence. The Chapel of Our Lady of the Afflicted, just around the corner from Liberdade's Church of the Hanged, is the centuries-old remnant of what was once the city's pauper cemetery. More recently, in the far north of the city, devotees built a new Chapel of the Afflicted at a deadly street intersection. And like the tombs of the thirteen souls, each of these sites is said to be haunted.

As I would come to realize, the thirteen souls are just one iteration of this broader devotion. In some ways, they are exceptional: the souls are rarely finite in number, let alone identified with distinct human remains tied to a historical event. But the thirteen souls' exceptionalism is also instructive. It points to the souls' defining qualities. The first of these qualities is that the souls are *indefinite*, by which I mean they are numerically plural and empirically ambiguous. No one prays to *a* soul but instead to kinds or categories of dead: the afflicted souls, the forgotten souls, the souls of the hanged. The souls' second defining quality is their *suffering*, whether in life, at the hour of death, or in the afterlife. Both of these qualities reflect the practice's historical place within the purgatorial culture that flourished in colonial Brazil. More important for understanding the contemporary devotion, they help us make sense of the practice's capacity for confronting social violence. If haunting is an "animated state in which a repressed or unresolved social violence is making itself known," as Avery Gordon writes, then the devotion to souls is another.[32]

In *The Work of the Dead*, the historian Thomas Laqueur suggests we live in an age of "necronominalism." "The namelessness of the dead, once so common, has become a moral rebuke that lists—and the encompassing category of 'unknown' as a kind of apology for not knowing—are meant to mitigate," he writes.[33] At the 9/11 Memorial in Lower Manhattan, the names of all 2,983 victims (including the six victims of the 1993 bombing) are inscribed in bronze.[34] No such lists exist at Edifício Joelma or at the tombs of the thirteen souls. Instead, a plaque at the base of a blue-and-white tile cross reads (fig. 1.3):

THE THIRTEEN SOULS
ONLY GOD KNOWS THEIR NAMES
REST IN PEACE
+ 2 FEBRUARY 1974 [*sic*]
FIRE AT EDIFÍCIO JOELMA

FIGURE 1.3 The Cross of the Thirteen Souls, March 2014. The plaque at the base of the cross has since been stolen. Photograph by author.

In February 1985, *Folha de São Paulo* reported that the "cross of Joelma in Vila Alpina became a pilgrimage site" two years earlier. Covering an outdoor mass on the eleventh anniversary of the fire, they reported that "a ceremony for the victims of the fire united some relatives and more than two hundred faithful." The report continued: "At the start of the ceremony, three doves were released by children dressed in white, an homage provided by the industrialist Antonio Bodanese, 52, in thanks for graces received. 'I was hospitalized for two years with a very grave disease and was about to die. I made a promise to the thirteen souls of Joelma and completely recovered,' he explained. Angelina Soares, 50, observed dozens of people praying. Her brother was buried there. 'I know that he is one of these souls that is granting me so many graces that give me consolation,' she commented."[35]

If Soares knew her brother was buried at the site, why didn't the city? If most of the fire's 187 victims worked for a single employer, Crefisul Bank, why was there no noteworthy attempt to name the fire's unidentified victims? Poor corporate recordkeeping, a lack of bureaucratic capacity, the limits of the state—we can only speculate. But absence and loss can be "productive rather than pathological."[36] "Death and departure cause obituaries and genealogies to be written, as they do tombstones. Etched on paper, names become mobile and acquire new lives, circulating beyond the grave," writes anthropologist Engseng Ho.[37] Absence and erasure make room for presence, opening up new spaces of possibility.

At the time of the fire, the devotion to souls was flourishing. In 1967, one reporter wrote that "on Mondays it is almost impossible to enter the church [the Church of the Hanged]" due to the large number of devotees there.[38] In 1974, six months after the fire, another noted the "great number of weekly visitors" at the church.[39] And more so than the cult of the saints, the devotion to souls thrives on ambiguity. Saints—even popular saints—are known. Their devotees relate stories of their devoutness, redemptive suffering, and miracle working. But as much as the sanctified are remembered to have suffered, they are rarely subject to such totalizing unknowability.

In contrast to the cult of the saints, the devotion to souls is a way of remembering forgetting. It thrives in the epistemological wound opened by neglect. And far from resolving this neglect, the devotion dwells in it, directing attention to agents of erasure and opening up spaces of possibility.

The Afflicted City

Argument and Organization

This book is a study of the devotion to souls in São Paulo. It asks how places become resonant with spectral presence, drawing devotees and ghost hunters alike. It asks why candles for thirteen unidentified dead burn alongside candles for the enslaved. It considers how devotees traverse the urban space of São Paulo and transform sites of death into places of devotion. It is also, then, a study of feeling and memory. Devotees pray because remembering the dead makes them "feel good" (*sentir bem*), as so many told me. They remember those they understand others as having forgotten, whether their own ancestors or the nameless multitudes known only by the nature of their suffering—the souls of the hanged, the souls of the drowned, the souls of the afflicted, the souls of the burned. And as I would come to learn, their practice evokes the memory of social violence in a city eager to forget.

Beyond the ethnography of a practice, this book is a study in urban religion. This is to say that São Paulo is not just the locus of this study but its focus. More than an inert backdrop against which the devotion to souls is staged, São Paulo is a vital organism that has shaped and been shaped by the practice. This view grew out of my research. As I spoke with practitioners and learned more about the haunted places where they prayed, I came to understand ghost stories as what Michel de Certeau calls "spatial stories."[40] The stories devotees told about the dead both described São Paulo and prescribed movement through it. By following the paths of their piety, this book aims to chart the city's affective topography, mapping the sites of spectral presence that mark its histories of violence, erasure, and neglect.

This book's argument begins with an observation: suffering and its relief drive the devotion to souls. Devotees pray to ease the affliction of the suffering souls, who have the power to help the living in kind. Mutual suffering sustains a relationship of mutual aid between the living and the dead.

While suffering is central to many religious practices—indeed, some scholars of religion have argued that religion is centrally concerned with appealing to superhuman powers to "confront suffering" or to avert misfortune and overcome crises—its shape varies.[41] And in the devotion to souls, it is marked by neglect. Devotees pray to the indefinite, suffering dead, whose individuality has been given over to collective designations like the afflicted souls and the thirteen souls. It is little wonder, then, that devotional sites are said to be haunted.

In this book, I argue that the devotion to souls is an embodied practice of mnemonic repair.[42] In sustaining a relationship of altruistic reciprocity between the living and the dead, the practice connects devotees' personal affliction with the memory of social violence in São Paulo. In so doing, the practice has engendered political movement, motivating devotees and activists to advocate for official recognition of historical injustice—especially, but not exclusively, as related to slavery and its afterlives—through interventions in São Paulo's built landscape.

In part I, "Orientations," I situate the devotion to souls in time and space. While this study is principally concerned with describing the devotion in contemporary São Paulo, the practice is not unique to that city or even to Brazil. It is widespread, if varied, throughout the Catholic world and was especially prolific before the turn of the twentieth century. Chapter 1 traces the contemporary devotion's antecedents, focusing especially on the purgatorial devotionalism of colonial Brazil. Defining features of today's devotion—like the emphasis on suffering, souls' capacity to help the living, and the custom of praying to the dead on Mondays—were set in this period. While the Catholic lay brotherhoods and other institutions that sustained the devotion weakened during the ultramontane reforms of the late nineteenth-century, the devotion survived and even flourished, becoming useful to Catholic authorities as a way of combating the new threat from mediumship religions like Kardecist Spiritism.

Chapter 2 locates the devotion to souls within the cultural geography of São Paulo. Though a transatlantic practice, the devotion to souls is also intensely local. Ghosts always are. Scholars sometimes speak of haunting as something that happens to nations and ages—the New World as haunted by the ghosts of colonialism or late capitalism as haunted by its "lost futures," for example.[43] But haunting is more than metaphor. What makes the ghost powerful is its immediacy, its palpable presence in specific times and places. Through the Chapel of the Afflicted and the Church of the Hanged—two "sites of memory" where the dead are densely present—this chapter argues that São Paulo is haunted by the ghosts of modernization. It tells the story of that modernization from the 1870s onward to chart the racial dynamics of memory and forgetting that underpin a devotional economy of affliction.

In part II, "Trajectories," I approach the devotion to souls as a vector for three types of movement. Chapter 3 focuses on *religious* movement. Near the end of the twentieth century, Brazilian social scientists coined the notion of "religious transit" (*trânsito religioso*) to characterize the country's shifting religious demographics. They suggested the concept as an alternative to the notion of conversion, one more appropriate to the pattern of Brazilians' continual movement between traditions. Building on that work, this chapter considers religious transit's ethnographic application. It goes beyond sociologists' focus on switching affiliation to consider how in São Paulo moving between religions means moving across the city. Proposing religious transit as an alternative to syncretism, it suggests how we might direct our attention away from metaphors of mixture and toward the movement of bodies through urban space.

Chapter 4 examines movement in the *affective* sense. Devotees say that devotional sites make them feel good. So does praying to the souls. This chapter develops my claim that mutual suffering—compassion, in the original sense of the term—underpins a relationship of altruistic reciprocity between the living and the dead. Exploring devotees' deep affective bonds with souls, this chapter considers the practice in relation to sympathy, care, and maintenance. Akin to what some social theorists have called "radical care," I suggest the devotion is a way of confronting the precarity engendered by Paulista modernity. Devotees visit devotional sites to remember the forgotten dead, as well as to alleviate the own afflictions. In so doing, the practice connects "selves, communities, and social worlds," linking devotees' personal suffering with the memory of social violence in São Paulo.[44]

In Chapter 5, I consider the devotion to souls in relation to *political* movement. As a ritual practice aimed at remembering the most vulnerable, one could argue the devotion is inherently (if implicitly) political. But beginning in early 2018, a series of changes to Liberdade's built environment coupled with a growing recognition of the neighborhood's Black history put the Chapel of the Afflicted at the center of an activist movement. Devotees, Black activists, and a loose group of laypeople interested in preserving São Paulo's cultural heritage joined in a movement to raise awareness about the chapel and restore its structure. But the alliance was also fractious at times, as disagreements exposed deep fault lines along questions of race and electoral politics in São Paulo. Set against the backdrop of the contentious 2018 presidential election, this chapter centers the voice of Black activists to frame the devotion to souls in relation to the politics of Black mourning. The postscript follows this movement through July 2023, as activist collectives negotiated with the municipal government and a local architectural firm over the construction of the Memorial of the Afflicted, raising questions about Black and Indigenous memory in Liberdade.

Sources and Methods

This book is primarily an ethnography of the devotion to souls in São Paulo. As the study of a ritual practice rather than a specific place, my fieldwork was necessarily multisited. In what follows, I focus on three key sites: the Church of the Holy Cross of the Souls of the Hanged, the Chapel of Our Lady of the Afflicted in São Paulo's Liberdade neighborhood (which I sometimes call "the Liberdade churches"), and the tombs of the thirteen souls in Cemitério Vila Alpina. In contrast to some of the other sites that are popular for the devotion to souls—namely, the Sanctuary of the Souls, which I also visited but appears less prominently in this narrative—the Liberdade churches and the tombs of the thirteen souls are each connected with violent events in the city's history, and that historical connection lends them ritual potency. As one devotee told me at the Chapel of the Afflicted, "People like to come here [rather than the Sanctuary of the Souls] because they want to go where people suffered, where you have to give light." Making sense of these sites requires understanding something of the city's history. But they are also places where people make sense of that history, where people reckon with past social violence and to make claims of historical presence.

Of my many secondary field sites, I most frequently visited the Spiritist Federation of the State of São Paulo (FEESP)—the largest and one of the most important Kardecist centers in Brazil. As I discuss in chapter 3, a substantial portion of the devotees I interviewed visited this center, and some volunteered regularly as mediums. This massive, nine-story structure offered no shortage of activities, but my most regular participation included a weekly course on Allan Kardec's *The Spirits' Book* and a months-long course, required for all volunteer mediums, called "What Is Spiritism?" Given Kardecism's influence in Brazil and its assertion of the possibility of communication with the dead, I attended FEESP to get a sense of institutional Kardecism's similarities with and differences from the devotion to souls. I also attended regular public ceremonies and weekly courses on "mediumship development" at the Exu Tranca Ruas Institute, an Umbanda center in the city's Northern Zone. As with FEESP, I began visiting the institute after speaking with a number of devotees who identified as Umbandistas and affirmed the importance of the souls of the dead within Umbanda. As one put it, "the cult of the souls is practically a thing of the *terreiro* (or center)."[45] My choice of the institute was largely a matter of access: in addition to its location near a metro stop, it held twice-weekly public ceremonies and offered courses several nights per week.

My research consisted of about twenty-six months of fieldwork in São Paulo between 2014 and 2023, plus years of following what became known as the Movement of the Afflicted via WhatsApp and video meetings from afar. Of each of my three main field sites, I spent the most time at the

Chapel of Our Lady of the Afflicted. This was partly due to a combination of my own curiosity and, starting in 2018, the emergent political movement at the church. And earlier on, it was also due to ease of access. The layout of the church made it easy to solicit interviews, and one of the chapel's administrators, whom I call Renata, was especially helpful in soliciting interviews. On Mondays, she would pull up a chair next to her desk for me to sit, and we would chat with each other and devotees as they came in to buy candles. Devotees trusted her. They spoke to her candidly about their troubles, and when Renata asked for interviews on my behalf, most were happy to oblige. Because of her position at the church, Renata was well-acquainted with its history, could speak to the ebb and flow of devotees, and was able to put me in contact with people she thought worth meeting.

My own positionality is relevant here. I am a white, cisgender, male scholar from the United States. For the most part, I benefitted from the unearned epistemological authority that centuries of colonialism have invested in white men from the North Atlantic, especially when soliciting interviews. I gained people's trust easily and had access to places I otherwise might not have. And when the movement around the Chapel of the Afflicted emerged in 2018, I was no longer just a participant observer. As I relate in chapter 5, my presence amplified tensions around race, especially as debates unfolded over Black representation and the extent to which the movement should emphasize the chapel as a site of Black history. My participation as a white man in what was becoming a predominantly Black (and later, Afro-Indigenous) social movement was challenging and often uncomfortable, for me and probably for others as well. It was also clarifying. The more time I spent with the Movement of the Afflicted, the more I aimed to write a book that would be a modest contribution to that work.

In what follows, I try to foreground what practitioners said and did. To that end, some of my richest early sources are the recorded, transcribed, semistructured interviews I conducted with 117 practitioners, principally in São Paulo but also Rio de Janeiro. Interviews ranged from as short as a minute and a half to nearly two hours.[46] Among the practitioners, 88 were women and 29 were men. This purposive sample may slightly overrepresent female participation in the devotion, but if so, not by much. Devotees were not predominantly of any race. I did not ask devotees about income, but based on the information they volunteered (about employment, level of schooling, residence, or even descriptions of their class status), I gathered that most were lower-middle to middle class. As far as I could tell, none of the devotees I met were destitute, though some lived in poor neighborhoods on the city's periphery. A substantial minority were lawyers, engineers, or other white-collar professionals.

I also interviewed activists involved in the movement to save the Chapel of the Afflicted and designate the adjacent lot as a memorial. Though I recorded and transcribed six of those interviews, I found informal conversations and participant observation more helpful for understanding both the devotion to souls and the emerging activist movements. Throughout this book, I only use quotation marks when reporting direct quotes (as direct as possible considering questions of translation), either from jottings or recorded interviews.

In addition to published sources like travelers' accounts and early histories of São Paulo, I also use archival materials to shed light on the history of the devotion. Most of this material pertains to my three main field sites. Newspaper records, housed either in the Arquivo Histórico Municipal de São Paulo (AHM) and the Arquivo do Estado de São Paulo (AESP) or online (via the papers' proprietary archives or with the Biblioteca Nacional), offer some of the richest historical descriptions of lived practice at each devotional site. And in chapters 1 and 2, I also make use of ecclesiastical correspondence, lay associations' statutes and founding documents (*estatutos* and *compromissos*), and other miscellaneous records in the Arquivo Metropolitano do Arquidiocese de São Paulo (AMASP) to get a better understanding of the devotion's place in the history of São Paulo.

Though largely ethnographic, this study begins with the past. That is because it is about the dead. While gone, the dead are evoked in our memory. The pain of their absence gives them a second life. In English, we call this feeling of loss nostalgia or longing. In Portuguese, it is known as *saudade*. Saudade is a cherished emotion in Brazil, one typically seen as essential to the Brazilian national character. While one can have saudades for anything from places to food, it is also an emotion closely associated with the dead; as the popular saying goes, "saudade is the presence of those who are absent." While similar to nostalgia, it is not seen as naive or cloying but profound and poetic. To call attention to this difference is to highlight that memory is socially conditioned. It relies on vocabularies and ways of thinking and being that are historically specific. To understand the devotion to souls, then, we have to understand something about the devotional culture from which it emerged—the baroque religiosity of the colonial period, in which Monday became known as the "day of the souls."

PART I | Orientations

CHAPTER ONE

The Day of the Souls

On Monday mornings, Liberdade Square bustles. Morning commuters emerge from the subway station and pour into the square. There some stop at newsstands or vendors who sell coffee and *salgados* (savory snacks), sitting on benches or along the low concrete walls that line the subway exit, eating and talking before heading off to school or work. Groups of tourists come to take pictures of the city's unique "Japanese neighborhood," and Paulistanos without formal housing often sleep in the square, sometimes asking for food or change. Trucks unload goods and produce for local stores and restaurants, and car horns blare on Liberdade Avenue, a busy four-lane road that runs along the west side of the square. Standing there across the street from the Church of the Holy Cross of the Souls of the Hanged, one can smell burning paraffin coming from the church's two candle rooms, where on Mondays, hundreds of visitors come to burn candles and pray to the souls of the indefinite, suffering dead.

The day of the souls transforms the Church of the Holy Cross of the Souls of the Hanged and the space around it. Its dark wooden pews, all but empty most days of the week, fill with congregants. Members of the church's lay brotherhood, identifiable by their green sashes, sit in the front. There they linger for most of the afternoon, sometimes taking the sanctuary floor to lead the faithful in prayer between masses. When not participating in mass, visitors pray before saints and write mass intentions or petitions to saints and souls on small gray forms. Some never even enter the nave, instead heading straight for the church's two candle rooms, both of which open directly to the street. Over the course of my fieldwork, a flower and an herb vendor regularly set up shop outside the church, selling their flora to visitors. Oracles cast cowrie shells or read Tarot cards for a fee. Casa de Velas Santa Rita (Santa Rita Candle House), a religious supply store adjacent to the church, opened early and closed late to sell candles to devotees.

"I have a son with mental difficulties," Luzia told me. We were standing outside the church, and I had asked her how she started petitioning the souls. As I would later find was common, Luzia began praying in a time of need. "He would run away, return, run away, return, and I never knew where he was." I asked her whether she had received any graces. "Nossa!" she said, in a common expression of astonishment (short for Nossa Senhora, or Our Lady). "My son disappeared for a year," she told me, explaining that even though she moved to a new apartment and had a new phone number, her son managed to find her. "Isn't it quite the coincidence?" she asked. Like many visitors at the Church of the Hanged, Luzia had been praying to the souls for decades—thirty years, she told me. Even though she did not typically go to mass, she said, "You can find me here every Monday, the day of the souls. I come every Monday, and I light two candles: one to petition the souls, one to thank them." She prayed to the afflicted souls and thirteen souls, linking her familial struggles to the violence of slavery and urban development in São Paulo.[1]

"I *really* believe," Luzia said. "Every Monday, I'm here at this time."[2] Luzia did not know why Monday was the day of the souls, and neither did most others I spoke with. It was a tradition whose invention was so distant it seemed timeless. For many, it was something obvious, something anyone raised Catholic knew. I would ask them how they learned the devotion. "Well, I'm Catholic," one devotee said, as if that were explanation enough.[3] Another told me, "I was baptized in the Catholic Church, catechized in the Catholic Church, christened in the Catholic church, and I came to know God via this path."[4] For them, the Monday devotion was as familiar as private devotion to Saint Anthony is to Catholics in the United States.

To make sense of São Paulo's devotion to souls, it helps to know something about why eclectic practitioners pray to the dead at sites of social violence and why they do so on Mondays. This chapter focuses on the last part of that question, asking why Monday—a day not conventionally thought of as having sacred significance—is dedicated to the souls of the dead. In a way, the answer is simple, if obscure: between the eleventh and thirteenth centuries, prominent liturgists like Jean Beleth and Sicard of Cremona affirmed that the suffering souls in purgatory received respite from Saturday to Sunday evening. They recommended the faithful pray on Mondays to ease the souls' suffering as they returned to the purgatorial fire. The custom took hold as confessors and preachers spread purgatorial devotions and designated Monday as a day for celebrating masses for the dead, cemetery processions, and the benediction of graves.[5]

Being that the Monday devotion to souls is not especially prominent throughout the Catholic world, why is it well known in contemporary Brazil? In this chapter, I offer two historical explanations. First, I suggest the devotion was an important part of the baroque Catholicism of the Portuguese colonial period, having become particularly popular during the eighteenth century. It was propagated within lay Catholic brotherhoods and promoted by ecclesiastical authorities and the Portuguese crown, principally Dom João V. Though brotherhoods faced reforms in the late nineteenth century, the devotion to souls remained an important practice. This brings us to the second reason for the devotion to souls' popularity: the rise of mediumship religions, particularly Kardecist Spiritism, near the turn of the twentieth century. In Brazil and other Catholic countries, it was a way to combat the growth of mediumship religions by offering an alternative means of ritually engaging the dead.

This history helps account for some of the contemporary devotion's defining features, such as practitioners' emphasis on suffering (both theirs and that of the dead), their belief in souls' capacity to help the living, and their preference for practicing the devotion in Catholic churches and on Mondays. These practitioners may not always be exclusively Catholic—Luzia, for her part, frequented a Kardecist Spiritist center and regularly read Kardecist literature—but from what I could tell, most see little friction between these ways of engaging the dead. Like Catholic saints, whose presence is also common in religions like Umbanda and Kardecist Spiritism, the souls are not strictly under the church's command. Purgatorial language offers a coherent religious idiom for talking about the souls, but like all language, it is fluid. It changes and escapes easy control. No one has a monopoly on the dead.

Purgatorial Antecedents

The cult of the souls was once widespread throughout the Catholic world. It thrived in France in the nineteenth century, a period the historian Michel Vovelle describes as a "great century for purgatory."[6] In Lombardy, Italy, a vibrant seventeenth-century devotion to souls, centered on the excavated bones of plague victims, alarmed church authorities. Church authorities were alarmed not because the faithful were praying *for* the dead but *to* them. The living petitioned the dead for favors, as if they were saints or the Virgin Mary.[7]

Shocked though church authorities in Lombardy may have been, the notion that the dead could help the living was not unique to the Italian peninsula in the seventeenth century. Early Christians, too, petitioned the deceased for help. "Let me suggest that there was something in the nature of Christian representations of the other world that seemed always to draw the living and the dead together," writes Peter Brown. "Each side—the living and the dead—was believed somehow to need each other. The dead, in particular, needed the living." It could also work the other way around. Brown relates that in the catacombs of San Sebastiano outside of Rome, third-century graffiti reveal that the living not only prayed for the dead but asked the dead to pray for them. "Januaria, take your rest well, and ask for us," one family scrawled into the plaster around the marble nameplate on the tomb of the departed.[8]

Remembering the dead was a way of asserting their place in the world of the living. But by the end of the fourth century, "the dead and the living . . . drifted apart." Bishops were suspicious of "views of the afterlife that seemed to present the dead as hovering in too comfortable a manner around the living." They railed against customs like picnicking at the grave, which "assumed too cozy a relationship between the living and the dead." Augustine, whom the historian Jean-Claude Schmitt calls the "true founder of the Christian theory of ghosts," was especially important in keeping the dead at bay. At a time when the fate of the postmortem soul was far from settled, Augustine forcefully argued against the possibility that the body or soul of the dead could appear to the living. At best, the living could see a "spiritual image" of the dead, but even then, these images might be introduced by demons and were thus always suspect.[9]

Though the dead and living may have drifted apart, clerics could not totally sever the bond between them. In fourth- and fifth-century Rome, the rich customarily buried their loved ones near martyrs' graves. The holiness of these saints was such that their proximity would help ensure the dead's entry into heaven. By the seventh century, the social elite would spend great sums to build monasteries and convents, what Brown calls "powerhouses of prayer on behalf of the souls of the departed." Knowing their tombs would be bathed in the "perpetual light of perfumed candles," thought to symbolize the glory of heaven, the rich could rest easy knowing prayer would spare them too lengthy a stay in the cleansing fires of purgatory.[10]

In the seventh century, liturgy for the dead—masses in the dead's name on the third, seventh, and thirtieth days after death—became common practice. The institutionalized commemoration of the dead was further developed four centuries later with the establishment of All Souls' Day on November 2. Tradition attributes it to St. Odilo, the fifth abbot of Cluny, who initiated the holiday sometime around 1030. Hagiographies of Odilo say a Sicilian hermit heard demons complain that the suffrages of Cluniac monks were delivering too many suffering souls from their torments. When he learned of the hermit's visions, Odilo instituted the tradition, and soon after, "an apparition of the dead pope Benedict, freed from the punishment of the hereafter through the suffrages of the Cluniacs, confirmed the validity of that initiative."[11] Cluny was influential; the holiday quickly spread throughout France, Germany, and England and was adopted as official doctrine in 1274.

The establishment of All Souls' Day roughly corresponds with the birth of purgatory, which the historian Jacques LeGoff dates to between 1150 and 1200. LeGoff describes purgatory as "an intermediary other world in which some of the dead were subjected to a trial that could be shortened by prayers, by the spiritual aid, of the living." The doctrine crystallized a set of preexisting ideas about souls and the afterlife, such as a belief in the soul's immortality and resurrection, its separation from the body at death, its punishment and purification via fire, and the possibility of its eventual entry into heaven. And it did so in a way that reformed the relationship between the living and the dead, by putting the church in a stronger position to mediate between the two.[12]

Lay Brotherhoods and the Purgatorial Devotionalism of Colonial Brazil

According to LeGoff, the triumph of purgatory relied on the establishment of customs and institutions that fostered solidarity between the living and the dead. Masses and prayer were the primary means of releasing souls from purgatory, and both could be costly. One way to ensure postmortem prayers said on one's behalf was to set aside money in a will. Another was to belong to a Catholic brotherhood or confraternity. These mutual aid societies were fundamentally concerned with death and the dead, and purgatory became increasingly important within them between the thirteenth and sixteenth centuries. And in the wake of the Counter-Reformation, brotherhoods specifically dedicated to the souls multiplied.[13]

Catholic lay brotherhoods (*irmandades* or, less commonly, *confrarias* in Portuguese) existed in Portugal since at least the thirteenth century and were still mainstays of social life in Brazil at the turn of the twentieth.[14] These guild-like groups were primarily organized along class and ethnic or racial lines and, less frequently, occupational ones. Membership in the prestigious Santa Casa de Misericórdia (Holy House of Mercy), for example, was only open to landed nobles who were "free of any Moorish or Jewish stock."[15] The Black Brotherhood of Saint Elesbaan and Saint Ephigenia in Rio de Janeiro, which was organized by Africans from the Gold Coast, Cape Verde, São Tomé, and Mozambique, explicitly excluded "blacks from Angola." Membership in brotherhoods, then, reflected and reinforced the social hierarchy in colonial Brazil. And for enslaved and freed people with limited means, it was a way of ensuring a good burial.[16] Without brotherhood membership, enslaved people risked their corpses being dumped in remote locations by masters or, only slightly better, the trench graves of Santa Casa de Misericórdia.[17] The social support offered by a brotherhood could be crucial for those who wanted to avoid that undignified end.

Beyond ensuring a good death, brotherhoods helped ensure the salvation of their members' souls. Members expended considerable effort and money not only organizing deceased brothers' funerals but also praying for and requesting masses in intention of the dead. Their statutes often explicitly mandated prayer for departed brothers, typically on a chosen day of the week, Sundays, or specific holy days (such as on Fridays of Lent and the holy day of the church).[18] Brotherhoods with a special interest in purgatorial souls, like the Brotherhoods of St. Michael and the Souls that were popular in Minas Gerais, usually reserved Monday for mass and prayer for the anonymous souls in purgatory.[19]

In the early eighteenth century, purgatorial devotions were also encouraged by ecclesiastical authorities and the king, Dom João V (1689–1750; r. 1706–50). A contemporary of the king noted that "since the first years of his government, an ardent devotion to liberate the souls from Purgatory shone in his spirit."[20] João V opened a running account to pay for masses for the souls in purgatory, and some sources suggest he ordered between 10,000 and 18,000 such masses annually—a number that increased to 700,000 in the final years of his reign. The expense prompted the common complaint that the king "sends the living to hell to take the dead out of purgatory." His zeal for the souls merely amplified a trend that had begun a century earlier—in Portugal, *alminhas* (roadside altars to the souls) and brotherhoods dedicated to the souls began proliferating in the seventeenth century. "The devotion to souls was so familiar and rooted in the religious practices of the Portuguese," writes one historian, that there was "a veritable pious dialogue between the world of the living and that of the dead."[21]

This "pious dialogue" between the living and the dead extended to Brazil. While the tradition of the *alminhas* was never imported from Portugal, purgatorial imagery flourished. Altarpieces and alms boxes were adorned with iconography of purgatorial souls, who are typically depicted as naked (and often white and young) bodies bathed in flame. Concern for the dead was also codified in ecclesiastical dictates. The First Constitutions of the Archbishopric of Bahia (1707), which served as the principal ecclesiastical legislation in the country for nearly two hundred years, states: "Conforming with the general custom approved by the Church, in our Sé Cathedral and parish churches of our archbishopric, will be made processions on the Mondays of [every] year for the dead." The document also encouraged the establishment of brotherhoods, "principally those of the Holy Sacrament, and of the Name of JESUS, to Our Lady, *and of the Souls in Purgatory*, when possible, and the capacity of parishes allows it, because it is good to have these Confraternities in every church." The souls in purgatory were an essential part of religious life in Brazil.[22]

"In Brazil, religion, or that which is so called, meets you everywhere and you can do nothing, observe nothing, without being confronted by it in one shape or another," wrote Thomas Ewbank. An English inventor of means, Ewbank chronicled his 1845–46 stay in Rio de Janeiro in his travel diary, *Life in Brazil*. The work offers a helpful account of lived religion in nineteenth-century Brazil. Though a Protestant who saw the Catholic Church as a "barrier to progress," Catholic devotionalism fascinated Ewbank. "It is a leading feature in public and private life," he wrote, and something that no careful observer could ignore.[23]

Catholicism pervaded Rio de Janeiro public life in the nineteenth century, and the souls in purgatory permeated lived Catholicism. Lodged in Catete, a neighborhood in Rio's Southern Zone, Ewbank was near the famous Church of Our Lady of Glory, which was built over a century earlier in 1739. "Four or five feet in front of the chapel door, a post is fixed in the pavement, and against it an alms-box, bound with iron and secured by a padlock. On the raised back a cup is painted, and under it heads rolling in flames. On the box is written, 'Esmolas para as almas'—alms for drawing souls out of Purgatory."[24] The dead were integrated into everyday life in other ways. "Numerous days on the calendar are marked with the word 'Alma,'" which indicated days advantageous for freeing souls from purgatory. Ewbank wrote that on every day but Sunday, alms collectors would go door to door and solicit funds for that day's masses. "Thus, in Catete, every Monday a man knocks at our door for a donation to release the imprisoned souls." This man was likely collecting alms on behalf of the nearby Church of Our Lady of Glory, where the devotion continues today.[25]

Ewbank was especially struck by an alms box outside a store that "presented the best piece of picture-writing I have met with." It depicted two infants, one Black and one white, screaming in pain while burning in purgatorial fire. "Passing travelers can hardly refuse a trifle to innocents thus beseeching them with screeches, tears, and uplifted hands," he wrote. Though a Protestant who thought Catholicism a barrier to progress, Ewbank never

The Day of the Souls 29

dismissed purgatory as a means of spiritual extortion. He seems to have intuitively understood the affective hold of purgatorial devotionalism. "Indeed, who of the faith can withstand invitations to shorten the purgation of departed friends," he asked.[26]

The coins that clinked in the coffers Ewbank described most likely funded masses not for friends but for anonymous souls. Historians have noted that the faithful were careful to distinguish between these nameless dead and those of their friends and family—a distinction that abides for contemporary devotees. Brotherhoods prioritized prayer that shortened their own members' purgatorial stays, and analyses of last wills and testaments show that testators consistently requested more masses for themselves and loved ones than for the anonymous dead. This makes sense. One of the main reasons for drafting these documents was to minimize one's own purgatorial suffering. Even though funding masses for anonymous souls was a way of earning merit, having masses said for oneself was more effective at hastening one's own salvation.[27]

Testators may have requested fewer masses for anonymous souls than for themselves, but that they spent any money at all on purgatorial souls suggests how important they were in religious life. Outside of last wills and testaments, these masses were typically funded by alms boxes, like those Ewbank described, or by special collections. In the Brotherhoods of São Miguel and Almas in Minas Gerais, for example, members passed around a *bacia das almas* (basin for the souls) dedicated exclusively to the anonymous souls in purgatory. They also reserved Mondays for prayer to these souls, praying to those of members on other days, like Sundays or at other designated times.[28]

Requesting mass was not the only way of coming to purgatorial souls' aid. The faithful also prayed for the souls—and petitioned their help—privately. Historians disagree about when the souls came to be seen as intercessors, but in Brazil, it seems devotees were petitioning the souls for help at least as far back as the eighteenth century, as evidenced by oblique references to the souls' intercessory powers in some brotherhoods' charters (*compromissos*).[29] The 1713 charter of the Brotherhood of Saint Michael and Souls of Caeté (Minas Gerais), for example, relates the "wonders that God has wrought in this world through the Souls in Purgatory." The *compromisso* of the Brotherhood of Saint Michael and Souls of Pitangui (1727) similarly mentions souls' "wonders." And during his visit to Brazil in the 1820s, the French botanist and traveler Augustin Saint-Hilaire remarked, "The souls are not only prayed for, but are invoked in order to obtain graces"—so much so, he thought, that the "devotion often degenerates into abuse," with people even asking the souls for help finding lost objects.[30]

The historical record does not offer much insight into what devotees were asking of the souls. The art historian Adalgisa Arantes Campos posits a theological explanation for this absence, suggesting that devotees thought it more appropriate to offer souls suffrages to swiftly move them through purgatory than to leave *ex-votos*, or votive offerings in gratitude for favors received. But at least for practitioners today, there seem to be few theological barriers to leaving written testaments or other objects in thanks to the souls. At certain sites, including Our Lady of Lampadosa in Rio de Janeiro and the tombs of the thirteen souls in São Paulo's Cemitério Vila Alpina, devotees leave behind the same kinds of *ex-votos* used at other Catholic shrines, such as wax body parts and signs thanking the souls. Nowadays, the biggest consideration seems more material than theological: most sites popular for the devotion to souls in São Paulo do not have spaces for leaving *ex-votos*. This may be an artifact of history. In contrast to saints, anonymous souls have typically lacked distinct burial sites at which to deposit material objects.

Still, even in the eighteenth century, devotees did occasionally leave written testimonies of the souls' power. For example, Campos relates a rare *ex-voto* from 1743 in which a devotee thanked the souls for help in saving his life after a violent attack.[31] This is not so different from what devotees say today. One of the most common things the devotees I met asked of the souls was protection from street violence. One described a story of two thieves who robbed nearby people but walked past her, almost as if she were invisible.[32] Though this partly reflects the social position of devotees, who are less likely to live within the "city of walls"—that is, the highly securitized world of wealthy Paulistanos—it is also because of souls' association with streets, paths, and wayfinding (and, by extension, the *orixá* Exu). As another devotee told me, "I ask God to carry the souls to heaven, and that when the souls are there, they intercede for me, to open up paths [*abrir caminhos*], to protect me—me and my family, my friends, the people I like, my animals."[33]

Souls and Spirits

The devotees I spoke with prayed to souls like the afflicted souls (*almas aflitas*), the holy souls (*almas santas*), and the blessed souls (*almas benditas*), all phrases historically used as shorthand for the purgatorial souls in Iberian Catholicism. Blessedness and affliction might seem mutually exclusive, but in purgatorial logic, the two go hand in hand. As Campos explains, the further the souls are on the purgatorial path, "the more holy, more lucid, 'wiser and more understanding,' and, necessarily, more 'afflicted.' It is exactly these souls, those that suffer most, that are most in need of suffrages."[34]

Though purgatorial theology shaped the practice, devotees today do not always believe in it. As Diana Walsh Pasulka has noted, the church has deemphasized purgatorial doctrine since Vatican II.[35] During my visits, priests rarely mentioned the purgatory during masses at the Church of the Hanged and nearby Chapel of the Afflicted.[36] While devotees regularly mentioned heaven and hell, they also talked about reincarnation, which has considerably more traction in Brazil than purgatory. Surveys have suggested that somewhere between 12 and 37 percent of the Brazilian public believes in the idea.[37] As far as I have been able to tell, no one has even thought to survey the popularity of belief in purgatory.

Freed from the fires of purgatory, the souls have proliferated. Table 1.1, based on a review of 180 mass intention forms collected at the Chapel of the Afflicted, illustrates devotees' creativity.

For most, phrases like *afflicted souls* and *blessed souls* were not synonyms but instead referred to different kinds of dead. By referring to these souls as "kinds," I mean to evoke the notion of kinship, a relationship between these different dead that we can trace to at least one "common ancestor": the souls in purgatory. In his work on religious language, the anthropologist Webb Keane helpfully notes that ritual recitations "often retain some marked linguistic or performance features, which testifies to their persistent connection to and difference from the prior—and distant—context." While ways of referencing souls suggest a once-pervasive concern with purgatory, they have become kinds of souls in themselves. Here we find a tension between devotees' diverse conjectures about the dead and the relative stability of ritual language. This stability is important. Whatever devotees think of purgatory, the phrases used to denote the dead are linked with a representational economy that connotes their suffering and need for relief.[38]

There is an illustrative outlier in table 1.1: *almas de luzes*, or "souls of lights [sic]." When I asked devotees about the difference between "soul" and "spirit," most said they were synonymous. "The soul is the spirit," affirmed one devotee.[39] "It's the spirit that God put in us," explained another.[40] But while both terms can signify an abiding essence that survives physical death, the terms index relatively distinct, if overlapping, religious idioms. Whereas "soul" has Catholic resonances and evokes suffering, neediness, purgatory, and intercession, "spirit" conjures Kardecist associations like evolutionary planes, progress, and goodness. While devotees often code switched, describing souls

TABLE 1.1 Types of souls mentioned in written requests

Kind of soul (Portuguese)	Kind of soul (English translation)	Count
treze almas	thirteen souls	14
alma do (fulano)	soul of (someone)	12
almas aflitas	afflicted souls	7
todas as almas/almas em geral	all the souls/souls in general	6
almas do purgatorio	souls of purgatory	5
almas necessitadas	needy souls	5
almas dos enforcados	souls of the hanged	4
almas abandonadas	abandoned souls	4
almas injustiçiadas	wronged souls	3
almas esquecidas	forgotten souls	3
almas desesperadas	desperate souls	3
almas benditas	blessed souls	2
almas afogadas	drowned souls	2
almas queimadas	burned souls	2
santas almas benditas	holy blessed souls	2
almas aflitas benditas	blessed, afflicted souls	1
as 7 correntes das almas penadas	the seven currents of wandering souls	1
todas as tres, todas as nove almas	all the three, all the nine souls	1
almas das suicidas	souls of suicide (victims)	1
almas dos antepassados	souls of the ancestors	1
almas de luzes	souls of light	1
almas assassinadas	murdered souls	1
almas dos moradores rua	souls of the homeless	1
almas criancas assassinadas	souls of murdered children	1
almas dos presidiarios	souls of the convicts	1
almas dos Aideticos	souls of AIDS victims	1
almas dos Cancerosos	souls of cancer victims	1
almas dos escravos	souls of the slaves	1
almas dos soldados	souls of the soldiers	1
13 almas penadas e enforcadas	13 wandering and hanged souls	1
as almas	the souls	1

Source: Complied from 180 petitions and mass intention forms collected by the author at the Chapel of the Afflicted in 2014. Note that some devotees submitted multiple petitions and/or listed litanies of souls on their petitions. As such, this table is meant to illustrate the kinds of souls to whom devotees pray more than indicate something about the kinds' relative popularity.

as "spirits of light" (*espíritos de luz*, a common way of talking about highly evolved spirits in Kardecist discourse), petitions to "souls of light" are rare.

In his ethnography of Palo Briyumba in Cuba, the anthropologist Todd Ramón Ochoa distinguishes between what he calls the "ambient dead" and the "responsive dead." Whereas the ambient dead are "an undefined and pressing mass made up of infinite numbers of unrecognizable dead," the responsive dead are discrete spirits who respond to the living.[41] Over the years, I occasionally saw references to the souls as *kalunga*, the Bantu word for the ambient dead used in traditions like Palo and Umbanda. But from talking with devotees, it seemed to me that the souls lay somewhere between these ambient and responsive poles—they are both nowhere and everywhere, no one but everyone, forgotten but remembered. Even their anonymity is partial: while one cannot petition an individual soul (though people do sometimes petition deceased loved ones), few make requests of "all souls," preferring instead the specific kinds I specified above.

With these blurred distinctions in mind, I want to suggest that the souls' opacity—their "rich indetermination," to borrow a term from Michel de Certeau—is part of their appeal.[42] It is also what allows the devotion to act as a practice of mnemonic repair. As we saw with the thirteen souls, the devotion offered a way to remember the forgotten and name the nameless, thus making space for the dead in the public imaginary. Personal hardship draws people to the souls who, in saturating sites of historical trauma, color the affective topography of the city. As devotees engage in this work of historical memory, they also draw on family histories, imbuing the souls with the qualities of familiar dead and vice versa. Because the dead are no one, they can be anyone, making our hardship theirs and their hardship our own.

The notion of kin also evokes the devotion's affective tenor. In contrast to the devotion to saints, devotees today see their relationship with the souls as one of mutual aid. It reflects the sociality engendered within the Catholic brotherhoods that thrived before the twentieth century. Devotees refer to the souls as "friends" and characterize their relationship with the dead as one of reciprocal altruism. This is an important point. Even though scholars have characterized the devotion as "magical" or "instrumental," these labels miss its emotional qualities. They focus only on what devotees ask for and pay too little attention to devotees' relationship with the dead. Friendship and instrumentality are at odds. As one philosopher has argued, "We love *all* our friends . . . 'for themselves' and not just what they do for us. 'Instrumental friendship' . . . is a contradiction in terms."[43]

To say the contemporary devotion to souls took shape within the baroque Catholicism of the colonial period is not to make any normative claims about its orthodoxy, then or now. One of my arguments in this book is that the devotion to souls is a vector for religious movement. While commonly practiced in Catholic spaces, devotees often incorporate discourse and practice associated with non-Catholic religions—often enough, in fact, to provoke approbation from some church authorities and lay practitioners. Still, because the dead are universal, the devotion can accommodate people of different and multiple faiths. I suspect that, for precisely this reason, Catholic clergy and lay elite have used it to catechize and indoctrinate. It offers a means of communing with the dead but one markedly different from the mediumship religions that, from the late nineteenth century onward, the church sought to combat.

The Wandering Dead

Purgatory may have gripped the minds of Brazil's faithful, but until the turn of the twentieth century, the Catholic Church was institutionally weak. In his preface to the second English-language edition of *The Masters and the Slaves*, Gilberto Freyre describes Brazilian religion as a "family Catholicism, with the chaplain subordinated to the paterfamilias, with a cult of the dead, etc."[44] The church's position as the established faith, funded through the crown's 10 percent tithe on everything produced in Brazil, did little to incentivize its independent organization (though the Jesuits, who founded São Paulo, had a strong presence in Brazil until their expulsion in 1759). From 1551 until 1676, there was only one bishopric (in Salvador), and until the establishment of the republic in 1889, there was only one archbishopric (also in Salvador). Furthermore, the Portuguese crown held the right to name bishops and censor the Vatican's acts and decrees under the arrangement of Royal Patronage (Padroado Real), established via a series of papal bulls between 1415 and 1515. In urban areas, brotherhoods were the dominant religious institutions. And though they were subject to ecclesiastical approval, they operated with little clerical oversight until the Romanization, or ultramontane, reforms of the late nineteenth century, which emphasized the authority of Rome and aimed to unify doctrine and practice among Catholics worldwide.[45]

So, while purgatory was influential in Brazil, the laity was never known for ultramontane piety. Purgatorial doctrine was not the only way of thinking about the dead, and while ecclesiastical authorities and the crown encouraged purgatorial devotions, they did not demand or strictly control them during the colonial and imperial periods. Likewise, popular healers and independent religious specialists regularly appropriated the church's ritual, language, and material culture in ways that roused the Inquisition's ire. For instance, Inquisition records tell of Domingas Gomes da Resurreicão, a native healer known for healing *quebranto*, or weakness caused by evil eye. "To combat it, he blessed the patient's whole body with his index finger and thumb or with the cross on his rosary." Domingas would say, "Two evil eyes have given it to thee, with three thou shalt be cured," before honoring the souls in purgatory.[46]

Ecclesiastical authorities have long been anxious about attempts at direct contact or communication with the dead, fearing the persistence of Roman and other pagan practice.[47] But inquisition records suggest necromancy was not uncommon during the colonial period. A Portuguese woman (who was banished to Angola after being convicted of sorcery by the Holy Office in 1713 and 1720) attended a client who sought her help winning over the heart of his beloved. She instructed him to pray: "Souls, souls, of the sea, of the land, three hanged, three dragged, three shot to death for love, all nine shall gather into the heart of so and so, shall enter, and such tremor shall cause her for the love of so and so, that she shall not rest, nor be still, save she say yes to his wish to wed."[48] Similar language appears in contemporary *simpatias* and prayers, such as in the example of a petition to "all the three all the nine" souls cited in table 1.1. And in a 1987 collection of Umbanda prayers, one prayer begins, "Souls, souls, souls, three that died for drowning, three that died of burning, three that died for love, gather all three, all six, all nine to jolt the heart of so-and-so."[49] This striking continuity speaks to both the stability of ritual language and the broad potency afforded to the suffering dead.

Fear of wandering souls or ghosts was common in Brazil and Portugal. From at least the nineteenth century onward, these souls were typically called *almas penadas*, a phrase alternately translated as "lost," "pining," or "wandering souls" (though it might be translated more literally as "suffering souls"). The phrase *almas penadas*—like *almas aflitas* and *almas santas*—probably has origins in Iberian purgatorial discourse. In that context it referred to souls' purgatorial peregrinations, not their earthly ones. In time, like those other phrases, it became divorced from this original context and came to refer to souls that wander the earth. It remains common today, even part of popular culture via Penadinho (Little Wanderer), a cartoon character similar to Casper the Friendly Ghost.[50]

Some scholars have pointed to belief in *almas penadas* as evidence of a "folk Catholicism" that was "not in harmony with salvationist Christianity, much less Tridentine Catholicism."[51] But the church is not a monolith. Augustine may have proposed a Catholic theory of ghosts that limited their appearances, but many Catholics have argued that purgatorial souls could both appear to the living in dreams and affect earthly matter. For example, in 1894, Victor Jouet, a brother of the Missionaries of the Sacred Heart, collected relics of purgatorial souls' impressions upon earthly matter, such as a handkerchief on which he asserted a soul left an imprint of its finger. He collected these relics in a small museum inside the Sacro Cuore del Suffragio, a church dedicated to the purgatorial souls, near the Vatican.[52]

Observers described customs that suggest how Brazilians understood the dead's movement through the physical world. In *Life in Brazil*, Thomas Ewbank related, "Soon as a person dies, the doors and windows are closed—the only occasion, it is said, when the front entrance of a Brazilian dwelling is shut."[53] The folklorist José Leite de Vasconcellos reports that in late nineteenth-century Portugal, "when someone dies, one must get rid of all the water in the house, because the soul can return there to bathe," similar to the contemporary prohibition on lighting candles for the dead at home for fear of attracting needy souls.[54] These ideas were common elsewhere in the Catholic world and sometimes aroused clerical disapproval. For example, in 1530, the Bishop of Verona lamented "the practice of uncovering the roof so that the soul [of the dead] can get out, something that suggests that the soul could be held back by a roof."[55]

Vasconcellos noted other precautions and prejudices related to the souls. Regarding *almas penadas*, he wrote, "It is believed the souls of great sinners are transformed into animals, wandering late at night through fields, as well as churches and cemeteries," and that "the souls of those who die without giving back what they owe must return to this world, by God's favor, and implore a friend or relative to give back the stolen thing." He also noted the prohibition on spitting on a flame, "because they are souls that go to purgatory; who spits is a Jew."[56] While I never heard devotees mention this dated anti-Semitic prohibition, many carefully guarded the flames of their candles, sometimes standing over them until their candles burned out. For them, the candle is more than a symbol: it is the souls' "lost light," and were it to be extinguished before burning through, the souls would be left in darkness.[57]

Purgatorial devotion offers a sanctioned way of communing with the dead. It also keeps the dead at bay. Theologians debated whether and when

The Day of the Souls 37

purgatorial souls could return to earth, but that there were debates at all suggests that agreement that the dead were safely cordoned off in heaven, purgatory, or hell. Some scholars argue that in periods where purgatory flourished, hauntings decreased.[58] Others suggest that Spiritualism was most successful in Protestant countries that lacked a purgatorial ritual for engaging the dead.[59] But I am not fully convinced that purgatory ever really succeeded at eradicating ghosts and spirits or that the correlation between Spiritualism and Protestantism is so clear. After all, Kardecist Spiritism came from France and was popular throughout much of Latin America at the turn of the twentieth century—particularly in Brazil, where the church worried much about Kardecist Spiritism, which gained a large following after its introduction in 1853, but had little success in combatting it.

Combatting Spiritism

The church maintained its position as the established faith for the duration of the Brazilian Empire (1822–89), but church-state relations soured by the empire's end. The advance of liberalism had threatened state support of the church throughout the Catholic world, and in places like Mexico, reformers were successful in separating church and state, nationalizing the Catholic Church's landholdings, and restricting the authority of church courts. The church reacted in kind. The reign of Pope Pius IX, in particular, marked a shift in the Vatican's attitude towards the place of the church in Catholic countries. Perhaps most famous for his 1864 *Syllabus of Errors*—which condemned heresies like liberalism, modernism, socialism, Protestantism, and secret societies—Pius IX was responsible for pushing ultramontane reforms that would centralize the Vatican's power and unify doctrine and practice. Even though Dom Pedro II banned the *Syllabus*'s publication in Brazil, the country was not immune from the Vatican's reforms.[60]

New religious trends like spirit mediumship also threatened the church. Soon after Kate and Margaret Fox's highly publicized spirit communications in New York in 1848, droves of curious people tried their hands at communicating with the dead. For some, the séance was just an amusing parlor game, but for others it was a scientific means of investigating the spirit world. Séance practices quickly spread to France, where Allan Kardec (née Hippolyte Léon Denizard Rivail) "codified" them via five books that elaborated the core of what he termed "spiritist" belief and practice. Kardecist Spiritism, more than Anglophone Spiritualism, spread throughout Latin America, where its French provenance lent it a prestigious air.[61]

While initially slow to respond, the Catholic Church became increasingly concerned with mediumship and metaphysical religions and issued progressively strict prohibitions on Catholics' engagement with them. In 1856, eight years after the Fox sisters' first reports of spirit communications, the Holy Office decried the "abuses of magnetism," clairvoyance, necromancy, and "other analogous superstitions" as "heretical, scandalous, and contrary to the honesty of customs," which "condemned spiritualism without explicitly naming it," as the historian Guillaume Cuchet points out. In 1864—the same year that Pius IX issued the *Syllabus of Errors*—the Vatican put several of Kardec's works and his periodical, the *Revue Spirite*, on the Index of Prohibited Books, where it joined works on mesmerism, hypnotism, and Swedenborgianism. Thirty-four years later in 1898, the church officially banned spirit communications, arguing that even communications made in good faith were not with the dead but with evil spirits.[62] Finally, in 1917, the church banned Catholics' attendance at any mediumship session, even as spectators.[63]

In Brazil, the bishops' concerns with mediumship religions dovetailed with the broader process of ultramontane reform. At the time, the emperor Dom Pedro II was still exercising his right to appoint bishops and priests under Royal Patronage, which the church vehemently resisted. Seven of Brazil's eleven bishops attended the First Vatican Council (1869–70) and returned to Brazil with an ultramontanist agenda, hoping to free the church of all state control. The church in Brazil quickly expanded the number of dioceses from twelve in 1891 to fifty-eight by 1920. At a local level, clergy exercised increasing control over the lay brotherhoods, which had long enjoyed relative autonomy. Charters drafted during this period, which (as always) were subject to ecclesiastical approval, typically required parish priests to attend brotherhoods' meetings and sometimes even be appointed to leadership posts.[64]

Spiritist séances arrived in Brazil as early as 1853, five years after the Fox sisters' first spirit communications. In 1865, Luís Olímpio Teles de Menezes founded the country's first Kardecist Spiritist center, the Grupo Familiar do Espiritismo, in Salvador da Bahia.[65] Two years later, the archbishop of Bahia issued a pastoral letter condemning the "pernicious errors of spiritism." Observant lay Catholics also vigorously condemned the doctrine. In an 1868 article in the Rio de Janeiro edition of *O Apostolo*, an ultramontane Catholic weekly, the author laments that in Salvador, a pious stronghold, the "false doctrine of spiritism . . . [the] science of Satan" had taken hold.[66]

Catholic denunciations of "spiritism"—which was a catchall term for a variety of spirit mediumship traditions and not just Kardecism—became more frequent and forceful near the end of the century, though they were still slow coming. The church seemed more preoccupied with modernism and freemasonry than potential religious competitors. Still, greater ecclesiastical organization following the establishment of the First Republic resulted in more coordinated condemnations of spiritism. In 1890, Brazilian bishops began regular meetings to coordinate church administration, after which they published their findings in pastoral letters (*pastorais coletivas*).[67] In the *Pastoral Coletiva* of 1904, the episcopacy issued its first collective statement condemning spiritism, mandating that "all Catholics abstain from the superstition and evils of spiritism" and that "in all seminaries is developed, in theology or apologetics, teaching against spiritism and other errors." This language was reproduced in later pastoral letters, including the influential *Pastoral Coletiva* of 1915.[68]

The *Pastoral Coletiva* of 1915 condemned spiritism as "one of the most pernicious, if not the most pernicious of all," threats to the faith. This document functioned as the Brazilian church's legal code and a "veritable reference manual for parish clergy" for the next quarter century and thus set the tone of Catholic orthodoxy in Brazil.[69] "Arm yourselves, priests, against this fatal enemy, guard your flock, so that they are not caught in the devil's web, those who pontificate on spiritism," it read. The letter forbade Catholics from attending spiritist centers and prohibited spiritist literature, for "*Spiritism* is the collection of all the superstitions and gimmicks of modern unbelief, that, denying the eternal punishment of hell, the Catholic priesthood, and the rights of the church, destroy all Christianity."[70]

As it condemned spiritism, the episcopacy also recommended the devotion to souls as a way of strengthening the faith. "We encourage all parish priests interested in the conservation and augmentation of Religion in their parishes to introduce and foment the devotion in suffrage to the souls of purgatory," read the letter. It promoted November as the "month of the souls" and encouraged clergy to inspire the faithful to commune with the souls "not only in November, but also other times over the course of the year, and remember frequently the souls of the faithful departed in their prayers."[71]

Guillame Cuchet argues that "the revival of purgatory formed the positive side of this anti-spiritualist policy." Treatises on purgatory published in France and Rome after 1855 announce the "dangers of spiritualism and contrast it with the 'healthy doctrine of purgatory.'" Similarly, the English *Catholic Times* suggested that praying for the purgatorial dead was a sort of "spiritualism sanctioned by the Church."[72] Brazil was no exception, and the *Pastoral Coletiva* of 1915 instructed priests to direct people away from spiritism and toward "a special prayer to St. Michael"—long associated with purgatorial devotionalism in Brazil, as the angel who swiftly ushers souls from purgatory to heaven—"to permit them to speak with a spirit of a specific person."[73]

Catholics' concern with the mediumship religions persisted well into the mid-twentieth century, and clergy and lay elite continued to promote the cult of the souls as a way of combating it. For instance, in the 1930s, a period of Catholic revitalization following Getúlio Vargas's rise to power, the lay Association for the Souls in Purgatory was formed in São Paulo, with the following objectives:

1. To help and console the souls in Purgatory.
2. To ensure help and consolation for members of the Association after their death if they are captive in Purgatory.
3. To work for the veneration of souls, to combat spiritism and to contribute to the splendor of the holy Church.[74]

Though the Association for the Souls was a lay organization, it may have reflected an institutional preoccupation rather than popular concern. Unfortunately, the only documentary evidence on the association that I know of is a three-page list of statutes. We have no sense of how long it lasted or how vibrant it was. The statutes show, however, that it was strictly controlled, even by the standards of the time. The parish priest was the only person eligible to serve as its director. He had to be present at all meetings, was the only one capable of admitting new members, and could dismiss members at will.

At the first National Conference of Bishops of Brazil (CNBB) in 1953, spiritism was a major agenda item, alongside issues of land reform and Catholic Action. During the conference, the episcopacy initiated a national campaign against the "spiritist heresy" and declared that "spiritism is, at the moment, the most dangerous doctrinal deviation for the natural religiosity of the Brazilian people. The bishops also decreed that spiritist propaganda had left Catholics under the "highly erroneous impression that it is possible to continue to be Catholic and adhere to spiritism." They likewise founded the Anti-Spiritist Division of the National Secretary for the Defense of Faith and Morals. Boaventura Kloppenburg, Bishop of Novo Hamburgo (a city in the southern state of Rio Grande do Sul), was appointed its head. Kloppenburg led the vocal charge against the mediumship religions for decades, publishing a series of books and pamphlets like *Why the Church Condemns Spiritism*, *The Black Book of Spiritism*, and *What Is Spiritism? Orientation for Catholics*.[75]

Kloppenburg not only saw suffrages as the appropriate means of engaging the dead but also prescribed the devotion to souls in purgatory as one of several means of combating the influence of mediumship religions. In a pastoral guidebook that republished the recommendations of the 1953 CNBB, Desidério Kalverkamp and Boaventura Kloppenburg recommended that priests work to "increase devotion to the Holy Spirit, to the Good Lord Jesus, to Our Lady, to the angels *and to the souls of Purgatory, as an antidote to the florescence of spiritist superstitions*." The authors argued these "very Catholic devotions and already very popular in Brazil" would displace spiritist practice and help ferret out closet spiritists by revealing who negated purgatory.[76]

A Living Devotion

The devotion to souls was an ineffective antidote to the spiritist poison. Writing in 1955, the Jesuit scholar Thales de Azevedo commented, "Throughout the country, no small number of people think their profession of adhesion to Catholicism reconcilable with the spiritist beliefs of Alan Kardec, which have become extraordinarily widespread."[77] Mediumship religions only became more popular after the disestablishment of the church under the First Republic in 1889 and as the twentieth century progressed. Kardecists faced some resistance from the medical establishment, who took umbrage with Kardecists' embrace of scientific discourse and healing practices.[78] And the state, at times, suppressed Afro-Brazilian religions, of which mediumship was a prominent feature. But neither Kardecism nor the Afro-Brazilian traditions faded with time. The devotion to souls, it seems, was no better at wiping out spiritism than the devotion to saints was in putting an end to *orixá* devotion.

The cult of the souls may not have been effective in combatting spiritism, but it remained integral to Brazilian Catholicism. Old churches were expanded and new ones built to accommodate it. The original Church of the Holy Cross of the Souls of the Hanged, for instance, was demolished and rebuilt at larger scale in 1929 to accommodate the throngs of faithful. Writing four decades later, curious journalists noted that on Mondays, the church's candle room was often too crowded to enter. Later, in 1955, the Missionaries of the Sacred Heart consecrated the large Sanctuary of the Souls in the Ponte Pequena to accommodate the "grand devotion to the souls in purgatory" in the parish. A large structure ever since its inception, the sanctuary was expanded in the 1980s with a new Chapel of the Resurrection, a massive candle room that can accommodate hundreds of devotees at once.[79]

Today, the devotion lives on outside of Catholic lay brotherhoods. While some brotherhoods, like the Brotherhood of the Holy Cross of the Souls of the Hanged, still pray to the dead on Mondays, they are not the prominent social institutions they once were. And neither the brotherhoods nor purgatory are central to the devotion. The *cruz das almas* is a common feature in Umbanda *terreiros,* where the souls—who are commonly associated with the *pretos velhos* and memory of slavery—remain integral. Both there and in Catholic spaces, prayer to the souls tends to be private and paraliturgical, and devotees' practice and their understanding of it can be idiosyncratic and heterodox.[80] But even those that reject purgatory have inherited elements of its devotional culture. While the cult of the souls has changed, its style of spiritual reciprocity is not so different—and cannot be understood apart— from the purgatorial devotionalism of prerepublic Brazil. As with back then, contemporary devotees pray to the dead on Mondays, hoping to ease the souls' suffering and, in so doing, alleviate their own. And in São Paulo, that means going to devotional sites like the Church of the Holy Cross of the Souls of the Hanged: places remembered for trauma, death, and the suffering wrought by slavery and modernization.

CHAPTER TWO

The Souls of São Paulo

After a Monday evening mass at the Church of the Holy Cross of the Souls of the Hanged in Liberdade, I was chatting with Nilton, a white man in his early sixties, about the church's past. Nilton was an influential member of the church's lay brotherhood, and a few people had suggested I ask him about the history of the place. As we stood in the nave beside a dark wood confessional, I told Nilton that I had visited the archdiocesan archives but couldn't find much. The archivist said it was because the Church of the Hanged isn't a parish church, I told Nilton. "Ha!" he said, seeming skeptical. "Most churches here were built in town squares and don't have any special history. But this church has a *history*, understand?" he told me, gesturing downward with both hands for emphasis. He suggested "the priests" suppressed this history because of the church's association with miracles, Black people, and popular religion. "They didn't want Chaguinhas to become a martyr," he said.[1]

Devotees know the Church of the Hanged as a site of death. It is named in commemoration of those whose lives were taken at a nearby gallows where, devotees told me, "enslaved Black people were hanged."[2] Of all the gallows' victims, Chaguinhas (Francisco José das Chagas) is the most well-known. A soldier stationed in Santos and a beloved native of São Paulo, Chaguinhas was sentenced to death in 1821 for inciting rebellion among his fellow native-born soldiers over poor working conditions, unpaid wages, and unfair treatment from their Portuguese superiors. Most of the rebel soldiers were jailed, executed in Santos, or exiled to Africa, but Chaguinhas and his coconspirator José Joaquim Cotindiba were brought to São Paulo for public execution. Cotindiba's hanging was routine. But according to popular lore, when Chaguinhas was hanged on September 20, 1821, the rope broke. The sympathetic crowd cheered, declaring it a miracle and begging Chaguinhas be pardoned. The authorities, callous to the crowd's cries, refused to commute his sentence. On the second attempt, the rope broke again. The crowd pleaded for his release, screaming, "*Liberdade!*" and "He's innocent!" Some accounts hold that he was finally hanged on the third attempt, when the executioner swapped the fiber rope for one of leather. Others say it took four tries to end Chaguinhas's life or that the executioner had to bludgeon him to death.[3]

After Chaguinhas's execution, two laymen, Olegário Pedro Gonçalves and Chico Gago, erected a simple wooden cross near the hill on which the gallows stood to commemorate Chaguinhas and the gallows' victims.[4] It became known as the Holy Cross of the Hanged. At its side, according to an early twentieth-century historian, was a "rustic table on which wax candles were burned every night, that, according to tradition, were neither extinguished by wind nor rain." After a few decades, the "pious souls that come there to celebrate religious services" built a small structure to house offerings of candles and flowers. Even after the gallows' hill was razed and the neighborhood was developed, the devotion continued, and in 1891, the diocese dedicated a chapel to accommodate the devotion. The chapel was named Church of the Holy Cross of the Souls of the Hanged. Soon, "this simple temple attracted an incalculable multitude of faithful, [who were] captive to a caring, popular veneration, burning votive candles, and celebrating annual festivals." Expanded four years later and then again in the 1920s (at which point people began referring to it as a "church") the Church of the Hanged remains one of the city's most popular sites for the devotion to souls.[5]

Like the Church of the Hanged, other popular São Paulo sites for the devotion to souls are said to be haunted. The nearby Chapel of the Afflicted was once part of the Cemetery of Our Lady of the Afflicted, which many devotees remember as the "cemetery of the enslaved" and the resting place of Chaguinhas. Residents of Liberdade report hearing screams coming from both churches late at night. Ghost hunters post YouTube videos of their visits to the Chapel of the Afflicted, where they measure the dead's movements with EMF meters and frequency scanners. For devotees and ghost hunters alike, these vestiges of a bygone era are privileged conduits between the present and past, between this world and the next.

Last chapter, I argued that suffering drives the devotion to souls. Here I consider how it draws the living and the dead together at sites of social violence. As the epicenter of Brazilian modernity, São Paulo has a reputation as an enemy of memory. Scholars have observed that during the city's mid-century boom, the relentless pursuit of progress meant "the demolition of anything that was old."[6] But urban erasure was not indiscriminate. Between mass European immigration, large-scale sanitation projects, and the automobilization of São Paulo, the city's business magnates, politicians, urban planners, and sanitation experts modernized São Paulo, transforming it into the standard-bearer of Brazilian industry and progress. Focusing on the Church of the Hanged and the Chapel of the Afflicted, this chapter traces the

FIGURE 2.1 The Chapel of Our Lady of the Afflicted, September 2018. Photograph by author.

outlines of São Paulo's spectral topography, suggesting how modernization continues to haunt the city.

The Chapel of the Afflicted

The Chapel of the Afflicted looks out of place. Hidden away at the end of a short, dead-end alley, the chapel's weathered gray facade contrasts with the neighborhood's "Japanese"-style lanterns and ornamentation (fig. 2.1). It was consecrated in 1779 as part of the Cemetery of Our Lady of the Afflicted, the first public cemetery in São Paulo and one of the first in Brazil.[7] Church burials were the norm at the time, and the cemetery was reserved for "slaves, victims of capital punishment, and the indigent."[8] Located near the Field of the Gallows (Campo da Forca) on the city's southern periphery, it was an early potter's field—a "cemetery of disappearance" where "the victims of lynching, hanging, and racialized violence [were] put in their place."[9] (See fig. 2.4). When the diocese parceled and sold the cemetery grounds in 1886, the Chapel of the Afflicted was the only structure that remained.[10]

Inside, the old, small chapel is a break from São Paulo's modern immensity. When I visited, short wooden pews cramped the nave, and crumbling, soot-stained iconostases lined its walls. Little had changed since the 1990s, when a fire destroyed the old altar. Its hastily installed replacement was mostly bare wood save for a few patches of white paint, as if a worker walked off the job one afternoon, never to return. The chapel's plaster walls were crumbling, and the hanging light fixtures were bent and fitted with antiseptic white compact fluorescent bulbs. Exposed wiring ran across gray ceiling planks that were stained brown with sap. But despite the chapel's sorry state, or perhaps because of it, devotees described it as "serene," "tranquil," and "full of good energy." Unlike the Church of the Hanged, which sits along the busy Liberdade Avenue, the Chapel of the Afflicted was relatively quiet. Mass punctuated the silence just once or twice weekly, usually on Mondays. For most of 2014, a devotional group visited on Monday afternoons to recite the Mil Misericordias (Thousand Mercies) chaplet, their continual call-and-response, "For the sake of his sorrowful passion / Have mercy on us and the whole world," sacralizing the chapel's soundscape.

On Mondays, devotees would walk in, sometimes chatting with Renata, one of the chapel's administrators, as they bought candles for the souls. Some prayed before Our Lady of the Afflicted or the images of saints throughout the nave. Even more prayed to the souls or to Chaguinhas. Some say Chaguinhas was imprisoned in the chapel the night before his execution, just like the others condemned to death at the gallows. To pray, visitors would typically light a candle for him in the chapel's candle room before returning to the nave to knock three times on a large wooden door, symbolizing how he met his end. Those who petitioned him wrote their requests on small pieces of paper—usually mass intention forms—which they folded and jammed into the door's crevices. Those who thanked him sometimes left flowers, wax body parts, or small metal plaques as *ex-votos* for favors received (fig. 2.2).

"I came to this church because a friend told me about it," Carla told me. "He's a person who works in a *terreiro*. He's from Candomblé. One day . . . he took me and said, 'Go there to the church of the souls and light candles for your ancestors.'" It was a hot day in mid-December, and Carla, a Black

The Souls of São Paulo 47

FIGURE 2.2 The Door of Chaguinhas, July 2023. Photograph by author.

woman in her fifties, was visiting the Chapel of the Afflicted to teach her young nephew how to pray to the dead. She explained that she first learned the devotion from her parents, who were longtime devotees. But she only began regularly praying to the souls during a time of crisis. "At the time, I was really sick, and I was having trouble with work," she said. "So, I managed to come every Monday. I came, I prayed to the souls, and I received a very big favor, which was my job."[11]

As she visited, Carla learned more about Chaguinhas and the chapel's history. "There's a whole history here in São Paulo, *here*," she said. As we spoke, her nephew sat beside her, quietly listening. "I was just telling him, up by Liberdade Square was the home of the gallows, the place where the slaves were hanged. And below, a big cemetery. There are all these bones down there, but as no one is interested in rescuing this history, no one mentions it. You put another ethnic group here, the Japanese, and it's *tudo certinho, tudo resolvido* [all proper, all resolved], as if the neighborhood never had Africans and Black people, despite that they were here for almost three hundred years," she said.

Carla had a point. Most Paulistanos know Liberdade as the "Japanese neighborhood," famous for its weekend street fair, where vendors sell

FIGURE 2.3 View down Rua Galvão Bueno, Liberdade, São Paulo, September 2018. Note the torii in the distance, as well as banners reading Boas Festas (Happy Holidays) and announcing 2018 as the Year of the Dog. The banners were sponsored by Bradesco, a national bank, along with the Associação Cultural e Assistencial da Liberdade (ACAL) and the Associação Cultural Nipo Brasileira de Registro (ACNBR, also known as Bunkyo), two groups that promote Japanese culture though large public events (sometimes featuring Japanese diplomats or members of the royal family) in Liberdade. Photograph by author.

tempura and huge dumplings the size of a child's fist. The neighborhood's distinct aesthetic is the result of a "Plan of Orientalization," first proposed by the journalist Randolfo Marques de Lobato in 1969. Implemented by the municipal government in the early 1970s, the plan sought to transform Liberdade into a tourist destination, "recuperating" it from "the degradation that has reached the center of São Paulo," as *Jornal Nippak* put it in a 2014 article.[12] Taking a cue from the Chinatowns of New York and San Francisco, the city installed stylized street lamps meant to look like paper lanterns (see figs. 2.1 and 2.3) and a large *torii* (a gate traditionally found at the entrance to Shinto shrines) over Rua Galvão Bueno, the neighborhood's main commercial street (fig. 2.3). It also replaced the neighborhood's plain sidewalks with tiles featuring *mitsudomoe*, an abstract shape of three commas in a whorl, and paid proprietors to update building facades in an "Oriental"

The Souls of São Paulo 49

style featuring a predominance of red.[13] Soon, Liberdade became a symbol of Japanese identity throughout the country.[14]

As the historian Ana Paulina Lee notes, Liberdade's overwhelming Japanese identity obscures its other histories. In addition to the neighborhood's Black historical presence, it veils the substantial Chinese, Vietnamese, Korean, and Taiwanese populations that live and work in Liberdade, as well as continued political tensions among *nikkei* (Japanese immigrants and their descendants) around the question of Okinawan identity.[15] To some extent, Liberdade's aesthetic identity reflects the numbers: today, the city of São Paulo is home to the world's largest Japanese diaspora. Japanese residents began settling on Rua Conde de Sarezas, a street on the northern edge of Liberdade, as early as 1912, and newspapers began referring to Liberdade as a "Japanese neighborhood" in the 1960s.[16] But Liberdade was not a primary destination for early Japanese immigrants, most of whom came to work on coffee plantations throughout the state. The neighborhood's Japanese identity only began to take hold nearly a half century after the start of Japanese immigration, following a series of demolitions that furthered the displacement of the neighborhood's Black residents in the 1940s and the opening of Ciné Niteroi, a Japanese-language cinema, on Rua Galvão Bueno in 1953.[17]

In the early twentieth century, Liberdade and adjacent neighborhoods like Bixiga and Bela Vista "had some of the city's highest concentrations of African descendants and bore deep ties to enslavement, abolition, and antiracist organizing."[18] Though not predominantly Black—around the time of abolition, no neighborhood in São Paulo was—the region on the southern fringe of downtown was home to influential *escolas de samba* (samba schools, or groups) like Paulistano da Glória and Escola de Samba Lavapés (in Liberdade) and Vai-Vai (in Bela Vista), as well as several Black social clubs, which in turn gave rise to the city's Black press and political vanguard (see map 2.1).[19] Modeled on the lay Catholic brotherhoods that were then in decline, these clubs "provided the financial support and social networks necessary for upward mobility." They also established what the historian Kim Butler calls the "social press," or newspapers focusing on local information and gossip and serving as a literary forum for Black writers. By the 1920s, these papers became venues for social criticism, political philosophy, and articulations of Black identity. Near the end of the decade, the newspaper *Progresso* was the first to embrace *negro* as a term of self-identity for all Black Brazilians, rejecting not only *preto* (then considered more polite) but also "the traditional distinction between blacks and mulattos."[20]

By the middle of the 1920s, social clubs' political tone sharpened. In 1926, the Palmares Civic Center (Centro Cívico Palmares, named after the famous *quilombo*, or maroon community, that lasted nearly a century in the Brazilian northeast) in Liberdade was the first to bring together social services and political action, such as a campaign against racial discrimination in the state police force. A few years later, in 1931, Arlindo Veiga dos Santos, a former participant in Palmares, founded the Brazilian Black Front (Frente Negra Brasileira), Brazil's first Black political party and national organization. Also located in Liberdade, it was an expansive institution and the one that would promote the use of *negro* most aggressively. In addition to its political organizing and publishing, the Black Front held social and recreational events, provided social services including medical care and a credit union, and ran businesses such as a beauty salon, barbershop, and dressmaker. Though it was relatively short-lived—the organization was forced to close when President Getúlio Vargas dissolved all political parties in 1937—the Frente Negra is recognized as a foundational Black political organization throughout Brazil.[21]

If Carla worried that Liberdade's Japanese identity made it seem "as if the neighborhood never had Africans and Black people," it was because none of this history was easily visible in Liberdade. While a large tower in Liberdade Square reminded visitors of Radio Taissô, a Japanese radio calisthenics program, nothing marked the former headquarters of the Brazilian Black Front, the Palmares Civic Center, or any of the other social clubs and samba groups that were once so prolific in the area. Neither was there anything to explicitly indicate that the square had been home to the gallows or that much of what is now central Liberdade had been a cemetery. That would begin to change four years later, due partly to an activist movement that Carla helped build. But in 2014, the Chapel of the Afflicted and Church of the Hanged were the only material reminders of Liberdade's Black history.

As far as I can tell, nothing in the historical record directly indicates that Liberdade's "Orientalization" was an explicit project of historical erasure. But it did not need to be. Since the late nineteenth century, urban reform was key to modernizing São Paulo. And as the historian Barbara Weinstein argues, the "color of modernity" was decidedly white.[22] Through state and national social policy, whitening ideology (*branqueamento*) justified for subsidizing the mass European (and later, Japanese) immigration that reshaped the country's racial demographics. It also informed urban "improvements" aimed at eradicating Blackness from the urban landscape. And even

The Souls of São Paulo 51

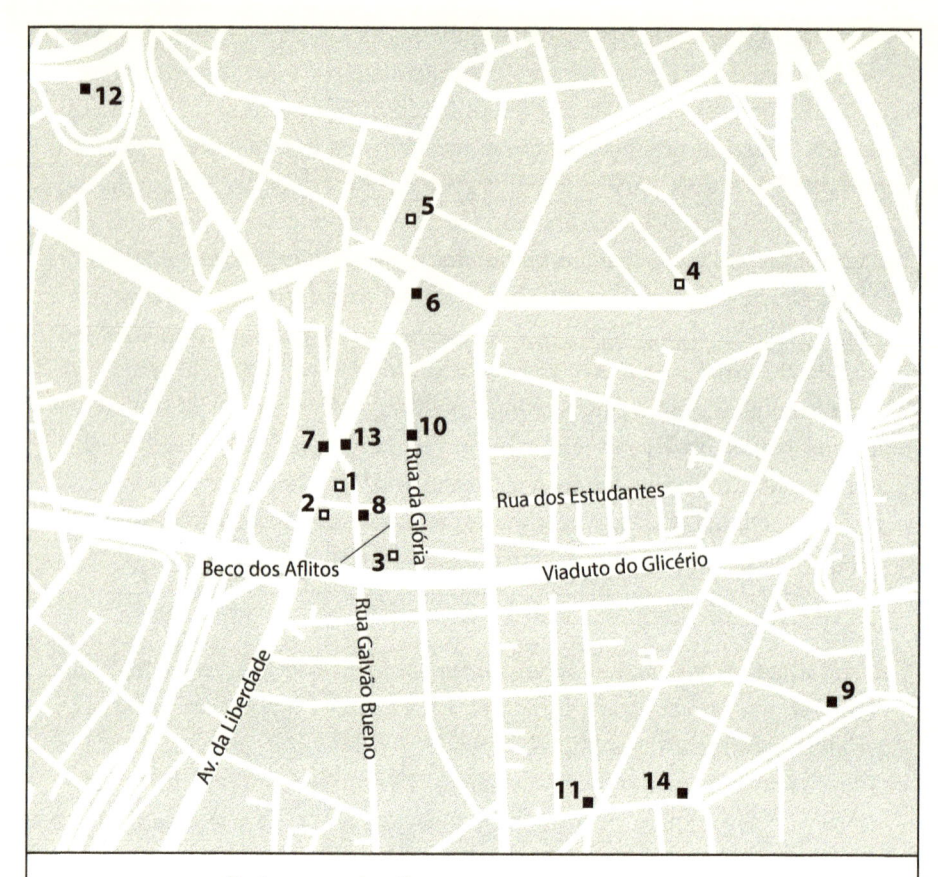

□ **Contemporary locations**
1. Liberdade Square (Renamed Praça da Liberdade-Japão in 2018, and Praça da Liberdade Àfrica-Japão in 2023)
2. The Church of the Holy Cross of the Souls of the Hanged
3. The Chapel of Our Lady of the Afflicted
4. Sé Cathedral
5. The Church of Our Lady of the Good Death

■ **Black historical sites (locations are approximate)**
6. The Church of Our Lady of the Remedies
7. The Brazilian Black Front (Frente Negra Brasileira)
8. Paulistano da Glória Samba School
9. Lavapés Samba School
10. Home of Madrinha Eunice (Founder of Lavapés Samba School)
11. Home of Antonio Bento (Abolitionist)
12. Palmares Civic Center (Centro Civico Palmares)
13. *Elite* (Newspaper of the social club Elite of Liberdade, 1924 location)
14. *Progresso* (Newspaper)

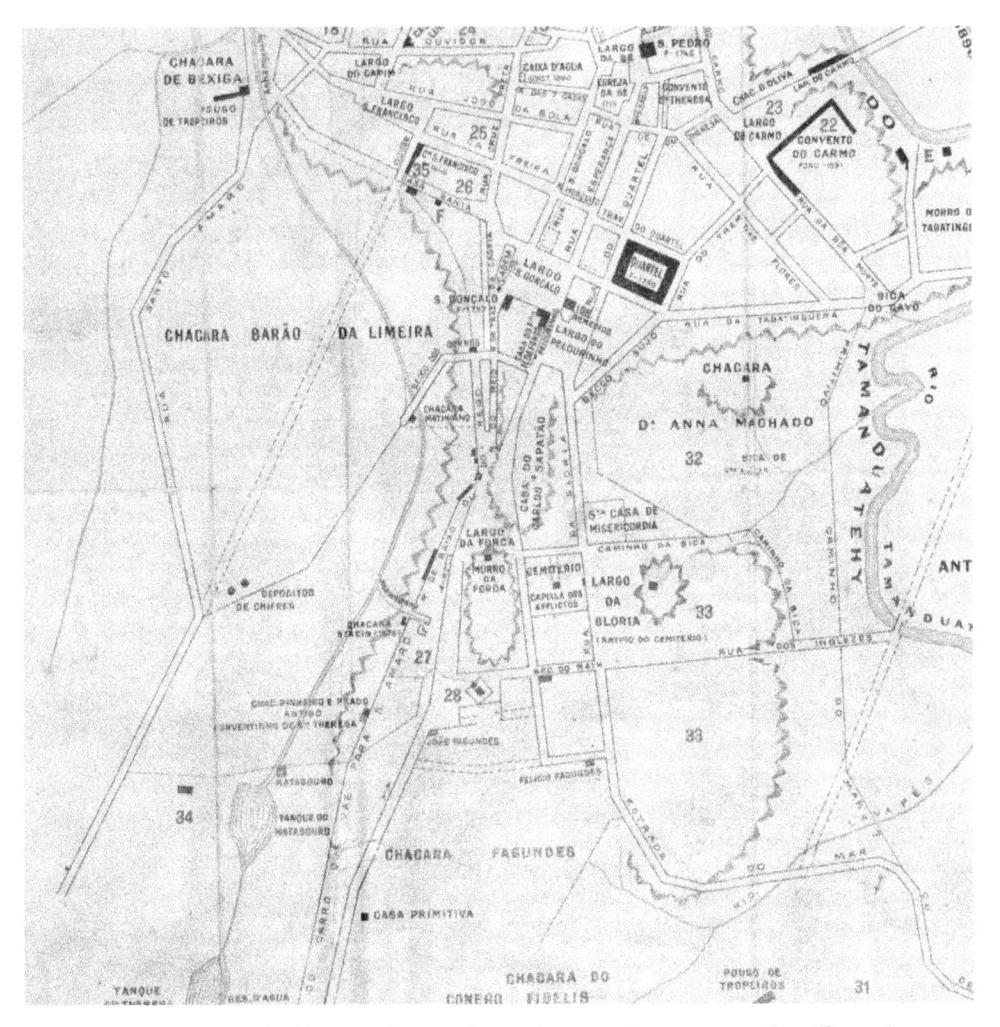

FIGURE 2.4 Detail of historical map of central São Paulo, 1800–1874, by Affonso de Freitas. Courtesy Museo Paulista, via Wikimedia Commons.

MAP 2.1 (*facing page*) Map of contemporary Liberdade with historical markers. Note that all markers for historical sites are approximate and are culled from a combination of primary and secondary sources. Some of those sources are in disagreement. For instance, contemporary sources commonly claim that the headquarters of the Black Brazilian Front is at the current site of Casa da Portugal (Av. da Liberdade, 602). However, the geolocation tool Pauliceia 2.0 (https://pauliceia.unifesp.br/portal/home) places what we know to be the organization's old address (Rua da Liberdade, 196) across from the northwestern edge of Liberdade Square. Here I favor that address, which seems more likely both based on historical maps and its proximity to the house of the abolitionist Antonio Bento and other Black social sites. For approximate locations of the other Black historical sites above, as well as many others, see Araujo, "A escola de samba"; Ferreira and Silva, "Mapas e Memórias"; Silva, "Territórios negros em trânsito"; Museu da Cidade de São Paulo, "Memórias Soterradas." Map created by author.

after blatant scientific racism fell out of favor, this racialized understanding of modernization crystallized assumptions about race, free labor, and modernization that would shape the trajectory of São Paulo's urban development and governance over the course of the twentieth century.

The Race for Progress

When the diocese parceled off the Cemetery of the Afflicted in 1886, São Paulo was in the midst of profound transformation. A decade earlier, the provincial administration of João Teodoro (1872–75) presided over what historians call the city's "second founding." In hopes of attracting wealthy planters to reside in the capital, his administration canalized rivers, demolished colonial landmarks, and built European-style parks and boulevards. The plan worked, and São Paulo became the financial hub of the coffee boom.[23] In 1872, São Paulo was the seventh-largest city in Brazil, with 31,385 inhabitants. By 1900, domestic migration and mass European immigration swelled that number more than sevenfold to 239,820.[24] Today, São Paulo boasts over 12 million inhabitants, making it Latin America's largest urban economy and the most populous city in the Americas.

For the region's elites—politicians, leading businessmen, and "prominent liberal professionals and men of letters"—European immigration promised a solution to two problems: a labor shortage and a population deemed excessively Black.[25] Planters began petitioning the provincial government to subsidize European immigration ever since 1850, when Britain's enforcement of its ban on the transatlantic slave trade drove up their labor costs. Most were convinced that Black people were constitutionally unsuited for free labor, and free Afro-Brazilians were understandably reluctant to work on plantations. So were potential immigrants. While a few thousand immigrants arrived through the 1870s, it was not until the mass flights of enslaved people from plantations in 1887, abolition in 1888 (Brazil was the last country in the Americas to abolish slavery), and the founding of the New Republic in 1889 that the trickle of immigrants turned into a flood. By 1914, over 1.6 million western European immigrants settled in São Paulo State alone, over 60 percent of whom had their voyages fully paid for by the state government.[26]

Elites hoped that European immigrants would whiten the population through a process of "constructive miscegenation." Influenced by scientific racism and Comtean positivism, elites saw the development of a coherent Brazilian race (*raça Brasileira*) as key to the success of the New Republic and the country's large Black population as a threat to its development. At the same time, they were reluctant to embrace North American–style white supremacy, in part because so many were mixed race themselves. Instead of promoting racial purity, prominent scientists and intellectuals tended toward a French strain of neo-Lamarckian heritability, which affirmed that acquired traits could be passed down through reproduction. While they believed that "superior" white genes would inevitably overcome "degenerate" Black ones, they hoped European immigration would hasten the process, with the new arrivals acting as "civilizing agent[s]" that would "improve the race."[27]

Immigration reshaped São Paulo. By 1893, foreign-born residents made up over half of the city's population.[28] By 1907, Italians alone outnumbered native-born Brazilians by two to one.[29] Managers preferred to hire immigrants for well-paying jobs in manufacturing and construction even though most of those immigrants arrived without any industrial experience. Shut out from industry, Afro-Brazilians were largely confined to domestic work, informal labor, and service jobs in the transportation and energy sectors.[30] Employment patterns shaped residential ones, as immigrants moved to new, "sanitary" workers' villages near manufacturing centers. Black Brazilians, on the other hand, settled in *cortiços* and *porões* (tenement-like dwellings and storage holds), in neighborhoods like Barra Funda to the northwest of the city center and Bixiga and Liberdade on its southern edge.[31] And while the city's Afro-Brazilian population grew in absolute numbers, it declined in relative ones, shrinking from about 16.5 percent of the total population in 1890 to just 8 percent in 1940.[32]

Japanese immigrants fit into elites' expanded understanding of whiteness. At first, most immigrants arrived from just four countries: Italy, Portugal, Spain, and Germany. But Paulista planters quickly soured on the new arrivals—especially Italians, who gained a reputation as lazy labor activists.[33] As Jeffrey Lesser explains, around the same time, Japan's Meiji government was exploring emigration as a way of dealing with food shortages and a restless rural population. Billing their subjects as the "whites" of Asia, Japanese diplomats promised their subjects were "everything Europeans were not: quiet, hard-working, and eager to become Brazilian." Supporters of Japanese immigration argued introduction of Japanese "blood" would "have a better result with our national population than [the introduction of] black blood or of any other nonwhite."[34] With heavy subsidies from the Brazilian and Japanese governments, about 189,000 Japanese immigrants settled in Brazil between 1908 and 1940, almost all in the state of São Paulo.[35]

If immigration was one way of whitening São Paulo, urban reform was another. In 1886, an expanded Code of Postures (Codigo de Posturas) aimed to push commercial and social activity off the streets, transforming them into spaces of "exclusive circulation." The legislation restricted *quitandeiras* (street produce vendors, who were then predominantly Black women) for "interfering with traffic" and prohibited open-air markets in the city center (which were frequented by Black residents) on the grounds that they were an "affront to culture."[36] It also outlawed the practice of *curanderismo* (healing) and "those who pretend to be inspired by some supernatural entity and predict future happenings that can cause serious apprehension in the spirit of the credulous" with a fine and eight to ten days in prison.[37] Soon after, the passage of the state Sanitary Code (1890) and creation of the Sanitary Service (1894) empowered state agents to visit *cortiços* and *porões* to look for the sick and compile statistics. Elites saw the dense, communal living arrangement of *cortiços* as vectors for disease, crime, poverty, and vice, all of which were associated with nonwhite groups. To shield themselves, they retreated into new, "sanitary" neighborhoods with names like Higienópolis (lit., "hygiene city").[38]

Brazilian governance in the early twentieth century was marked by a zeal for "sanitation-eugenics."[39] Buoyed by the remarkable success of campaigns against smallpox, yellow fever, and the bubonic plague in Rio de Janeiro between 1903 and 1909, Brazil's ascendant and "naively optimistic" medical class turned its attention toward combatting "degeneration" (from the Latin *degeneratus*, meaning "away from the race or kind") in all its forms: poverty, crime, prostitution, and even women's work.[40] As with immigration, neo-Lamarckian genetics provided a scientific justification for urban intervention; if acquired traits could be inherited, then engineering a salubrious environment was key to improving the race and national progress.[41]

Politicians were not shy about "making the link between race, progress, and urbanization," writes Lorraine Leu.[42] Washington Luís, who served as mayor of São Paulo before rising to president of the state and then of the Brazilian republic, described in 1916 the city's Carmo floodplain as a vast, disease-ridden blight that housed "slime of the city, in disgusting promiscuity, composed of vagabond *negros*, of *negras* swollen by excessive drink, of vicious miscegenation, of unspeakable vestiges . . . all dangerous."[43] Canalizing the river and turning the area into a park would remedy these maladies, advancing "beauty, cleanliness, hygiene, morality, security, finally, civilization and São Paulo's spirit of initiative." A few years later, in a speech at the 1922 World's Fair, Brazilian president Epitácio Pessoa was even more explicit. Celebrating the razing of Morro do Castelo, a predominantly Afro-Brazilian neighborhood in Rio de Janeiro, he announced, "Our latest sanitation project, modeled after the most progressive examples, visibly facilitates the strengthening of the race and increases its productive capacity."[44] Like immigration, urban intervention was a critical tool in the modernization and "whitening" of urban Brazil.

As part of these interventions, São Paulo city officials also took aim at prominent Black "sites of memory"—the historian Pierre Nora's term for places that "anchor, condense, and express" collective memory and identity.[45] During São Paulo's "third founding," mayor Antônio Prado (1899–1911) enacted a series of sweeping reforms that included installing electricity infrastructure and streetcars, canalizing the Anhangabaú and other waterways, widening streets, and razing *cortiços*. The city also went after the Church of Our Lady of the Rosary of Black Men in the old city center. Built by a Black brotherhood in 1737, the church was a historic site of Black organizing and religious expression. It was also a long-standing target of the white elites, who were intrigued and appalled by the "torpidly lascivious swaying of hips" at *batuque* dances in front of the church. In 1872, the city expropriated a series of buildings adjacent to the church and, in 1893, removed a public fountain from the square against the protest of locals. Under Prado's reign, the city finally demolished the church in 1903 to make way for an expanded square, which is now home to the city's stock exchange.[46]

Beginning in the 1930s, urban-planner-turned-mayor Francisco Prestes Maia (in office 1938–45 and 1961–65) transformed the city yet again. In what the sociologist Teresa Caldeira calls "the most famous undertaking of the municipal government in the beginning of the century," Prestes Maia's 1930 Avenues Plan (Plano de Avenidas) laid the foundation for São Paulo's developmental trajectory for the next half century. Inspired by the Garden City movement and "decentrist" urbanism, the plan entailed building a series of wide radial avenues to encourage growth in new suburbs.[47] It de-densified the center through demolition and redevelopment, prompting real estate speculation and higher rents that priced out working classes. By the 1960s, the city's population density was cut in half, and its population was reorganized along a "center-periphery model," in which poor and disproportionately Black residents were pushed out to precarious neighborhoods (favelas) on the urban periphery.[48]

Like Antônio Prado before him, Prestes Maia targeted Black sites of memory. After being demolished in 1903, the Church of Our Lady of the Rosary of Black Men was rebuilt in Paissandu Square, where it was consecrated in 1906. As Andrew Britt details, Prestes Maia's original Avenues Plan called for demolishing the rebuilt church even though it was not near any of the avenues slated for expansion. In its place, he proposed building a monument to Duque de Caixas, a white nineteenth-century military general and politician.[49]

While the demolition of the Church of the Rosary never happened, during his first term as mayor, Prestes Maia set his sights on another Black church: the Church of Our Lady of the Remedies. Located on the northern edge of Liberdade, the Church of the Remedies was a historic center of abolitionist organizing and museum of slavery. Its demolition was not specified in the original Avenues Plan. But according to one of the mayor's contemporaries, Prestes Maia "wanted to demolish the Church of the Remedies . . . and arranged the grounds to do so."[50] In his revised plan, Prestes Maia called for a widened avenue and expanded square that would require the church's demolition, which he justified on the grounds that the church was "of debatable historical and artistic value."[51] His claim was a dubious one: as Britt shows, at the same time as Prestes Maia doubted the church's artistic value, he sought to acquire the famous Portuguese-style blue-and-white tiles from its facade.[52] Against widespread objections (including from major newspapers), the mayor went ahead with the Church of the Remedies' demolition in 1942–43. The demolition, Britt argues, "comprised part of a planned project of forgetting, animated, though perhaps not exclusively motivated, by anti-Black racism."[53] And in animating modernization, this "spatial project of forgetting" also enlivens the city's ghosts.

Modern Ghosts

"This church . . . I've heard it said that this church has a sad story, really very sad," Beatriz told me. We were at the Church of the Hanged, where Beatriz, a white neo-Pentecostal woman, had just ascended from the candle room. "Once there were lots of slaves in the country. Here, when slaves were old, they were no longer useful, no longer able to work on the farms of the rich men here, the coffee plantations, they sent them to be hanged here, in this place. So this, this hurts our hearts . . . because they were Black, understand?" Tears came to Beatriz's eyes, and she had trouble speaking. "Very heavy," she murmured. She took a few deep breaths and regained her composure. "And they say, people say, that passing here at certain times at night, one can still hear screams and sounds of terrible suffering. Because when they grew old, they were brought here and hanged. It's because of this that [the church] has this name . . . because there was a lot of suffering in this place."[54]

Ghosts are born of failure.[55] Haunting, writes Avery Gordon, "always registers the harm inflicted or the loss sustained by a social violence in the past or present."[56] It also signals an unwillingness or inability to reckon with that violence. By some counts, São Paulo has the largest Black population of any city outside of Africa, with over 4 million Afro-Brazilian residents.[57] And on the eve of abolition, São Paulo Province had some of the highest numbers of enslaved Africans anywhere in Brazil.[58] Despite this, "dominant popular and academic representations have long cast the city of São Paulo as a non-Black, immigrant metropolis whose growth had little to do with slavery."[59] Thanks to mayors like Antônio Prado and Prestes Maia, its built landscape reflects that racialized vision. In contrast to port cities like Salvador and Rio de Janeiro, where heritage sites like the Pelourinho and Cais do Volongo memorialize slavery and Black history (albeit in ways that sometimes obscure more than they reveal), São Paulo has done little to acknowledge its slaveholding past.[60]

In *How Modernity Forgets*, the anthropologist Paul Connerton argues that forgetting is a structural feature of capitalist modernity. "A major source of forgetting, I want to argue, is associated with processes that separate social life from locality and from human dimensions: superhuman speed, megacities that are so enormous as to be unmemorable, consumerism disconnected from the labour process, the short lifespan of urban architecture, the disappearance of walkable cities," he writes. The reification intrinsic to capitalist production has been universalized to the point of affecting the urban landscape. Destroyed and rebuilt according to the frenzied logic of the "temporality of consumption," the modern city has become like a commodity. Without a stable geography, the city's shifting sands leave nowhere for memory to dwell.[61]

But if modernity forgets, its amnesia is uneven. "Forgetting, like miscegenation, is an opportunistic tactic of whiteness," writes Joseph Roach.[62] The history of São Paulo's modern amnesia illustrates what scholars of the Black Atlantic have long argued: that modernity and whiteness were entangled from the start. As Michel-Rolph Trouillot put it, modernity requires "an alterity, a referent outside itself, a pre- or nonmodern in relation to which the modern takes its full meaning."[63] In the urban context, modernization has entailed eradicating perceived atavisms from the landscape. So it was that in 1905, Júlio Mesquita, the founder of the newspaper *O Estado de São Paulo*, could praise Mayor Antônio Prado for taking away the city's "traditional loincloth"—that is, erasing its Indigeneity—and transforming it into "a testament to civilization, [which] seduces and attracts intelligent foreigners."[64]

The problem for aspiring moderns is that the past can never be banished. As Bruno Latour writes, "The past remains . . . and even returns. Now this resurgence is incomprehensible to the moderns. Thus they treat it as the return of the repressed."[65] Though Latour was not talking about ghosts or haunting, he might as well have been. Freud famously described the uncanny—in German, the *unheimlich*, or "unhomely"—as "something that was long familiar to the psyche and was estranged from it only through being repressed."[66] Though similar to the feeling of fright or dread, the uncanny has a "specific affective nucleus" that distinguishes it from those terms. Like a word repeated until it loses all meaning, uncanny things suffer from an excess of familiarity, so much so that they become distant and strange.

At once strange and familiar, the Chapel of the Afflicted is an example of what Anthony Vidler calls the "architectural uncanny." Throughout the twentieth century, journalists periodically rediscovered the chapel, celebrating it as a rare oasis within São Paulo's desert of memory. But their praise was often elegiac, tempered with a sense of melancholy. "Sometimes it seems that São Paulo is nothing more than a city of the rigid lines of skyscrapers and people who rush through the streets in an immense frenzy: the city is an enemy of peace and tradition," began a 1943 article in the *Correio Paulistano*. "However, hidden like an oasis among the city, there are certain places that even the Paulistano seems to have forgotten. The church hidden at the end of the Alley of the Afflicted is one of them, giving us the impression of having been forgotten by time, resting in its sad fate, trying to 'unremember' [*deslembrar*] its wretched episodes."[67] Caught between memory and forgetting, between haunting and holiness, the chapel captured the anxiety over what Vidler calls the "fundamentally unlivable modern condition."[68]

WHAT IS THE GHOST? The scholarly literature tends to treat specters as signs—for the lingering presence of the past, for the social experience of the place, or even for the "limitations of many of our prevalent modes of inquiry."[69] When Jacques Derrida coined the term in his 1995 book *Specters of Marx*, the ghost offered a way of describing and diagnosing "the moments in which the present—and above all, the current present . . . of the postmodern end of history, the new world system of late capitalism—unexpectedly betrays us."[70] Since then, this theoretical bearing has generated a rich critical vocabulary for describing "that which acts without (physically) existing."[71] In particular, haunting has become a powerful way of describing how past structural violence echoes through the present, such as with slavery and its afterlives. It can also be a way of describing the anticipations that shape current behavior, like Marx and Engels's "spectre of communism" or the dystopian dread of sentient artificial intelligence.[72] In each case, time opens and collapses, and something once thought far off is now immanent. If spectral language works, it is because the ghost is both there and not, "really present" but empirically elusive.

But the ghost is also an object of experience. Some people see or otherwise sense ghosts. Even more talk about them, seek them out, or avoid them. People who work in Liberdade told me stories of chairs moving by themselves and ghosts rifling through stockrooms.[73] The Church of the Hanged and Chapel of the Afflicted are both regular stops on haunted tours of the city, and the latter features prominently in *Spectros*, a Netflix series about the revenant dead in Liberdade. Ghost hunters and spirit mediums say that the dead cling to Edifício Joelma and the tombs of the thirteen souls, anchored there by the weight of their suffering.[74] Other markers of modernity—the Municipal Theater, built under the Prado administration; Edifício Martinelli, the city's first skyscraper; Edifício Copan, the city's famous wave-shaped high-rise built by Oscar Niemeyer—are said to resonate with spectral presence.

We can do social theory without being squeamish about the supernatural. Social analysis and spectral phenomenology are hardly at odds. If anything, São Paulo's ghosts suggest one way that otherwise abstract social forces can impinge upon lived experience. Recent anthropological scholarship has detailed some of the ways in which São Paulo, like all Brazil, is figuratively haunted by slavery. For instance, in *The Anti-Black City*, Jaime Amparo Alves persuasively argues that São Paulo civil society is constituted through anti-Black policing and social policy.[75] Liberdade's ghosts tell us something about how this violence has shaped the affective and mnemonic topography of the city center. And taken along with the specters of places like Edifício Joelma, the Copan, and the Anhangabaú River, they suggest how slavery's afterlives are fettered to São Paulo's history of modernization.

While we tend to think of ghosts as malignant, "spectral presences can be enabling," writes Julia Obert. "They assert the body as an active interface with the city rather than mere flesh to be bluntly corralled by the dictates of urban planning."[76] In São Paulo, O Que te Assombra? (What Haunts You?) leads free antiracist walking tours through the city center. In a city dominated by car culture, a walking tour is itself a subversive act—especially in the *centro*, which has a widespread reputation as a bastion of crime and drug abuse. As Michel de Certeau has argued, walking in the city can be a way of reclaiming it, of resignifying spaces in ways that upend the meanings ascribed to them by power.[77]

The Souls of São Paulo 61

If ghost stories are one way of engaging the past, the devotion to souls is another. And through the mechanism of intercession, it affords the possibility of forging a relationship of mutual aid between the living and the dead. To be sure, souls, like ghosts, can be harmful. In contrast to saints, devotees are wary of lighting candles to souls at home. They also are careful not to leave *promessas* unfulfilled and to avoid falling into debt with the souls. But as we have already seen, the souls' suffering also enables them to help the living. And by drawing together the living and the dead, the practice affords the possibility of mnemonic repair. The dead sustain the living, and through their regular practice, the living sustain the memory of the dead.

EARLY IN MY FIELDWORK, I interviewed Emilia, a seventy-seven-year-old Black woman who was a member of the Brotherhood of the Church of the Hanged. She lived far away, in a city nearly two hours outside of São Paulo by bus. While in good health, Emilia walked with a cane, and the journey could not have been easy. She told me she had a cross for the souls in her yard, where she sometimes lit candles. When I asked why she came here, all the way to São Paulo, she matter-of-factly replied, "It's because here is where the slaves were hanged, right?"[78] A few weeks later, I asked a similar question of Claúdia, an older Black woman who had been petitioning the souls for help with her son. "I come to these two churches [in Liberdade] because for me, this place is strong, because here passed the hanged, the slaves, and everything. So, I'm really devoted, because back then, one of mine was also a slave," she said.[79]

In the 1960s, well after Liberdade's Black social clubs had dissolved, the devotion to souls remained a site of Black sociability. In an interview with the anthropologist Alexandre Kishimoto, Fernando Penteado, a journalist and sambista with Vai-Vai samba school, related how on Mondays, "three, four, five thousand people gathered" near the Municipal Theater before heading to the Church of the Hanged. It was a time for flirting and planning for the weekend, but also devotion. "There's a religiosity behind this. Lighting candles for the souls, asking for protection for the week," Penteado told Kishimoto. "It wasn't like: 'Oh, I'm just going for the sake of going, just flirting.' No. Even though people were flirting, they would still stop in the church. Some would even go down to Aflitos, where there is a chapel. Because for us, in the Black community, that place has a lot of meaning. That territory is very significant for us."[80] Similarly, Rosemeire Macondes, the niece of sambista Madrina Eunice, emphasized the churches as a site of ancestral presence. She said that every Monday, she accompanied her mother and grandmother on visits to the Chapel of the Afflicted and Church of the Hanged to "light candles for the holy blessed souls . . . for these ancestors that passed away." For them, "every Monday was sacred," she said. In "Rootedness: The Ancestor as Foundation," Toni Morrison reflects on the central presence of the ancestor in African American literature. "These ancestors are not just parents, they are sort of timeless people whose relationships to the characters are benevolent, instructive, and protective, and they provide a certain kind of wisdom," she writes. And if the ancestor is foundational, then the absence of the ancestor is frightening and destructive. "When you kill the ancestor, you kill yourself."[81] Neglecting the ancestor means neglecting the past, which in turn means neglecting community and one's commitment to bettering its future.

During our first conversation, with her nephew at her side, Carla explained the devotion to souls in relation to this ancestry:

> I was explaining to him [her nephew] that it was the slaves who built this church here in 1700, and right there is the little room of Chaguinhas, where people stayed before being hanged. They stayed there, imprisoned, they prayed, and before being hanged . . . they had this ritual of the souls. And so the question of my devotion comes to this: I have this habit of the cult of ancestors, of praying for the ancestors, because I believe when they are well, I'm well too . . . because you're a part of them. That's to say, I have, I must have a trace of my mother, of my grandfather, of my great grandfather . . . you always carry something. People don't die. If you have a child, the child will eternalize you by some trace. Skin, hair, something. The person doesn't die. There's a cycle of life that's continuous, and we don't take account of this continuous cycle of life [often enough]. So, the cult of the souls is exactly this.[82]

While Carla sometimes distinguished between the souls and ancestors — "My ancestors are one thing, and the souls another," she said at one point — she also collapsed this distinction. For her, praying for the ancestors was also a way of praying *with* them, of maintaining the tradition of those who came before. Through the devotion, Carla "carried something" from her ancestors into the present and passed it on into the future.

Of course, the memory of the gallows means different things to devotees. As far as I could tell, white devotees were less likely to invoke the memory of slavery at the Liberdade churches. Some denied its importance altogether. For example, at the Chapel of the Afflicted, a fifty-one-year-old white charismatic Catholic named João told me he lived far from Liberdade. I asked him if he visited because of the church's history. "No, no, no, no, no! I don't care about the history of the churches. Because when I came, I didn't know anything about the history. I didn't come knowing of the great respect for souls, for Chaguinhas, for the hanged, and so on. I came for me, myself. It's necessity, necessity," he said.

In contrast to João, other white devotees invoked the chapel's history but in a more generic sense. For them, the chapel evoked what J. Lorand Matory calls "modernist nostalgia"—that is, "the longing, in the midst of an urbanizing and industrializing society, for a bucolic past world of personalistic and emotional attachments."[83] It was a curious relic of the past, charged with good feeling. While I did not know it at the time, the tension between these different registers of memory would intensify four years later, when a movement emerged to save the Chapel of the Afflicted, whose structure was threatened by construction in an adjacent lot. Still, however these devotees might have related to the past, their very presence affirmed the chapel as a privileged place to pray to the dead. And in so doing, it helped mark the chapel as a site of memory.

WHEN DEVOTEES LIKE Carla comment on memory—or its concealment—they are also making political statements. In his well-known essay on sites of memory (*lieux de mémoire*), Pierre Nora distinguishes between memory and history. While scholars have largely put this distinction aside, it can be instructive. For Nora, "memory is life." In contrast to history—the deadened, professionalized representation of the past—memory is "affective and magical," "open to permanent evolution," and "blind to all but the group it binds."[84] Put another way, memory is less about fidelity to the past than the affirmation of identity in the face of historical erasure. When Carla told me, "It was the slaves who built this church in 1700," it hardly matters that she mixed up her dates or that her claims about who built the church are not based on archival research. The question is rather how she and others mobilize the past to "understand and discursively present themselves to make community in the present."[85]

Looking at photos of old São Paulo, one is struck by how little the sprawling, twenty-first-century metropolis resembles the modest city of the late nineteenth. The city's old topography never stood a chance of survival. As its population swelled and São Paulo took its place as the epicenter of Brazilian modernization, successive waves of demolition and development remade its landscape several times over. Its rivers were canalized, its verdant spaces paved over, and most of its old buildings razed. The Field of the Gallows, the neighborhood where Chaguinhas was hanged, once marked the city's southernmost limit. Today it is near the center. Rechristened as Liberdade, its thick history has been hidden by the stylized lanterns and building facades that came with the neighborhood's Orientalization. But while easy to miss, these memories dwell there still, conjured and vitalized by devotion to the suffering dead.

The stories devotees tell about the dead are also a way of talking about São Paulo. Memories not only inhabit spaces but inflect devotees' movements through them. Sites of memory, says Nora, depend on the will to remember, and the act of remembrance is always a return. As Paul Ricœur writes, "To remember is to have a memory or *set off in search of a memory*."[86] Remembering is doing something. Telling stories about the souls is a means of mapping the city—of both describing it and prescribing movement through it. Paulistanos are famous for being always on the move, and in part 2, we examine their religious movement and its consequences.

PART II | Trajectories

CHAPTER THREE

Religious Transit

"I began on a doctor's suggestion," Maria said, "Dr. Efrem. I don't know if you already heard of him." I had not, and I wondered if I heard correctly. Why was Maria telling me about a doctor? We were standing outside the Chapel of the Our Lady of the Afflicted, where Maria had come to pray to the souls of the dead. "I went to his office, I had some health problems, and he said to come here," she said. Dr. Efrem recommended Maria pray a *trezena*, or thirteen-week prayer cycle, to the thirteen souls. "He gave me a pamphlet and told me to follow the pamphlet, and I came here to pray." And it worked, she said. "I got such marvelous things, things I really needed." Her health improved, and business got better. Within a year, she managed to purchase two properties she had her eye on. Maria had been a devotee ever since.[1]

Though baptized and confirmed Catholic, Maria described herself as "Kardecist Catholic." She said she began visiting Kardecist centers as a teenager and now most often visited Perseverança, a large Kardecist center in the city's Eastern Zone known for its humanitarian work. She had always been curious about religion, she said, and became even more so when she "sort of lost her footing" following her divorce. Then she went everywhere—spiritist centers, neo-Pentecostal churches, even Kingdom Halls of Jehovah's Witnesses. "I'd go here; I'd go there. A friend would call, and I'd go!" she said. Eventually she toned down. "I understood that I have to be with my own faith," she said, "that my church is inside me."

Still, Maria remained deeply attached to the Chapel of the Afflicted. "I have faith in these prayers, and I believe that *here* . . . I don't know, there's something here in this place," she said. "I don't know how to explain it, but I feel it has a strong energy." Like the other devotees I'd met, Maria saw the chapel as a special place, a refuge from São Paulo's chaos, where one could pray in peace. As was common among white devotees, she knew little about its history but described it as a special place for accessing the dead.

Last chapter, I considered how popular sites for the devotion to souls are saturated with the memory of trauma and suffering, owing in part to devotees' prayers. Here I consider devotees' urban trajectories. To this end, I employ what Brazilian scholars have called religious transit (*trânsito religioso*), which they have used to make sense of the country's shifting religious demographics. But whereas most literature on the subject has focused on switching affiliations, I explore religious transit's ethnographic utility for understanding eclectic devotees' movement through urban space. My point is that practitioners like Maria do not only code switch between Catholic and Kardecist idioms but that they also move between particular places—between *this* church and *that* spiritist center—for specific reasons. When practitioners talked about their devotion, they spoke concretely. They talked about taking to São Paulo's streets, crossing the city, and petitioning the dead at sites of suffering.

Suffering shapes the spatial trajectories of the living and the dead. This is to say that religious movement is inextricable from movement in the affective sense. Practitioners pray to the dead for different reasons, but almost all start from a place of vulnerability. They seek the souls' help with everyday problems like finding employment, legal troubles, and family strife. To quell their affliction, as well as that of the souls, they travel to certain sites of social violence on Mondays to petition the indefinite, suffering dead. And according to devotees, the souls also move, traveling toward candles to "come get a bit of the flame" and ease their otherworldly anguish. The play of mutual suffering and its relief draws together the living and the departed.

While death is singular in its inevitability, the revenant dead are many. The shape they take and the places they dwell depend on how people in the present confront the past. Understanding the devotion to souls requires not just attention to space and affect but their conjuncture in memory. As a pit grave for paupers, enslaved Africans and their descendants, and the gallows' victims, devotees remember the Chapel of the Afflicted as the "cemetery of the excluded," home to the socially dead. It is fitting, then, that devotees go there to pray to the souls. Whether or not they know the chapel's past, their devotion is part of the social framework that sustains its memory. The practice, then, suggests how we might think of religious transit as not just about shifting patterns of affiliation but also the mnemonically generative movement of sentient bodies through urban space.

Eclecticism and Syncretism

During a course on mediumship development at a large Umbanda temple in São Paulo's Northern Zone, the instructor required a few students to pose questions to the rest of the class. One asked the class about the difference between religion (*religião*) and religiosity (*religiosidade*). After a few other students gave rambling speculations that tried to work out the difference, the instructor offered clarification. Religion, he said, is a system, while religiosity is about practices. He then illustrated the distinction with the example of going to a Catholic church to light candles to the souls. "Do you need to be Catholic to do this? No," he said. "This is an example of religiosity."[2]

By that point, I had become used to seeing Umbanda and Candomblé practitioners at the Liberdade churches and tombs of the thirteen souls. When I visited the Chapel of the Afflicted over the course of 2014, Renata, then the chapel's administrator, would often say, "This church is *bem mística* [very mystical]," telling stories of apparitions or afflicted souls appearing to people in dreams. One day, just after I had finished interviewing a devotee who was interested in Kardecist Spiritism, Renata turned to me. "See," she said, "I told you this church is very mystical! The people who come here—they say, 'I'm Catholic and spiritist' or 'I'm Catholic and Umbandista.' But you already know it's like that, right?"[3]

I had to agree. Like Maria, over two-thirds of those I interviewed at the Chapel of the Afflicted identified as non-Catholic or as Catholic and something else too, or said they were Catholic but frequented non-Catholic religious places. Several even described themselves as "eclectic" (*ecléctica/o*), using a term common in both discussion of religion in contemporary Brazil and the country's intellectual history.[4] Renata did not mind this eclecticism, but she disapproved of visitors bringing the material culture associated with other traditions into the chapel. "Did you see the *oferenda* [offering]?" she asked me one morning, referring to an offering someone had left in the candle room. I had—when I arrived that day, the chapel's janitor showed me a shallow tray of popcorn wrapped in white cloth. He said it was probably in offering to Obaluaê, the Yorùbá *orixá* associated with health, sickness, and cemeteries. "I don't have any prejudice against these religions," Renata said, visibly annoyed. "But the church isn't the place to leave an offering. And I don't want to clean it up." She said she used to scold those who left behind offerings, but the priest who then served as chaplain had told her to stop. Just throw out the offerings after they leave, he said. Renata complied but did not see why some people insisted on leaving things for spirits there, in a Catholic church.[5]

Offerings to *orixás* and Umbanda spirit entities are common at devotional sites. Burial sites are places of *axé*, or spiritual power, and appropriate for petitioning certain kinds of gods and spirits. For years, the large lower candle room at the Church of the Hanged had prominent signs reading, "IT IS

NOT PERMITTED TO LIGHT COLORED CANDLES." Early in my fieldwork there, I asked a church employee about the ban, knowing full well it was meant to dissuade devotions associated with Afro-Brazilian religions. "We recycle the wax," he answered, "and we can't recycle colored wax. It's only this." So I asked about the *mães-de-santo* casting cowries out front, asking why they set up shop there rather than, say, the more spacious and highly trafficked square across the street. Rodrigo gave an embarrassed smile. "Look, Mike," he laughed, "in Brazil, everything is mixed." He then described Brazil as a mixture of three races—the Portuguese, Africans, and Indigenous tribes—whose religions mixed accordingly.[6]

"In Brazil, everything is mixed." It was an interpretation I would come to hear often. As Stephen Selka observes, "Perhaps more than any other country in the Americas, Brazil is known for its cultural eclecticism and religious syncretism."[7] The devotion to souls would appear to be a case in point. While typically practiced in Catholic churches, as the anthropologist Patricia Birman notes, the devotion "counts on the significant presence of practitioners of Umbanda, Candomblé, and spiritists more generally."[8] Material traces like offerings or colored candles for Afro-Brazilian gods and spirits render these practitioners' presence visible, as does their comportment. Umbanda practitioners, for instance, are known to exit candle rooms facing inward so as to not turn their backs on the holy. Used in this sense, *syncretism* would seem to plainly designate "religion out of place."[9]

But as scholars have long noted, syncretism is a problematic term. It "essentializes too much," implying pure and prior essences that degrade through mixture.[10] This criticism stems in part from syncretism's historically pejorative usage, particularly by seventeenth-century Protestants, to lament Indigenized churches, which they saw as novel corruptions of an implicitly authentic European Christianity.[11] For these and other reasons, many social scientists have abandoned the term in favor of others like "hybridity" or "creolization." But as some critics have argued, these synonyms are similarly flawed: both are only intelligible in contrast with purity, and each conjures problematic associations with biological speciation and racial identity.[12]

In 1967, the historian Robert D. Baird wrote, "Although seldom defined, the term [*syncretism*] is usually assumed to be abundantly clear, even though examination of its usage reveals that it is used in various and conflicting ways." A half century later, the term is still unclear, alternately referring to everything from ostensible religious syntheses and religion out of place, to social or historical processes of mixture, to individual religious eclecticism. This ambiguity lends syncretism considerable explanatory purchase, as it permits an elision of description ("*that* is syncretic") and explanation ("and it's due to a historical process of syncretism"). In Brazil, this elision takes consistent form. In a tenacious "blood-based logic" enshrined by early-twentieth-century studies of New World acculturation, scholars and laypeople alike continue to posit that Brazilians mix religions because they are essentially mixed.[13] As one historian offhandedly claimed, "Mixing white, indigenous, and black blood, it is as if Brazilians had been 'condemned' to syncretism."[14]

But at places like the Church of the Hanged and Chapel of the Afflicted, it seems clear enough that Catholicism, Candomblé, Umbanda, and Kardecist Spiritism are not syncretizing of their own accord. Rather, eclectic devotees with varied religious commitments are coming to this particular church—a place known as "the church of the souls" and a site of social violence—to pray to the suffering dead.

Religious Transit

Last chapter, I introduced Carla, the longtime devotee and self-described Black *militante* (militant activist) I met at the Chapel of the Afflicted. She told me that while her parents were devotees, she started visiting the chapel because her friend "from Candomblé" told her about it. Curious about her mention of Candomblé, I asked her about her religious affiliation. "If it were the census, I'd say spiritist. I'm of a more spiritualist line," she said, indicating her affinity for Brazil's different mediumship traditions. "I can go to a Candomblé *terreiro*, just like I can come to a Catholic church. You don't necessarily have to have *the* religion," she said. "You have to be where you feel good, where you have a connection [*tem trânsito*] with something that you think is more elevated."[15]

Note Carla's spatial, affective language. She first responded in terms of affiliation, as was appropriate to my question: "What is your religion? How would you answer on the census?" But she quickly spoke of traveling ("I can go to," "I can come to") to religious places (like Candomblé *terreiros* and Catholic churches) that engender feelings of well-being and connection ("You have to be where you feel good, where you have a connection with something"). In interviews, other devotees made similar comments. "I feel good when I come here," said Iwi, a third-generation Japanese woman in her early fifties. Iwi had only started the practice a few months earlier, having also been recommended by Dr. Efrem.[16]

As we were talking, I noticed that Iwi was wearing two necklaces: one with a small, gold Medal of St. Benedict and another with a bronze medallion with the eight trigrams of the I Ching around a yin and yang symbol. When I asked about them, Iwi explained, "I walk [*Eu ando*] with both of them. This Medal of St. Benedict, I put it on as soon as I get up. This other is . . . I'm a practitioner of Tai Chi. This here has a symbol, the yin and the yang, the inside and outside. So then, everything leads to one thing, to a path [*caminho*]. That's why I'm a very open person, very eclectic [*muito eclética*]. So, for me, everything is valid. Everything that does well, everything that makes me feel good, is valid, no?" I told her that I heard other devotees say similar things, telling me they might go to, say, a Buddhist temple and spiritist center on the same day. "The doors are open," she affirmed. "The doors are open."[17]

In the late twentieth century, Brazilian scholars began to describe the country's religious dynamics in terms of religious transit (*trânsito religioso*). The timing coincides with dramatic changes in the Brazilian religious landscape. Between 1980 and 2010, evangelical Protestant affiliation grew exponentially—from 7.8 million to 42.3 million—as more Brazilians than ever declared themselves "without religion" and Catholic affiliation reached an all-time low.[18] At the same time, scholars began to question the utility of conversion for understanding these changes. Conversion implies a "radical break and shift from one fixed identity marker to another," ill-suited to characterize individuals' "often-subtle" fluctuations between religions.[19] Religious transit, on the other hand, is meant to be less definitive and more processual, signaling continual change rather than largely stable and exclusive religious identities.

While its proponents have cast religious transit as broadly useful for understanding religion in contemporary Brazil, most work on the subject has focused on switching affiliation.[20] This is due at least in part to the influence of Ronaldo de Almeida and Paula Montero's "Trânsito religioso no Brasil," which, to my knowledge, was the first study to quantify religious switching in Brazil.[21] Using data from a nationally administered questionnaire that asked respondents their current religion and the one in which they were raised, the authors find that about 26 percent of the Brazilian population switched their religious affiliation. The authors suggest Catholicism is a kind of "universal donor" that is losing adherents most rapidly in Brazil, particularly to the Pentecostal churches. Pentecostals, on the other hand, seemed to switch to "without religion" (*sem religião*), while Kardecists tended to revert to Catholicism. This shows that religious transit is not random but "occurs in precise directions, depending on the institutions involved."[22] Pastors of the Universal Church of the Kingdom of God, for instance, are skilled at using language and ritual familiar to practitioners of Catholicism, Kardecist Spiritism, and Afro-Brazilian traditions to attract new adherents.[23]

As helpful as quantitative studies of religious switching can be, they have been limited by some of the assumptions about religion that get baked into survey design. As Almeida and Montero note, the questionnaire data they analyzed captured neither multiple affiliations nor successive switching.[24] Neither did it distinguish between affiliation and participation (which is understandable, given that the survey was meant to gauge cultural influences on sexual comportment and attitudes toward HIV/AIDS).[25] This approach privileges Protestants, whose religious identity tends to be consistent with participation.[26] It also reproduces the rigidity inherent to conversion, which religious transit, in emphasizing "rapid comings and goings," was meant to overcome. This, of course, is no coincidence: both the notion of conversion and the quantitative measures used in census and other surveys were born of a western European and North American sociological idiom that has historically presumed stable, singular religious identities.[27]

The assumption of consonance between religious participation and affiliation means that survey data rarely, if ever, accurately represent the prevalence of Brazil's mediumship religions. As various scholars have noted, Candomblé practitioners are often also Catholic and have historically identified as such on the census. Kardecist Spiritism is similarly underrepresented in survey findings. As with Umbanda, which first emerged among Kardecists in the state of Rio de Janeiro in the 1920s, there are different levels of participation in most Kardecist institutions. Their services are often free, and at larger centers, one can casually drop in to consult with mediums and listen to lectures. Furthermore, the basic tenets of Kardecism have become broadly familiar to Brazilians via high-profile mediums like Chico Xavier, popular films and telenovelas with Kardecist themes, and "spiritist novels," which claim to relate stories narrated to spirit mediums from the beyond.

While sociologists have developed increasingly nuanced measures of religious participation, here I want to consider the possibility of religious transit's ethnographic application. I echo Miriam Rabelo's suggestion that "a far more complex picture of religious trajectories and of their relation to religious change emerges when space is turned into an object of explicit reflection."[28] After all, this is the basic meaning of "transit": moving *across* (from the Latin *trans* + *īre*), from one point or place to another. It also more closely reflects what devotees like Carla and Maria did. When they talked about their religion, they told me about the places they went. They told "spatial stories" that organized and ranked different places, making "sentences and itineraries out of them."[29] I like this place but not that one; I feel good here but did not feel a connection there; I come here to remember; I go there to forget. In the devotion to souls, not all places are the same.

"I HAD AN EXPERIENCE WITH THEM; it's just that I didn't like it," Maria said, reflecting on her visit to the tombs of the thirteen souls in Cemitério Vila Alpina. "It worked, but it didn't. I got what I wanted, but I didn't," she complained. "It's like, when God gives, he doesn't take away." She was evasive about what she asked for and what happened, but she hinted it had something to do with her marriage. "I didn't feel a *sintonia divina*," or "divine syntony or resonance," at Cemitério Vila Alpina, she told me. "Not everyone who burned to death has reached a level of evolution where they can help you," she said.[30] Nowadays, she only petitioned the dead at the Chapel of the Afflicted. "The little chapel has a very good energy," she told me. She still prayed to the thirteen souls but distinguished between the "thirteen souls of Joelma" and the "thirteen souls of the Chapel of the Afflicted." Maria did not know who these latter souls were or how they died. The details seemed unimportant to her. She just knew that at the Chapel of the Afflicted, she "feels safe."[31]

In colloquial Portuguese, to have transit (*ter trânsito*) with something is to have a connection or influence with it. This usage invites us to consider the affective dimension of religious transit. As Sarah Ahmed writes, "we move toward and away from objects through how we are affected by them."[32] Maria's movement was not strictly between religions but between "affective spaces" of felt difference. Affect, Kevin Lewis O'Neill points out, is both corporeal and intersubjective.[33] What distinguishes São Paulo's most popular venues for the devotion to souls is not so much that they are Catholic—Cemitério Vila Alpina, after all, is a municipal cemetery—but that they are places where practitioners say they feel good. And in what might seem like a contradiction, devotees' good feeling is linked to their feeling closer to and more connected with the suffering dead. Maria never doubted the existence of the thirteen souls of Joelma, only that she did not feel a "divine resonance" with them. This affectively charged perception of the dead's presence in ritual space guided her urban trajectories and accounted for why she now only prayed to the souls at the Chapel of the Afflicted.

Urban Trajectories

In São Paulo, moving between religions means moving across the city. "We live here, and we can go to a ton of places," Cecília told me. "We have access!" The anthropologist Maria José de Abreu notes that São Paulo's size, density, and intense commercial activity "demands mobility and agility, not only in the circulation of information, goods, and people but in the traffic between this and other worlds."[34] Its roadways and public transit infrastructure also allow for relatively easy movement between different religious sites. Cecília was a forty-seven-year-old Black woman who described herself as a video game "fanatic." She was telling me about Seicho-no-Ie, a Japanese new religion that has a large center in Jabaquara, a neighborhood in the city's Southern Zone. Though far from her home, its location near the final metro stop on the blue line—the same line that passes by the Chapel of the Afflicted—made it easy to access, and Cecília went there often. For her, the Seicho-no-Ie message resonated with the devotion to souls. "There in Seicho-no-Ie, without having gratitude for your ancestors, for people who have already died, for your family, there's no way you're going to have happiness," she said. Sometimes Cecília's mother, a committed spiritist, chided her for going. "I tell her, 'I follow everything that is good for me,' understand?"[35]

When we met that August afternoon, Cecília had just finished her shift at the Spiritist Federation of the State of São Paulo (FEESP), the largest and most influential Kardecist Spiritist center in the city and probably in all Brazil. She volunteered there three days per week, administering visitors *passes*—fluidic "passes," a Kardecist healing practice with roots in mesmerism. Over coffee and cake, Cecília told me she tended to be "very agitated" in her "movements," always anxious and unable to sit still. Though she still suffered from anxiety, FEESP was able to help. Now she could calm down, she said. Brazilian Kardecists have a highly developed vocabulary and set of ritual practices for dealing with certain mental disorders, which they argue are often the result of "obsessing spirits." This was the case with Cecília. Through ritual "disobsession," she said, "the federation was able to indoctrinate the spirit that stays with me, [the spirit] that leaves me agitated.[36]

FEESP was a popular destination among devotees of the souls. About one in five of those I interviewed at the Church of the Hanged and Chapel of the Afflicted told me they visited it. Though it was relatively close to the churches—about a kilometer walk away—its popularity among devotees was probably more a testament to FEESP's influence than indicative of its being part of a devotional circuit. Its nine-story headquarters in central São Paulo is the biggest and busiest in the city. Its long operating hours, central location, proximity to public transportation, and ample parking make it especially accessible. FEESP also has substantial media reach, including through a weekly cable television program and a publishing house that prints books, a monthly magazine, and a twice-monthly newspaper.[37]

FEESP serves an impressive number of visitors. One of the federation's directors told me the center had over 7,000 volunteers working to provide "spiritual assistance" to upwards of 9,000 visitors on weekdays and 15,000 on Saturdays.[38] Even if inflated, these numbers are plausible. When I met Cecília, she said she helped give *passes* to about four hundred visitors in two hours. During my visits, the Department of Orientation and Routing (DEPOE) was always busy. It was most visitors' first stop, where they would visit a medium that would diagnose any spiritual afflictions. This is to say that in contrast to the devotion to souls, visitors to FEESP rarely ritually engaged or incorporated the dead themselves. Rather, they sought guidance from mediums, who would prescribe a course of treatment that typically involved some combination of lectures and *passes* over several weeks for minor problems, and spirit disobsession for more serious ones.

Cecília had been volunteering as a medium at FEESP for nearly twenty years and practicing the devotion to souls for over thirty. When she prayed to the souls, she said, she always visited the Chapel of the Afflicted. It was family tradition that stretched back to her grandparents. She said that her grandfather told her, "The souls always answer our prayers [*atendem os nossos pedidos*]." Her father was also an ardent devotee, and it was he who taught her how to pray to the dead. "'You go there to the church; take a candle. Hold the candle,' he said. 'Don't put the flame to the underside of the candle,'" which some people do to melt its wax to keep the candle upright. "'Hold it, put it down, and light it,' he said. 'And never forget to pay your promise [*pagar sua promessa*] after what happens. When you need relief, ask the souls.'" Cecília began visiting in earnest when she was sixteen to plead with the souls to save her parents' troubled marriage. She said it worked then and, again later, when she asked the souls for help finding a job.[39]

Cecília rarely visited the Church of the Hanged. While I met a few devotees who regularly prayed at both churches on Mondays, most visited one or the other. For all their shared history and spatial proximity, no formal administrative structures link the churches. They belong to different parishes, and for as long as I have known them, members of the Brotherhood of the Holy Cross of the Souls of the Hanged have rarely participated in events at the Chapel of the Afflicted.[40] In a way, the churches are redundant—both are colloquially known as the "Church of the Souls," and devotees understand both as appropriate places to petition Chaguinhas. Devotees' preference for one over the other often came down to habit and feeling. Some liked the tranquility of the smaller chapel or preferred the baroque ornamentation of the

Church of the Hanged or had opinions about the kind of people who visited either church. "The people that go there [to the Church of the Hanged], lawyers . . . They're powerful and acquisitive people," Cecília told me. What's more, she said, "There at the Hanged, you light a candle, and they put it out. They don't have respect," Cecília told me. "I want the souls to be able to enjoy the light for at least a little while, so I come here."[41]

I was intrigued by Cecília's attention to candles. Devotees take various precautions with candles, such as not using candles that have fallen over, not lighting one's candles with the flame of another candle (at least without asking permission), and not lighting candles at home. But Kardecists tend to discourage the ritual use of candles. "Spiritists never use candles," one of FEESP's directors told me. "They're not necessary."[42] In Brazilian Kardecist discourse, this is often presented as a simple matter of fact. For example, on the frequently-asked-questions page of its website, the Brazilian Spiritist Federation states: "Spiritist practiced is realized with simplicity, without any exterior worship, according to the Christian principle that God must be adored in spirit and truth. Spiritism does not have priests, nor does it adopt or use in its practices: altars, images, floats, candles, processions, sacraments, concessions of indulgence, canonicals, alcoholic or hallucinogenic drinks, incense, smoke, talismans, amulets, horoscopes, cartomancy, pyramids, crystals or any other objects, rituals, or forms of exterior worship."[43]

Allan Kardec himself had little to say about candles, but the prohibition makes sense in the context of Brazilian spiritism. As was the case elsewhere in Latin America—including in Mexico, where Francisco I. Madero was guided by spirits as he challenged Porfírio Diaz and then mounted a successful presidential campaign—spiritism enjoyed prestige as a French import ever since the founding of the country's first Kardecist center in 1865.[44] FEESP remains overtly Francophile, to the point of holding French-themed events featuring French flags and typical foods. More broadly, centers aligned with a de facto Kardecist orthodoxy are marked by the performance of modernity through the heavy use of European classical music; a kind of "deritualization" (which, drawing from Catherine Bell, we might define as the explicit denial that a given practice constitutes ritual); an emphasis on progress, evolution, and rationality; and the insistence that Kardecist practice is scientific. As always, race is at issue here, since Kardecist modernity is often defined in contrast to "less evolved" spirits and traditions—namely, those associated with Afro-Brazilian religions. The attitude toward candles is just one example of boundary work, as Kardecist institutions both historically and today sought to distinguish themselves from Catholicism and Afro-Brazilian mediumship religions by eschewing those traditions' perceived ritual excesses.⁴⁵

Cecília was aware that her devotion to souls transgressed Kardecist norms. "No, they don't light candles. That's why my mother is against me coming here," she said. "My mother doesn't like lighting candles, but I light candles for the souls, for the saints. . . . But spiritists don't light candles; it's true." I pressed her on the tension, asking how she reconciled it with her work as a medium at FEESP. "I'm spiritist, but I cannot leave [the church completely]. I was raised Catholic." In a later conversation, she explained, "I'm not going to change the way I think because of Kardecism. Souls need light. They need light, so you light a candle. I'm not going to change because of Kardecism. It's like I told you: there are people who go to FEESP, learn all this, then go to a center with *pretos velhos*." Why should they give up their practice? Why should she? "You can't. You can't. You can't just deny them." Cecília was bound to the souls, and this connection drew her back to the Chapel of the Afflicted, week after week.⁴⁶

If suffering binds the living and the dead, it also shapes souls' trajectories through the world. Last chapter, I argued that modernization haunts São Paulo, anchoring the souls to the places and things that register historical trauma. But while spectral presence is stronger at some sites than others, the dead are potentially anywhere. That is why devotees avoid lighting candles for souls at home. "At home is dangerous. . . . The people say you can't light candles for souls at home," Maria told me. While devotees assured me there was no problem in lighting candles for one's guardian angel at home, the souls are different. While some are "spirits of light," others are needy, imperfect, and in the world. "The souls are around. So they can enter your house. Candles for the souls you have to light in the church," Maria said.⁴⁷ With only two exceptions, the devotees I interviewed all agreed. "It's said that there's a danger to lighting candles at home, [which is] the souls will go there in search of light, or a spirit will come to get the light of the candle," Cecília told me.⁴⁸ All too human, they are apt to cause trouble if not treated with proper care.

Souls' mobility, then, motivates the trajectories of the living. Devotees go to the souls rather than encourage the souls to travel to them. One can see why some observers have described the practice as a "pilgrimage," even though devotees are typically local and rarely use such language.⁴⁹ When I met Cecília, I asked her whether she had visited the Sanctuary of the Souls, a large church in the Armênia neighborhood built by the Missionaries of the

Sacred Heart in the middle of the twentieth century to accommodate "a great devotion to the Souls of Purgatory. . . . principally by people less favored by material luck."[50] Close to the subway and boasting a large parking lot, the sanctuary is both easily accessible and able to accommodate many more devotees than the Liberdade churches. Its candle room alone is larger than the Chapel of the Afflicted. Cecília told me she knew it but preferred the Chapel of the Afflicted. "Here is where people like to come . . . because they want to go where people suffered, where you have to give light," Cecília explained. "All around here was a cemetery. There's Corporal Chaguinhas. . . . That's why people like to come here," she said.[51]

Saudade: The Presence of Absence

No word better captures the complex mix of emotions evoked by prayer for the dead—the sadness and longing for those who have gone but also the indulgence in this sadness—than *saudade*. Despite the stereotype of Brazilians as "poor but happy," as Nancy Scheper-Hughes points out, "much of the literature written by Brazilians about themselves eventually returns to the subject of 'Brazilian sadness' and melancholy." Even the "reckless surrender to *carnaval* . . . is a necessary corrective to the sadness and melancholy of the everyday."[52] It is a far-reaching sentiment: one can have saudades for people and places but also "particular smells, foods, colors, or sensations from the past that were associated with poignant events and loved ones." But the death of a loved one, more than anything else, provides "the most potent source of *saudades*."[53] In São Paulo's cemeteries, those "gardens of memory," this lapidary sentiment is ubiquitous.[54]

Rather than depression to be avoided, saudade is described as a bittersweet yearning for the beauty of what was. Saudade "unites and attaches . . . To evoke *saudades* protects and conserves; indeed, it enshrines memory. *Saudade* has been described as the ultimate nourishment of love . . . it strikes and is felt inside, in the heart and chest of a person."[55] In both English and Portuguese, emotion has kinetic associations and etymology. "Motion" is part of the word, all the way back to the classical Latin. In colloquial usage, we speak of profoundly emotional events as "moving," both internally ("Seeing images of starving children, I was moved to tears") and regarding action in the world ("to devote my life to ending hunger").[56] Saudade is no exception. It prompts action, enshrining memory through recall and repetition. It is an emotional place to which one returns. That is why it is so evident at sites of memory like cemeteries and churches.

Devotees do not just have saudades when they visit the Church of the Hanged—they go there to evoke the feeling.[57]

"[I light candles for] some friends I've lost and family, like my uncle. When I'm here, I feel good. Particularly. And I even feel that the other side is well," said Bruno, one of the few younger devotees I met. A São Paulo native in his late twenties who described himself as "a kind of eclectic dude" who likes "a little of everything," Bruno talked about his experiences reading Allan Kardec and Chico Xavier, Brazil's most famous spiritist medium and author, and even his visits to a Seventh Day Adventist church that his father frequented. Unlike most others, Bruno did not make requests to the dead. "I only ask for blessing," he said. "The fact that you're remembering, recalling the someone that did right by you, it leaves you with even more saudade . . . and I feel in that moment it's doing me well. So, I think that's cool."[58]

The devotion to souls can be a way of coping with loss, but it is not meant to provide decisive closure. It is instead a practice of maintenance and care, meant to sustain relationships in the face of unbreachable distance. And, as seen with Cecília, the affective ties engendered by the practice can mean maintaining it in the face of potentially conflicting religious commitments. Even those who have moved away from the church remain devotees out of their deep feeling for the indefinite, suffering dead, who they consider trusted friends and partners. As Cecília told me, she could not just deny the souls. They had helped her, and she felt obligated to retain a relationship with them. The pull of saudade endures, like the marble and granite into which the word is so often engraved.

Devotees' affection for the souls might seem surprising. In contrast to beings like Catholic saints, *orixás*, and Umbanda entities, the souls lack individuality and personality. They do not manifest in spirit mediumship, and material culture like scapulars, images, and home altars are not common to the practice in contemporary Brazil. But as I suggested in chapter 1, souls' ambiguity makes them relatable. As no one in particular, they are potentially anyone and everyone. "Saints are saints," one devotee explained, "but souls are like us. They're closer."[59] Devotees spoke about the souls with intimacy and warmth. "I call the souls my friends," Carla told me. "I have a very strong relationship with them. The thirteen souls, the afflicted souls—they're my friends."[60]

As the indefinite dead, the souls absorb devotees' saudades for departed loved ones. Robert Orsi suggests "family dynamics are one spring of sacred presences—saints and the Mother of God draw on the intimate histories of relationships within family worlds (always as these are shaped and inflected by culture and society). The saints borrow dimensions of their identities from family members who in turn become associated with particular saints."[61] These same dynamics pertain to contemporary Brazilian devotees, whether of the souls, saints, or *orixás*. But in the cult of the souls, the familial dimension is especially pronounced. That is because members are not just associated with the dead—they often *are* the dead. While distinct from the souls, when family members die, they become incorporated into devotees' Monday prayers.

Last chapter, I introduced Beatriz, a white neo-Pentecostal woman who prayed at the Chapel of the Afflicted. Beatriz explained to me that she prayed for the sake of her "disincarnated" mother, who had been a committed devotee. Pressing her on her use of that word, which is used by Kardecist Spiritists to refer to the dead, Beatriz revealed that she practiced Kardecism before converting to Evangelicalism thirty years earlier. She explained that while she agrees with her church's doctrine that Christ is the only savior, she thought the souls of the dead—especially those who suffered in life—could help the living.[62] She told me that she was unwilling to forsake her parents' memory and eternal well-being out of fidelity to her church. And while she prayed to the familial dead, she told me, she also prayed the Novena to the Afflicted Souls, whom she petitioned for help.[63]

The familial element adds to the devotion's affective intensity. Family tradition transforms devotional sites into familiar places. And the familial dead, too, can become objects of devotion. They have a special place in the Monday practice, distinct from the anonymous collectives of suffering souls that are the devotion's primary object.[64] As Carla explained to me, "My ancestors are one thing, and the souls are another." She, like others, addressed her ancestors individually, by name, rather than just glossing them under "the souls."[65] And for the most part, neither Carla nor the others I interviewed made petitions (*pedidos*) or promises (*promessas*) to the familial dead. Some said they asked departed loved ones for help but more in the manner that one would seek advice from living family or friends. "Oftentimes you pray and suddenly dream about a person important to you, and he shows you some path," one devotee said. "I think, since they have already experienced many things we experience, they know what path to take."[66]

The demographics of devotees are relevant here. Like Carla, Beatriz, and Maria, most of the devotees at São Paulo's major devotional sites are middle-aged or older, and about two-thirds are women. Some learned the devotion from friends or from seeing a novena left at a church. But a plurality of the devotees I interviewed learned the practice from parents and grandparents at a young age, even if they only came to consider themselves devotees later in life. Their age also means they are familiar with death, often of the parents or grandparents who taught them the devotion. The practice, then, activates different kinds of memories. It can be a way of recalling the history of a place, but also one's youth. Devotees talked about standing alongside parents and grandparents as children before the burning heat of candles learning how to pray to the dead. But the devotion is not only about the past. It is a way of engaging the deceased as they are now: disembodied, immortal souls who are powerful to help the living.

Memory, J. Z. Smith points out, "is a complex and deceptive experience. It appears to be preeminently a matter of the past, yet it is much an affair of the present."[67] So it is with saudade, a "contradictory feeling linking universes which were usually viewed as disconnected—the material and spiritual, the past and the present."[68] The devotion to souls is a way of recalling the past in service of the present and future. It is an effort to realize desire through memory. Smith continues his observation by noting that, although memory "appears to be preeminently a matter of time, it is as much an affair of space."[69] That is why devotional spaces matter. They are places where devotees go to remember, to get closer to the suffering dead.

NEXT DOOR TO the Church of the Holy Cross of the Souls of the Hanged, there is a *loja esotérica* (esoteric store), Casa de Velas Santa Rita. The store is divided in half. The half closer to the church sells rosaries, images of the saints, crucifixes, and white candles. The farther half sells herbs and crystals and minerals, images of Umbanda spirits and *orixás*, and colored candles. The owners of the store started out by selling candles to devotees and later founded a factory that produces Catholic and Afro-Brazilian religious images, in an effort to cater to their clientele.[70] Early in my research, I asked the owner why he thought it was so common for people to burn colored candles and leave images of *orixás* at the Church of the Hanged. "Not everyone who died there [at the gallows] was Catholic," he said. I initially dismissed his explanation as too simple, but he raised an important point: the Liberdade churches are places where the dead were present. And as Robert Orsi observes, the church has a perennial "problem with real presence: controlling access to it."[71]

Prayer for the suffering souls, and even the purgatorial souls, has never been restricted only to Catholics. We have already seen how Inquisition records report sorceresses who conjured the souls ("of the sea, of the land, three hanged, three dragged, three shot to death for love") in acts of love magic. Crosses or "houses" for the souls are common within some Afro-Brazilian ritual spaces, particularly those of Umbanda.[72] And Dr. Efrem, the homeopathic doctor who recommended that Maria pray to the thirteen souls at the Chapel of the Afflicted, told me he recommended it to "thousands" of others. He was a devotee himself and identified as Jewish and spiritist. "I frequent a spiritist center," he said, "but I am also Catholic. It's sort of, ah, a mixture. I have a crucifix, images of Christ." The doctor was not a renegade bent on transgression. He distinguished between religions and between religion and his medical practice. But he insisted all these things were means to a set of related ends—health, well-being, and peace.[73]

By employing the notion of religious transit, I do not mean to reify religious traditions and fix boundaries only to demonstrate transgression. But I think we can fairly acknowledge that religious institutions often promote styles of discourse, cultivate religious identities among followers, enforce theological boundaries, and position themselves both spatially and ideologically in relation to other religious and secular things. Like Dr. Efrem, the devotees I spoke with acknowledged these boundaries even as they crossed, collapsed, and contested them. I agree with scholars of Black Atlantic religion who have argued it is not the scholar's job to verify claims about religious origin or authenticity.[74] But it is the scholar's place to acknowledge those claims and take them seriously.

The devotees who visit the Chapel of the Afflicted and the Church of the Hanged are not always Catholic. Why, then, go to a Catholic church to light candles for the dead? Devotees gave different reasons, but most were related to affect. The Liberdade churches made them feel good, because these places had a special connection with the suffering souls. Drawn by affection for the suffering dead—as well as the desire to relieve their own suffering—devotees cross the city to pray at spaces of trauma and death, affecting those spaces in the process. They come bringing light and prayer, hoping to ease the souls' affliction. They also bring their hopes and anxieties, their memories and their saudades, and their personal religious histories and different ways of understanding the dead. And they go feeling better—if not always better, then more deeply bound to the dead.

Religious Transit

CHAPTER FOUR

Sympathy for the Dead

"She asked for the means to build a *terreiro*, and now she's come to pay her obligation," Bruna said, gesturing toward Olinda, her *mãe-de-santo*. Olinda was standing near her silver Renault and talking on the phone. "That is, she came to give back what she got." Bruna had just finished leaving popcorn and small plastic cups filled with coffee on the tombs of the thirteen souls in Cemitério Vila Alpina. Large trees shaded the area where we stood, and we could hear *sabiá* (a kind of thrush) singing their famed birdsong. Bruna and her *mãe-de-santo* were visiting São Paulo for a few weeks, having traveled from Manaus, a city in northern Brazil, to participate in Afro-Brazilian religious festivals on the São Paulo coast. They also came to thank the thirteen souls. "What is paying an obligation?" Bruna asked. "It's a matter of giving thanks, really."[1]

Bruna called Olinda over to us and introduced me as a researcher. Olinda was reluctant to talk, saying they had to go soon but could answer a few questions. "Can I smoke a cigarette?" she asked. "For me, talking without smoking . . ." Lighting a Dunhill, Olinda told me about herself. She was born in the northeastern city of Fortaleza to a Pentecostal family, and her mother thought she was possessed by a demon. "The pastor told my mother to give me to someone else. She gave me away." Eventually she encountered Zé Bruno, an Umbanda master who told her she was not afflicted by demons but rather that she was a spirit medium. "That I had spirits of the depths with me," she explained. Under his guidance, Olinda said, she was initiated into Umbanda at seven years old and stayed in his center for twenty-one years. In time, Zé Bruno told her to follow her calling and "find other religions." She sought initiation in Candomblé and said her new *terreiro* in Manaus incorporated "all of my roots: Umbanda, Angola [Candomblé], and Ketu [Candomblé]." And, she added, "it has a space for the thirteen souls."[2]

I had thought these things were forbidden in Ketu Candomblé. When I began to say as much, Olinda interjected. "No! Pay attention! I have roots from twenty-one days of birth until seven years, and I can't throw this all away. Now, everything has to have its place. I have a big place, and saint has its place, and the souls have theirs. The place for the church of the souls is the church of the souls. I can't abandon my roots. . . . I'm not going to throw this all away. When it's the day for Candomblé, it's only Candomblé. When it's the day for Umbanda, it's Umbanda. I don't mix. If I leave something to the side, it's because the people of Candomblé don't cultivate *caboclos* [spirits of Indigenous people] or souls."

Before being initiated into Candomblé, Olinda's *pai-de-santo* told her, "You have to get rid of all this if you want me to initiate you," referring to her work with the souls and Umbanda entities. As scholars like Stefania Capone have documented, moving from Umbanda to Bantu (or Angola/Congo) Candomblé to Ketu (or Nagô) Candomblé is common in Brazil as spirit mediums seek increasing prestige.[3] Nagô Candomblé has a reputation as "authentically African" and more powerful, and Olinda's *pai-de-santo* was enforcing Nagô orthodoxy, which discourages ritual contact with *eguns*, or spirits of the dead, which are thought to be ritually contaminating and deeply dangerous. But like many others who follow this trajectory, she refused to give them up altogether.[4] "I said, 'If you want to initiate me, you're going to have to accept it, because I'm not throwing anything away.' Because this here gave me my life." She was attached to the *caboclos* and the souls. "They sustain me, and I feel good. My family, thank God, my children are well. None are addicted to drugs; they're all good parents. I won't let anyone stop me, because I came from these roots."

We have already seen how the play of suffering and relief enlivens the devotion to souls. Devotees visit places and engage in practices at places marked by social violence—places that, in a seeming contradiction, make them feel good. They also go to places associated with the people and beings important to them: the Pentecostal church frequented by a sister, the Kardecist center where a mother volunteered, the Catholic church where their ancestors prayed to the dead. Like Olinda, they return, drawn by obligation, to "give back what they got." And when Olinda gave back to the souls, she brought things with her: popcorn for the *orixá* Obaluaê and coffee for the *pretos velhos*, which Bruna left atop the souls' tombs.

Last chapter, I suggested religious transit as a way of talking about how devotees move between religious spaces. Here I want to call attention to movement in the affective sense. One of my arguments in this book is that the souls' suffering is marked by neglect. No amount of prayer or candlelight can fully ease their affliction. Exploring the exchanges that sustain devotees' relationships with the dead, this chapter considers the practice in relation to what Hiʻilei Julia Kawehipuaakahaopulani Hobart and Tamara Kneese call "radical care"—that is, "a set of vital but underappreciated strategies for enduring precarious worlds."[5] Operating through obligations of mutual aid, the devotion engenders a felt sense of sympathy between the living and the dead. In so doing, it offers one way of living through the "brokenness of the broken world."[6] But while melancholic, the devotion is not defined by despondence. Rather, devotees' enduring ties with the dead call our attention to the work of maintenance and care that are critical to sustaining material and spiritual worlds. And centering maintenance—of built and natural environments, of practices and traditions, and of "relationships between heaven and earth involving humans of all ages and many different sacred figures together"—can help us understand religious and political change alike.[7]

Sympathy

Like Olinda, other devotees have built their own altars or chapels for the souls. While most of those I met said they avoided lighting candles for souls at home, most agreed that yard shrines are permissible (though few have the space to build them). As far as I could tell, these yard shrines extend the devotion rather than privatize it, since devotees who have them tend to also visit churches. In chapter 2, I related my conversation with Emilia, a seventy-six-year-old Black woman who was a member of the Brotherhood of the Holy Cross of the Souls of the Hanged. Though she had her own shrine, she told me she traveled to the Church of the Hanged every Monday to pray to the dead, "because here is where the slaves were hanged, isn't it?"[8] The same goes for Umbandistas, who may propitiate the souls at a *cruzeiro das almas*, or "cross of the souls," inside their temples. Thiago, an Umbanda medium I met at the Chapel of the Afflicted, told me he visited because "an Umbandista who does nothing for the souls is not an Umbandista."[9]

In May 2015, devotees in Tatuapé, an industrial neighborhood in São Paulo's Eastern Zone, built a chapel to the thirteen souls. The chapel was part of the New Spiritualist Brotherhood, a religious center whose director described it as having "roots in the African religious matrix." Visiting one Monday afternoon a few weeks after the chapel opened, I was greeted by Isabelle, one of the center's volunteers. After I waited for a few minutes at the entrance, sitting across from a small altar to the *pretos velhos*, Isabelle led me into the chapel—a long white narrow room with a window along the right side. It was plainly adorned, with a few potted plants and a picture of Santo Antonio on the left wall. There was a single wooden bench for devotees. The altar was also simple: thirteen wooden crosses, each about a foot tall, hung along the back wall. Five small tables in front of the altar each held an image of a Catholic saint: Our Lady of Fatima, St. Michael, Our Lady of Aparecida, Saints

Cosmas and Damian, and Saint Anthony. To the left of them, an empty vase sat atop a Doric column. Thirteen small glass cups of water lined the wall, and though they were also empty at the moment, Isabelle said the cups usually had candles in them.[10]

Isabelle told me that José, the center's director, had to take care of a few things before speaking with me. While José struggled to rescue his cat from one of the center's rafters, I asked Isabelle about her experiences with the thirteen souls, whom she identified with the thirteen unidentified victims of the 1974 fire at Edifício Joelma. She affirmed the souls' power. "Everything I asked, I received," she said, using the same phrasing I had heard from other devotees. "Whenever I talk about them, I get goosebumps. Look." She held up her arm and showed me. As she talked about some of the favors she received—help finding work, help buying a house, help with unspecified health issues—she shuddered, getting goosebumps again. Genuflecting, Isabelle brought her palms together in prayer and thanked the souls.

After Isabelle left, I sat in the chapel alone for a few minutes while waiting for José. Hearing the hiss of spray paint, I peered out the window and saw a volunteer spraying a row of thirteen white candles with gold paint. When José entered, dressed in shorts and a black T-shirt, I could see the tattooed inscriptions of his religious commitments: on his left forearm, a black and red band in homage to Exú; on his left inner wrist, a black outline of Brazil; on his right calf, images of Ogum and Iansã. José explained that the New Spiritualist Brotherhood is not "only Umbanda or Candomblé," like many mediumship-based religious centers in São Paulo. He said, "We embrace spirituality." He explained that his mother, who was a *benzedeira* (a blesser, or folk religious healer), taught him about the thirteen souls when he was young.[11] He never gave up devotion to them, teaching it to others who visited his center. Even before the chapel's opening, the devotion to the thirteen souls formed one of the pillars of the center's ritual life, with the group regularly visiting the souls' tombs in Cemitério Vila Alpina. In time, its members' gratitude to the souls was so great that they felt compelled to build a chapel in the souls' honor.[12]

As José talked, I was curious to hear what he made of the place of suffering in the devotion. Like the other devotees I had met, he sometimes referred to the thirteen souls as generic "spirits of light" and sometimes as the fire's unidentified victims. It seemed like there was a tension, so I pushed José on this. I asked what he thought of the thirteen souls' suffering at the moment of their death and how it related to their holiness or power to help the living. "There's an empathy, really," he suggested. "For example, charity is empathy—you have to put yourself in the place of another person. I think so, that there's a relation of empathy. I think every spirit, after reaching a universal consciousness of things, perceives our earthly suffering, and this generates empathy. But there's nothing obligatory."

I have suggested the devotion to souls is a way of grappling with suffering, and José's comments highlight how this emotional engagement can generate empathy. Neuroscientists have distinguished between two types of empathy: affective and cognitive. Affective empathy is a kind of "emotional contagion" in which our perception of others' emotions produces similar states and physiological responses within us. It appears to be neurologically distinct from cognitive empathy, which is the ability to understand others' emotional states and loosely synonymous with theory of mind. The devotion can arouse both. As we spoke, José's empathy for the thirteen souls seemed to me more like the latter. But many devotees had visceral, involuntary bodily reactions as they spoke about the souls—their voices quivering, their eyes filling with tears, their breathing short and shallow. Some were so overcome with emotion during our conversations that they found themselves unable to speak.[13]

Though writers often contrast sympathy and empathy—such as by describing sympathy as feeling *for* versus empathy as feeling *with*—there is no widely agreed-upon distinction between the terms.[14] *Empathy* is a newer word, generally dated to the early twentieth century, where it began to be used among psychologists writing in German and English. Its etymology accounts for its predominance in contemporary scientific writing, where *sympathy* is rarely used. But sympathy has an older history, and one more closely aligned with social thought and religious practice. Sympathy was the quintessential social emotion for moral philosophers like Adam Smith, who asserted it as the foundation of moral behavior among otherwise autonomous individuals. Used in this sense, sympathy is akin to "affective empathy" but also extends beyond it. As Robert Cox notes, Smith's use of the term had occult resonances. For him, sympathy was not just "fellow feeling" but a "powerful, primal force of nature, a mutual attraction between bodies."[15] Both connotations of sympathy (*simpatia*) are common in Brazilian Portuguese—so much so that *simpatia* can denote magical rituals or formulas, especially those used to *amarrar* (tie or bind) one to the objects of one's desire, such as wayward lovers and indecisive fiancées. The souls are sometimes integral to such incantations, and at the Chapel of the Afflicted, I found printed *simpatias* that incorporated prayers to the dead, including the Novena of the Afflicted Souls and Prayer to the Thirteen Souls.

Donovan Schaeffer describes religion as a "hybrid system, a set of embodied practices for the production of affects."[16] And since emotion is inexorably social, those affects can generate, magnify, and reflect affective *ties*. With respect to the devotion to souls, José suggested how the practice depends on this felt sense of connection. "Every time you pray, you create a spiritual bond with [the souls], and they manifest themselves. You don't need to be a medium, because they can enter into your dreams" or sometimes even the physical world, he said. "Here, for example, we honor the souls, we pray and make *pedidos* [petitions], and all our prayers were answered. Manifestations are commonplace; sometimes we hear heavy footsteps, and no one is there."[17] Like North American evangelicals who "learn to hear God" through regular prayer or Lucumí practitioners who forge affective ties to the dead via mimesis in what Elizabeth Pérez calls a "hermeneutic of sympathy," the devotion recalibrates practitioners' perceptions, attuning them to the souls' subtle manifestations: goosebumps on the skin, a shift in the shadows, chance street encounters, a spell of good luck.[18]

In *Society of the Dead*, Todd Ramón Ochoa describes how Isidra, a Cuban Palo practitioner, discerned the presence of the dead in bodily events "like the fluttering of her heart, breathlessness, goose bumps, and chills across her neck."[19] While I have suggested that the souls sit somewhere between what Ochoa calls the "ambient dead" (or *kalunga*) and "responsive dead"— that is, the undifferentiated mass of dead that permeate the world versus the discrete spirits who respond to the living—the ways devotees talked about the dead were not so different from Palo practitioners. To some extent, this is not entirely surprising, given the influence of Congo religion in Brazil. Some practitioners of Afro-Brazilian religions explicitly identify the souls with *kalunga*, for instance. And as we have already seen, even observant Catholics sometimes draw from different religious idioms in describing their relationship to the dead.

Practitioners' involuntary bodily responses suggest one way that devotees sense the souls. The practice transforms practitioners, binding the living and the dead and inculcating the souls' presence into practitioners' bodies, sometimes becoming part of their bodily habitus.[20] Carrying the souls—or the *orixás* or *caboclos*—changes the way one carries oneself. Even those who frequent non-Catholic institutions continue to practice the devotion in churches and cemeteries out of a sense of obligation and attachment to the dead, which can include the parents and grandparents who had been devotees. This "sense" is sensory: affective ties are felt, generated by and generative of emotion.

Power and Proximity

Affect also helps make sense of the souls' reputation for efficacy. That is because souls' ability to answer prayers is linked to their proximity to the living. Like the saints, whom Peter Brown has elegantly called the "very special dead," these somewhat-less-special dead are able to help devotees. That they are less special makes them even more accessible (for, as Smith argued, sympathy arises from social proximity) and potentially more powerful.[21] Similar to what Elaine Freitas calls "precarious saints"—that is, morally questionable figures whose holiness may be fleeting—the souls' efficacy is owing to their lowliness, not in spite of it. As beings who "need light," helping the living is their path to redemption.[22]

Devotees commonly explained the souls' ability to help the living in terms of intercession, which is familiar by way of the cult of the saints. At the Spiritualist Brotherhood, José told me that the devotion to the thirteen souls "grew in São Paulo because people sought their intercession . . . and obtained miracles." Later, he explained the process: "You make a request; you solicit their intercession. And the Catholic belief says the souls need prayer, need supplication, so they can be comforted."[23]

I typically asked devotees why they thought the souls had the power to help the living, which was something of a provocation. Several chastised me for assuming souls have power of their own. As one said, "Look, they do not have any power at all. People say . . . I don't know, because I've never disincarnated, but it is said that they go to the Son of the Father, Jesus Christ, and ask. They ask him. . . . They go and intercede with the Son, the Son intercedes with the Father, the Lord of all, he who created everything."[24] Similarly, another explained, "It's not they [the souls] that help. They can intercede for you. I believe it's like this—they intercede and bring your petition to other spirits, like Jesus." She then likened intercession to navigating a corporate bureaucracy, a familiar way of understanding power.[25] "A firm has a director, right? And then it has a manager? And then a supervisor, for you who are there below and can't speak with the director or the manager. You have to speak with the supervisor, and the supervisor goes there in the manager's office and says, 'Look, Junia wants a raise.' And the manager says, 'I'll go see with the director if we can give her a raise.' I think there's a scale like that."[26]

In Catholic theology, intercession is "the act of pleading by one who in God's sight has a right to do so in order to obtain mercy for one in need." However, it "differs from all other species of prayer because the benefit sought is for another."[27] That the saints, angels, and Mary can intercede for the living has been dogma since the Council of Trent. But as I noted in chapter 1, the souls' ability to intercede has been contentious, rankling clerics who preferred the relationship between the living and the dead be one of selfless giving with no expectation of recompense rather than one of reciprocity. But Brazilian clergy promoted seeking souls' intercession since at least the middle of the nineteenth century, and the *Catechism of the Catholic Church* clearly states that "Our prayer for [the dead] is not only capable of helping them, but also of making their intercession for us effective."[28]

But the doctrine of intercession falls short of capturing how devotees understand souls' ability to act in the world. After all, if souls' power were limited to intercession, why avoid lighting candles to them at home? Even devotees who invoked intercession tended to describe the souls as more extensive entities, confined neither to purgatory nor heaven. For example, after talking about intercession, José, the Spiritualist Brotherhood's director, suggested the thirteen souls "exist in a parallel world to the earth, which isn't material, but in some way they have control over the materiality of things here on earth. . . . They manipulate this plasma, this thing of terrestrial life."[29] Other devotees offered similar explanations, which drew from Kardecist Spiritism's "harmonial," sympathetic theology to explain souls' action in the world.[30] Maria, the devotee I introduced last chapter who prayed to the thirteen souls at a doctor's recommendation, suggested, "It's as if the blessed souls were people like us. That's why I think they're here with us; they're present. They know what you need and I need, as if they were friends." Likening the souls to Patrick Swayze's character in *Ghost*, she said that if you need something from someone, the souls will go to them, "blow," and "move themselves rapidly" to get that person's attention.[31]

What matters is that the souls, whether in purgatory or "here with us," are close. They are like the living, intimate through their familiarity with everyday struggle. And though most resonant at sites of suffering, the souls' efficacy partly stems from their ability to move through the world. At the Chapel of the Afflicted, I met Tereza, a sixty-year-old Black woman who credited the thirteen souls with saving her son from an illness that nearly killed him. A street vendor who operated without a license, Tereza sought the souls' protection from drunks, thieves, and the police alike. "Let's suppose I'm there selling with my cart and the police are there. If they come running, I can only think, I can walk right past them without them seeing me, or they see me but don't arrest me. . . . I say, 'Ready [*pronto*], my souls, and now? Do I go? Do I stay?' . . . I know that I really believe, and I say the souls are my friends," she said.[32]

One of the most common devotional aids at the Liberdade churches is the Novena of the Afflicted Souls (see this book's frontispiece). On any given Monday, it is easy to find dozens, if not hundreds, of these novenas, nine copies of which devotees bring each week as they come to pray to the dead. Unlike the professionally printed Prayer to the Thirteen Souls, this novena is typically handwritten or photocopied. As such, it is open to continual change, an endless set of versions without any obvious original. But for all their differences, every version of the novena I have seen emphasizes the souls' suffering and ability to help the living. Each of the twenty-six iterations I encountered instructs its users to pray at a church, to bring nine copies of the novena, and to light a candle for the souls. And in violation of the church's prohibition on attributing "the efficacy of prayers or of the sacramental signs to their mere exhibition or performance, apart from the interior dispositions they demand," the novena unfailingly assures its users, "Who does not have faith will be moved by what will happen. . . . It is so moving that by the third Monday, you will see your petition [*pedido*] answered."[33]

As with the English verb petition, in a religious context, *pedido* conveys a posture of beseeching humility on behalf of the petitioner. The anthropologist Renata de Castro Menezes describes this as the "etiquette of the *pedido*," or the way to ask. As seen in the Novena of the Afflicted Souls, the language of the pedido is stylistically distinct from everyday speech, often employing a formal tone, established partly through the use of the pronouns *tu* and *vós* (you), common in Catholic oratory but rare in everyday speech in southeastern Brazil. Menezes notes that petitioners lavish superlatives on the beings they petition, calling figures like Saint Anthony "glorious" (and the souls "so powerful"). They are careful not to ask for too much or for superfluous things, as well as to be thankful for graces received.[34] At the Chapel of the Afflicted, Renata explained that devotees often framed questionable requests in oblique terms: for example, if a mother disapproved of her daughter's partner, she might ask that the souls help her daughter's application to a foreign university.[35]

The *promessa* (promise) is another way of seeking help of souls and saints and somewhat different from the pedido. The language around the promessa tends to be more transactional: whereas one "gives thanks" after a petition has been answered, one "pays" a promise. It acts like a promissory note. The terms of the promessa are usually more extreme than those of pedidos and are often dictated by desperation: "If you heal my child, I'll visit every Monday for ten years." And like debts, promessas are transferrable. As a wealthy white practitioner who had been visiting the Church of the Hanged for about three months explained to me, "My mother, ah . . . made this agreement with the souls that, every time I close a good deal, I would come here and light a candle. So she made this promise, and it's only me that has to pay!" She laughed at her predicament, continuing, "Every time I close a good deal, I have to come here . . . for the rest of my life!"[36]

Debt shapes the cult of the souls in other ways. While I was hanging around the administrative desk at the Chapel of the Afflicted, a devotee approached Renata and asked to buy eight candles. As she had just bought a pack of eight candles not ten minutes earlier, Renata asked her what happened. "One of them fell over," she explained. Renata tried to give her a candle free of charge. "No, I need all eight [at once]. It's a ritual." When Renata offered a package of eight for free, the devotee insisted on paying.[37] I thought little of it until months later, when another devotee paid Renata with a one-real note, a denomination no longer in circulation. Though valid, Renata thought it was not and gave it to me, laughing. Devotees will scrounge up change if they need to and will rarely take candles for free or on credit. "They're not worried about owing me money," she said. "They don't want to be in debt to the souls."[38]

Even though Renata had clued me in to devotees' concerns about being in debt to the souls, she resisted seeing the devotion as merely transactional. I once asked her if there was any significance to the number of candles people buy, suggesting that maybe some bought more in hopes of currying the souls' favor. "Michael, you ask impossible questions," she said. But after thinking about it for a moment, she said that sometimes devotees buy more candles *after* receiving a favor, as a way of showing thanks. "It's not just an exchange," Renata said, but more like a "seeking" or a "day-to-day conversation." It could be that Renata was trying to put a good face on the devotion, perhaps to contrast it with the neo-Pentecostal churches we had been talking about earlier, which she characterized as money-hungry "aberrations." But in other conversations, she insisted that the practice was not an instrumental exchange with the souls. "It is not magic," she insisted.[39]

Fair enough. But whereas fleeting commercial transactions close out relationships, debt maintains them. Note the kinds of debt distinctive to the promessa versus owing money for candles. As a moral obligation, the promessa incurs a debt of gratitude. At the tombs of the thirteen souls, Bruna put this clearly enough: "What is paying an obligation? It's a matter of giving thanks, really." These "relationships of gifting, obligation, and exchange" are common to Catholic (and Afro-Brazilian) devotional culture, and they suggest the extent to which economic ideas structure and reflect relationships between humans, gods, and spirits.[40]

But devotees' resistance to borrowing candles intended for the souls is not a question of obligation or gratitude. Rather, this custom points to the thin difference between souls and ghosts. Souls and ghosts are typically described in relation to privation, such as the "needy souls" or, in the Buddhist context, "hungry ghosts." This relationship abides in social theory; Slavoj Žižek, for instance, calls ghosts "the collectors of some unpaid symbolic debt," and Avery Gordon writes, "The whole essence, if you can use that word, of a ghost is that it has a real presence and *demands its due*, your attention."[41] Borrowing from the dead upsets the terms of exchange, transforming souls from grateful debtors into vengeful creditors seeking recompense.

The question of debt also points toward the relationship between economy and social violence. In chapter 2, I argued that São Paulo is haunted by modernization. In his ethnography of anti-Black violence in contemporary São Paulo, Jaime Amparo Alves makes a persuasive case that the city's "neoliberal urban governance is marked by necropolitics," in which "spatial segregation, mass incarceration, and killings by the police are all constitutive dimensions of the reproduction of the order." Sites like the Liberdade churches illumine the city's necropolitics, as well as the ways in which those politics are inextricable from an economic system in which the prosperity of some relies on the biological and social death of others.[42]

These pregnant exchanges between the living and the dead depend on and reinforce the souls' affective intensity. Last chapter, I suggested the devotion is animated by the tension between restlessness and peace, suffering and relief, and haunting and devotion. Devotions of all kinds trade on difference, especially between superhuman and human and heaven and earth. But whereas, say, the devotion to saints or the Virgin Mary involves exchanges that "educe a benevolent state, a cluster and conjuncture that is generative of fortunate possibilities and dispositions," the cult of the souls is more afflicted, marked by melancholy and despair. Put another way, the souls demand a specific disposition of the living, one different from that of saints. They require care.

Care, Maintenance, Repair

"I love my mother, still, a lot," said Beatriz, the neo-Pentecostal devotee I introduced in chapter 2. "I do everything that she liked, for her. I bring candles for her. I request mass for her. I pray for her. Our Father, Hail Mary—all these things for her. But I'm evangelical, the World Church of the Power of God." A white woman in her fifties, Beatriz had been raised Catholic and practiced spiritism before joining an evangelical church. "If the denomination I go to knew, they would say something like, 'You're not evangelical. You're between two things,'" she said. But her parents were devotees, as were her grandparents. And she had to ask herself, "What if they're missing all that they did before?" Praying to the souls was a way of carrying on family tradition.[43]

A month earlier, Beatriz had returned to her hometown in the northeast to take care of her mother's tomb. It was a mess. "Everything broken, all ugly," she said. "So I went there, fixed it up, put down nice ceramic [tiles on the tomb], and made it beautiful. I put a plaque with the date she was born and the date she died; she disincarnated." She did the same for her father and brother. "The evangelicals say you don't need to do it because [the dead] are sleeping" until the bodily resurrection, Beatriz said. "They say it's just throwing your money away. For me it's not. For me it's a matter of respect."

In recent years, "care has reentered the zeitgeist." Hobart and Kneese trace the term's recent rise to the 2016 US presidential election, after which "op-eds on #selfcare exploded across media platforms" and prominent activists like Angela Davis "explicitly tied social change to care."[44] Later, the COVID-19 pandemic highlighted what feminists have long argued: that care and care work are as undervalued as they are indispensable. The pandemic also prompted attention to enduring disparities in care due to issues of affordability, access, and bias on behalf of medical health professionals. Amid cascading political, health, and environmental crises, care has emerged as an urgent "'ethico-political' commitment to the neglected and oppressed and a concern with the affective dimensions of our material world."[45]

Hobart and Kneese define *care* as "a relational set of discourses and practices between people, environments, and objects that approximate what philosophers like Adam Smith and David Hume identify as 'empathy,' 'sympathy,' or 'fellow feeling.'"[46] But in distinction to these other terms, affliction shades the word. In early usage, *care* denoted "mental suffering, sorrow, grief, trouble," as well as lamentation and mourning.[47] As Judith Butler notes, mourning pulls us beyond ourselves. It cannot be planned. It comes in waves. "What grief displays," she suggests, "is the thrall in which our relations with others holds us."[48]

The point of care thinking is not to dwell on loss but to understand "how the world gets put back together." Attending to care's material dimensions thus means taking seriously the work of maintenance and repair. Water systems, road infrastructure, software programs, gravesites—all these things are built once but must be maintained for years, if not centuries. In an era obsessed with innovation, focusing on maintenance and care is more than a theoretical choice; it is also an ethical and political one. As Shannon Mattern writes, "This is an exciting area of inquiry precisely because the lines between scholarship and practice are blurred. To study maintenance is itself an act of maintenance. To fill in the gaps in this literature, to draw connections among different disciplines, is an act of repair or, simply, of taking care—connecting threads, mending holes, amplifying quiet voices."[49] At the most basic level, "engaging with care requires a speculative commitment to neglected things."[50] But it also requires cultivating "a deep wonder and appreciation for the ongoing activities by which stability (such as it is) is maintained."[51]

Maintenance can also be a way of understanding religious change and even innovation. It is not stasis. As Steven Jackson notes, repair maintenance and repair are "sites for some of [innovation's] most interesting and consequential operations." Despite the myth of the innovative genius, some of the most defining technologies of contemporary life, such as the internet, emerged from collective, patchwork efforts.[52] In a maintenance-centric approach, innovation and change appear as continuous, processual, and relational rather than bursting forth in "moments of quasi-mythical origination."[53]

Centering maintenance over origins can offer a finer-grained view of religious creativity and change. As I discussed last chapter, the question of origins has long frustrated the study of religion. This has been especially so regarding African-inspired religions, which tend to be imagined in relation to a putatively stable point of origin. In this thinking, the most "authentic" traditions are those that hew most closely to an imagined tradition, such as of Yorùbá religion prior to colonial encounter or the slave trade. Change thus gets dismissed as either syncretic aberration, due either to innovative individuals (like Zelio de Morães, a white spiritist widely recognized as a, if not the, founding figure of Umbanda) or "corrosive" social forces (like racial mixture or urbanization, which Roger Bastide argued led to the ostensibly unprincipled mixture seen in Bantu-inspired religions).

Concerning religion as in technology, maintenance can lead to innovation. In maintaining her parents' tombs and praying the devotion, Beatriz was forging a way of being religious that cut against evangelical norms. We can say the same for Olinda as she moved from Umbanda to Candomblé.

When I solicited an interview from Olinda's *filha-de-santo*, Bruna, at the tombs of the thirteen souls, she demurred, telling me, "You should talk to Olinda. She has more baggage than me." In colloquial Brazilian Portuguese, baggage is not merely a burden but all that which accrues with experience. Olinda had been praying to the souls and cultivating her caboclo before being initiated into Ketu Candomblé and refused to "throw this all away." Affectively bound to these beings, she brought the caboclos and souls with her as she built a Ketu Candomblé *terreiro* and brought the *orixás* and *pretos velhos* to the tombs of the thirteen souls.

In the midst of movement, then, maintaining affective ties to souls and spirits can precipitate change. In "Moving between Religions in Brazil," the anthropologist Miriam Rabelo traces the trajectory of Lurdinha, a *mãe-de-santo* in Salvador da Bahia. Like Olinda, Lurdinha moved from Umbanda to Candomblé and did not want give up the caboclo and *exu* spirits that the "orthodox" Candomblé houses consider syncretic aberrations. Rabelo argues that whereas the African *orixás* are distant and superior, "caboclos and exus like to mingle with humans; they drink, smoke, chat, and give advice." Adepts form "very personal and affectively charged bonds with these spirits." Perhaps even more so than the souls, they become friends. "It is the force of these affective ties, rather than the persistence of beliefs, that sets syncretic work in motion," Rabelo argues. When priestesses like Lurdinha and Olinda found *terreiros*, they maintain ties with old spiritual friends, incorporating them into these new ritual spaces.[54]

We find similar affective accumulations in other Black Atlantic traditions. For example, Elizabeth Pérez tells of Ashabi Mosley, the head priestess of a Lucumí house temple in the South Side of Chicago. Before her initiation into Lucumí (more commonly known as Santeria), Ashabi was initiated into Palo Monte, the "Kongo-inspired Afro-Cuban religion," and was a practitioner of Puerto Rican Espiritismo. She and her followers celebrated these traditions within the temple, and Ashabi maintained a *nganga*—"a cauldron that contains the organic, mineral, and manmade sacra" of Palo Monte—in an alcove near the bathroom. Pérez observes that the *nganga*'s spatial marginalization reflected its subordinate position to Palo Monte in the temple. But while subordinate, its presence suggests that like Olinda, Ashabi could not just abandon her roots.[55]

When devotees move between religions, they carry things with them. Sometimes these things are material culture (like colored candles or cups of coffee), but they can also be beliefs (like reincarnation or spiritual evolution), practices (like homespun prayers and *simpatias*), and bodily comportments (such as always exiting holy places while facing inward). It might be more helpful to say that devotees bring configurations or assemblages—of belief, practice, comportment, and material culture, as well as experience, emotion, doubts, and fears—when they move.[56] While exactly *what* is brought changes, depending on the person and the context, my point here is that we all have baggage. No one travels alone.

AT THE NEW SPIRITUALIST BROTHERHOOD, José likened the devotion to souls to charity. In the context of the practice, that language has a distinctly Christian ring; according to the Catholic Church's Sacred Congregation of Indulgences, offering all one's merits and suffrages to the purgatorial souls is a "Heroic Act of Charity."[57] But the care engendered by the devotion is rarely so unidirectional: more than just charity, it resembles the mutual solidarity of Catholic lay brotherhoods.[58] This sense of solidarity came across in my interview with Carla, whom I introduced in chapter 2. As she taught her young nephew to pray to the souls at the Chapel of the Afflicted, she told him, "You have to care for those who care for you." And in 2018, as she mobilized activists to save the Chapel of the Afflicted, she would argue that caring for the church was not only about maintaining a crumbling building but the "restoration of a people." For her, the ancestors were the foundation for asserting Black presence, and caring for them was a political act.[59]

In their influential article, "Toward a Feminist Theory of Caring," Bernice Fisher and Joan Tronto suggest that affection precedes caring. "Love and affection connect us to others; caring about assumes a connection with others," they write. "Thus, caring about is an orientation rather than a motivation." While this might be true in most cases, we can cultivate care for others. Just as care workers can grow attached to those under their care, so can devotees come to call the souls their friends. More than just an orientation, maintenance and care are social practices that can generate affect, not just harness or direct it.

The suffering dead, I have suggested, can never be fully laid to rest. Caring for them can encourage what de la Bellasca calls "an ethico-political commitment to neglected things." But the devotion to souls' politics is not fixed. While it is tempting to assume that praying to the souls of the socially dead inevitably engenders liberatory politics among devotees, scholars of religion are well aware that while religious practices might shape politics, they rarely determine it. In the nearly nine years I spent at the Church of the Hanged and Chapel of the Afflicted, I met fervent Catholic traditionalists, monarchists, supporters of center-right parties like the Brazilian Democratic

Movement (MDB) and Brazilian Social Democracy Party (PSDB), and militant leftists. Theorists sometimes talk about affect as ineffable—a precognitive, prelinguistic force that hovers just below conscious awareness. And to some extent, I think it is fair to say that places like the Chapel of the Afflicted are places of emotional intensity. But I want to resist the notion that there is an unbreachable divide between affect and semiosis. As much as we may be "driven by forces outside language," I agree with Sasha Newell that signs are the "principal manner by which affect transmits between bodies."[60]

If signs can transmit feeling, they can also generate, quell, and channel it. In chapter 2, I talked about how racialized ideas about progress and modernity shaped urban development in São Paulo. With few old buildings that evoke São Paulo's Black history, the Chapel of the Afflicted stands apart. But while São Paulo's *movimento negro* has roots in the Black press that emerged in the early twentieth century, it was only in the twenty-first century that Black activists embraced the Chapel of the Afflicted as a politically important site of memory. Emphasizing the power of the place, they allied with devotees in a fight to repair the long-neglected chapel and call attention to Liberdade as a center of Black cultural production. Doing so was part of a broader project of mnemonic repair that aimed for a fuller accounting of slavery and its afterlives. Put another way, what became known as the Movement of the Afflicted was a movement to produce and mobilize affect. Unfolding over the course of the Brazilian 2018 presidential election, the sometimes-faltering efforts of this uneasy activist coalition highlight abiding tensions over race, electoral politics, and representation that mark the contemporary political moment in southeastern Brazil.

CHAPTER FIVE

The Politics of Mnemonic Repair

We were on our way to the Church of Our Lady of the Good Death when it started to rain. It was September 20, 2018, the 197th anniversary of the execution of Chaguinhas, the rebel soldier turned popular saint. Chaguinhas and the others executed at São Paulo's gallows are said to have prayed to Our Lady of the Good Death before they met their ends, and we planned to retrace their steps in a candlelight vigil through Liberdade that would end at the Chapel of the Afflicted. At around 8:00 p.m., when the funeral cortege was scheduled to start, attendees were hanging out in a large room inside the church that served as an event space, chatting and eating snacks they had purchased from two women at a small table. Others readied stilts, instruments, and a portable loudspeaker in a narrow hall that opened to the street. But the rain was coming down hard, so we waited.[1]

The procession was part of a movement to save the Chapel of the Afflicted. Devotees had complained of the chapel's disrepair for years, lamenting its crumbling plaster walls, moldy smell, and altarpieces eaten away by termites.[2] But they were prompted to action in 2018, when construction in an adjacent lot shook the chapel violently, causing deep cracks to open along its walls. Fearing the chapel's imminent collapse, Renata and four other devotees formed the União dos Amigos da Capela dos Aflitos (Union of the Friends of the Chapel of the Afflicted, or UNAMCA). The group's first action was to publish a strongly worded open letter objecting to the "deplorable state of the Chapel of Our Lady of the Afflicted" and calling on the municipal government, city, and state historical preservation authorities and the archdiocese to protect it from further damage. At least at first, their letter fell on deaf ears. The archdiocese was slow to respond, and preservation authorities were initially unconcerned that the new construction would structurally damage the chapel.[3] But soon, the movement brought together devotees, Black activists, and a more diffuse group of people interested in preserving the city's cultural patrimony. The movement grew quickly. By the end of August, over eighty people joined the WhatsApp group chats used for organizing. Though fewer attended regular meetings, a core group of active members sustained its work, helping plan events like that evening's cortege to raise awareness about the chapel's plight.

For many in attendance that evening, saving the Chapel of the Afflicted was part of a broader struggle. "The idea of having the cortege for Chaguinhas was precisely to establish a connection with the history of the Black movement," Abilio Ferreira told me. A journalist, author, and Black activist who led the planning for the cortege, Ferreira explained that the event was meant to evoke the annual Night March for Racial Democracy (Marcha Noturna pela Democracia Racial), an important vehicle for Black activism in São Paulo since its founding in 1996.[4] The Night March traditionally began at the Church of Our Lady of the Good Death, which its organizers once described as guarding "the lament of condemned slaves."[5] Processing by torchlight under the cover of darkness, the protest was inspired by a dream, in which its organizer saw enslaved "Black rebels fleeing through the forest, illuminating their paths with torches, wearing Black." A performance of fugitivity on the streets of São Paulo, the cortege would draw from this Black activist repertoire by joining protest with devotion to call attention to the two churches, as well as other significant Black historical sites like the Church of the Hanged and the Church of the Remedies, in a solemn, candlelit vigil.[6]

This chapter follows the lead of activists like Carla, Ferreira, and Aloysio Letra to examine the devotion to souls in relation to contemporary Black activism and the politics of mourning in São Paulo. Throughout this book, I have argued that devotees' supplication of afflicted souls has been integral to sustaining memory at sites of slavery in the face of the racialized erasure characteristic of Paulista modernity. In this sense, devotion at the Chapel of the Afflicted and the Church of the Hanged has had a latent or implicit political cast; as the anthropologist Christen Smith writes, "If death is also racialized and deliberately executed by the state, then it has an inherently political meaning."[7] But when I began my research in 2014, while devotees like Carla recognized the Liberdade churches as significant sites of Black memory, there was no organized, collective effort to promote them as such or as relevant to a broader politics of reparations. Though there were some stirrings of movement over the next few years, it was not until 2018 that a confluence of changes to Liberdade's built landscape precipitated the formation of a coherent activist movement that would assert the chapel as a site of Black memory and repair.

Beginning with a discussion of a conflict on the night of the cortege for Chaguinhas, this chapter dwells on contentious politics of mourning and memory. Bringing together devotees, Black activists, and what one organizer called the "patrimony people" (i.e., a loose collection of people interested in preserving historical sites), organizing for the cortege led to an internal conflict over race and protagonism within the movement. This conflict, in turn, pointed to deeper questions about what—or, perhaps more accurately, whose—memory the chapel should evoke. When Black activists first became involved in the months before the event, a minority of vocal participants (namely, white conservative devotees) were suspicious. They tended to understand the *movimento negro*, or "Black movement," as a monolith and an instrument of the radical Left. This partly reflected the times. In September 2018, the country was in the throes of a divisive presidential election that would result in the far-right candidate, Jair Bolsonaro, winning the presidency. But the divisions within the movement also spoke to abiding issues of anti-Blackness in São Paulo, which manifested as a debate over whether the group should "focus" on saving the chapel or a broader role in confronting "the ghosts of racial tension that haunt the nation."[8]

In the end, the work of Black activists transformed the parochial cause of saving the Chapel of the Afflicted into an expansive one. By framing the chapel's neglect as symptomatic of a long history of anti-Blackness in Brazil, they made the movement legible within national and international discussions about Black life, death, and representation. The chapel, whose restoration is underway as of this writing (May 2024), might have been "saved" by devotees alone. But the flood of media coverage that followed—including numerous articles and televised segments in major news outlets, a Netflix series that portrayed Chaguinhas as a Black man, public debates, and films—grew largely from Black activists' successes in promoting the Chapel of the Afflicted and the Cemetery of the Afflicted as sites of Black memory. When archaeologists discovered human remains in the lot next to the chapel in December 2018, Ferreira and his peers sought the "preservation of the archaeological collection and memory of the Black men and women who lived in this region during the period of slavery." In so doing, they sought mnemonic repair—an idea I adapt from Salamishah Tillet's notion of "mnemonic restitution" to call attention to interventions in the built landscape aimed at furthering the project of reparations—as they challenged the city's amnesia around slavery and sought to complicate exclusionary myths about São Paulo's history to assert Afro-Brazilians' right to full participation in the city's and country's civic life.[9]

Contention at the Cortege

Waiting for the rain to stop, I sat down at a plastic table with Renata and a photographer, a white woman from Rio de Janeiro who would go on to vote for Bolsonaro. We were making small talk when Aloysio Letra came over. An "artist, composer, and activist of the *movimento negro*," Letra explained to me he got involved with the UNAMCA because he saw Chaguinhas and the Chapel of the Afflicted as "important markers of Black history in the city of São Paulo."[10] He referenced both in his music and activism, and though he did not consider himself a devotee of the souls, he participated in UNAMCA's meetings and was instrumental in mobilizing young Black activists for the cortege.

Letra came with delicate news. Crouching down to meet us at eye level, he said he had spoken with some of the activists who intended to march that evening, and they suggested we reschedule the procession due to the rain. Renata looked over at me in shock. I laughed in resignation, having arrived from the United States that morning for the event. But despite Letra's politeness—he was communicating a message, not a command—the photographer was furious. "I'm sorry, Aloysio, but no!" she said, voice raised. "I came from Rio [de Janeiro], Michael came from Massachusetts—"

"I came from Guaianases," said Letra. He held up his forearm and slapped it. "I'm Black," he said and walked away.

Guaianases is a predominantly Black neighborhood in São Paulo's eastern periphery, about two hours from the city center by public transit.[11] I knew that by invoking his neighborhood and the color of his skin, Letra was calling attention to the photographer's privilege, as well as my own. I was irritated with the photographer's insensitivity and decision to speak for me. Not knowing where Letra had gone, I got up and excused myself, pacing the church and waiting for something to happen.

Until then, the evening's festive air hid the rifts that had come to divide the group over the past few weeks. At least on the surface, what was at issue were disagreements over the group's strategies and priorities. Whereas a few devotees, all of whom were white, wanted the group to "focus" on saving the chapel, others thought it imperative to highlight the chapel's Black past. Carla, who had been a key figure connecting devotees and Black activists, argued that the group must recognize the chapel was "built by enslaved, depersonalized Africans and Black people." Aloysio Letra joined in, explaining that for *negras* and *negros*, the chapel is a "means to an end": reparations. He thought white devotees' insistence on "maintaining focus" was a way to "submit *negros* to a hierarchy and depoliticize Black presence." The conversation got heated. In the days before the event, an especially vocal white male newcomer accused others of *mimimi* ("me-me-me," a pejorative dismissal of identity politics), made racially insensitive remarks, and posted homophobic memes. One of UNAMCA's earliest and most important members, a white person (who, like many white Brazilians, could claim some African heritage) got frustrated to the point that they refused to participate in the September cortege.[12]

With the presidential election less than three weeks away, it was a polarizing moment in Brazil. In late August, the country's highest electoral court barred former president Lula (Luiz Inácio Lula da Silva) of the leftist Workers' Party from running due to his earlier conviction on corruption charges. Since April, Lula had been campaigning from prison and was leading polls by about twenty percentage points when his candidacy was prohibited by the country's top electoral court. Without Lula at the helm, the party was struggling. Though it was clear enough that the charges against Lula were politically motivated—leaked text messages showing collusion between anticorruption prosecutors and a federal judge would later lead to the Supreme Court annulling the charges—even Brazilians on the left acknowledged the party's widespread implication in corruption scandals. And with just over a month before the election, the party struggled to transfer votes to Lula's replacement, former São Paulo mayor Fernando Haddad, a relative unknown on the national political stage.

With Lula out of the way, Bolsonaro, a far-right congressman from Rio de Janeiro, took the lead. Dubbed "The Trump of the Tropics" by the international press, Bolsonaro had a reputation for making offensive comments and his vocal nostalgia for Brazil's military dictatorship. His candidacy, like the broader Brazilian new right (*novo direito*), was defined in opposition to the Workers' Party. Bolsonaro's supporters called him "the legend" (*o mito*), venerating him as a politically incorrect savior who would wrest Brazil from the Workers' Party's legacy of crime, corruption, and cultural Marxism.

Wary of getting ensnared in electoral animus, some of UNAMCA's founding members discouraged participants from talking about politics. "We never had an interest in speaking to party politics," one of its leading members told me. He knew the chapel well. As a longtime devotee of Chaguinhas and the souls, he was aware of devotees' varied political sympathies and told me he feared that taking a partisan stance could facture the group. He was also sensitive to UNAMCA's relationship with the archdiocese, which the group had already provoked by implying it had neglected the chapel. He worried that if UNAMCA appeared openly political, they would further alienate the church and hurt the movement's cause.[13]

But politics were inescapable in the fight to save the chapel. This was partly because the national elections were totalizing, and mass-forwarded political memes inevitably made their way to UNAMCA's WhatsApp groups. But it was also because of the obvious reason that "any movement of the people is political," as one of the group's members admitted. Social movements are necessarily a form of contentious politics; they engage governments in the making of collective claims that, "if realized, would conflict with someone else's interests."[14] UNAMCA's most immediate claim was straightforward enough—they sought to block construction in the lot next to the chapel by appealing to relevant patrimonial organizations at the city, state, and national levels. Achieving this goal meant forming alliances with other activist groups, reaching out to legislators, and petitioning government agencies. It also meant building public support through events like the cortege for Chaguinhas and the Night March for Racial Democracy. And since the group welcomed anyone who wanted to participate, questions of activist strategy were often inseparable from commitments to broader political objectives.

At its inception, UNAMCA's founders conceived of the movement as a collective (*coletivo*) that would welcome anyone with an interest in saving the chapel. Their initial aims were narrow: they sought to save the chapel from collapse and, in time, ensure its renovation. But while the founders recognized the chapel as an important marker of Liberdade's Black history—two of the five founding members were Black, and all of the founders knew the chapel's history well—at first, UNAMCA did not publicly frame the chapel's plight in terms of race. That changed when Abilio Ferreira got involved. Ferreira learned of the movement from Carla, who supported it but thought "the racial debate was lacking." Since she was living in another city for work, Carla encouraged Ferreira to "foment this debate." They had known each other for decades. Even though Ferreira had not yet visited the chapel, the movement appealed to his long-standing interest in "the Black subject in the production of urban space." He got involved soon after UNAMCA published their first open letter, and soon after, other Black activists joined the cause.[15]

According to one of UNAMCA's members, the involvement of outside activists initially caused a "certain estrangement." While UNAMCA "was happy to bring together the *movimento negro* . . . [devotees] and the 'patrimony people,'" this member told me, the chapel's rector objected to the involvement of people who did not frequent the church. Some devotees shared the priest's objections and argued that Black activists had no claim on the chapel. While there was no steadfast racial divide—the priest then serving as chaplain was Black, as were many devotees—the most vocal objections to working with Black activists came from white devotees. One white woman told me that Letra was doing this for himself. She said that, for him, everything was about race; everything was about Black and white. Insisting that, "in Brazil, we're all Black," she made the common rhetorical move of invoking historical miscegenation to dismiss assertions of Black identity and the persistence of colorism in Brazil.[16] Another white member implied that Black activists were sowing division. "If we unite instead of divide," he said, "the world could be better!" His message, which was somehow intended to justify a transphobic joke he had just made earlier, ended in nationalist platitudes. "The [Brazilian] flag can unite all and end prejudice of all hues!" he said.[17]

These conservative white devotees tended to see Black activism as intrinsically partisan or outright illegitimate. Even Renata, who was typically conflict averse, complained, "*o movimento negro é coisa do PT*" (roughly, "that the Black movement is something typical of the Workers' Party"). The white member who urged the group to unite instead of divide saw identity politics as "radicalism" and implored the group to reject the "communist left." This kind of rhetoric was typical of the country's new Right, which equated social justice movements with the Workers' Party and attacked both as "cultural Marxism," or ideological cover for the advance of communism. And after the nationwide protests of June 2013 — a movement that various observers agree was critical in the emergence the new Right — conservatives increasingly embraced campaigns like Escola Sem Partido (roughly, School without Political Parties), which aims to rid schools of the ideological "indoctrination" of the "intellectual and political left."[18]

Conservative devotees' dismissal of Black activism likewise reflects the long-standing illegibility of Black protest and political action to white-dominated civil society. As João Costa Vargas argues, the different varieties of mass gatherings of 2013 illustrate this clearly enough. On the night of June 13, a severe police crackdown on a modest protest against bus fare hikes left hundreds of people injured, including bystanders and journalists. The next morning, images of Giuliana Vallone, a young white journalist for *Folha de São Paulo*, appeared all over the media, her right eye swollen shut and bleeding profusely from being shot with a rubber bullet. Brazilians were indignant, and within days, people of all political stripes took to the streets. On June 20 alone, over 1 million Brazilians demonstrated in around eighty cities across the country, protesting everything from the cost of the 2014 World Cup to general indignation over corruption and "politicians."[19]

As Vargas notes, by this point, the Workers' Party had lost much of its support from the white middle class. While their grievances were often articulated in terms of being fed up with corruption and mismanagement of the economy, they were also due to the wide-ranging reforms implemented by the Workers' Party, many of which reduced inequality and poverty and eroded the historic privileges enjoyed by the white middle class. A quota-based affirmative action system mandated a certain number of positions in universities and public sector jobs for Black and Indigenous Brazilians; the formalization of domestic labor made housekeepers, who were almost considered a right by the middle and upper classes, more expensive; and Bolsa Familia, a cash-transfer program to poor families, inspired "Welfare Queen"-type complaints.[20] So, even though most middle-class Brazilians were hardly fond of leftist anarchist groups like the Movimento Passe Livre, which organized the initial June 2013 protests, they nonetheless recognized those (predominantly white) protestors as airing legitimate political grievances.

Contrast the public reception of the June 2013 protests with that of *rolezinhos* late that year. These "little strolls" were "large gatherings of young, mostly Black (negros and pardos) impoverished residents of peripheral neighborhoods." Though similar gatherings happened as far back as the 1980s, they became a phenomenon and "national fixation" in the final days of 2013, when thousands of young people gathered in the city's shopping malls to hang out and flirt. The location is important, since in São Paulo and other major cities where violent crime (and "talk of crime," to borrow Teresa Caldeira's phrase) is part of everyday life, malls are seen as safe spaces of middle- and upper-class consumption.[21] While not political in any obvious way, the *rolezinhos* tested "the degree to which Brazilian spaces of relative affluence are able to absorb large concentrations of Black people. In this very simple yet effective manner, rolezinhos become metaphors for Black integration," writes Vargas. The public backlash was fierce: in a Datafolha poll, 82 percent of respondents were against *rolezinhos*, 77 percent "thought rolezinhos were about causing gratuitous mayhem," and 73 percent thought the military police—the force responsible for its crushing suppression of the protests earlier that year—"should be proactive in quelling rolezinhos."[22] In some instances, these events (or even rumors of them) led to police and vigilante violence that resulted in the deaths of young Black men. Vargas argues that, as part of a "white spatial formation," the São Paulo public square "is not inviting or enabling of demands based on Black subjects' experience." Vargas and other scholars have taken this point even further, arguing that (white) protestors are legible because the "Black protestor, qua Black, is not."[23]

It was in this fraught historical context that Black activists saw calls to leave politics aside as a way of silencing Black voices. For instance, a week before the cortege, one prominent member tried to ease the tension within the group by imploring that they maintain "focus" and leave aside issues not relevant to the chapel. Letra took the message personally. "My focus is saving the chapel, reaffirming Black presence, history, and ancestrality in Liberdade, and seeking reparation for the population of its original peoples, Indigenous and Black," he said. "The racial discussion is the context for our work." Soon Ferreira joined in, suggesting that debate and conflict was part of the work, not something to shy away from. "Our cause is itself debate," he wrote. "It's conflict in the face of historical omission by the Church and the state. The attempt to silence, to stifle, to gag people is—more so than conflict or debate—violence. Believe me: it will do no good to save the walls of the chapel without saving their meaning."[24]

Rua da Glória (Glory Street)

On the night of the cortege, after the photographer threw her tantrum and Aloysio Letra left the table, word started to spread that we might not march. It wasn't clear who would make that decision or how. Back inside Our Lady of the Good Death, I kept peering outside to check the weather, since the rain had been intermittent. In the background, I could hear the thirty-some congregants in the nave praying the rosary, their words resounding through the church.

After about ten minutes, Abilio Ferreira called the room's attention. "There's a question of whether we should march tonight, and this is a decision that must be made collectively," he said. We agreed to put the decision to a simple majority vote. At that point, only about half of the people who had come for the cortege were in the room. Seventeen voted to reschedule, and eleven, including me, voted to march. I couldn't discern any clear logic to the vote. To my surprise, one of UNAMCA's white members voted to reschedule, and Letra voted to march, holding up two hands and a foot to show his enthusiasm. "It's close," Letra said, "but, well, we'll reschedule." Letra said a few words in closing, and it seemed the night was coming to an end.

Letra stepped back from the circle and began packing his things. A few participants gave short speeches to affirm the movement's significance and thank everyone for coming. When they finished, Letra began to sing.

> *Estou enterrado na Rua da Glória*
> *Lembre de mim se passar por aqui*
> *Sou fato oculto da tua história*
> *Mas veja ainda estou aqui*
> *Mas veja . . .*

[I'm buried under Glory Street
Remember me if you pass through here
I'm a hidden fact of your history
But see, I'm still here
But see . . .]

It was "Rua da Glória," Letra's samba about Chaguinhas. Walking back into the circle, he took the hands of the people beside him as he sang, holding them up as a signal for us to do the same. The song hand become popular among devotees, and many of those present knew the words. We joined hands, and some began harmonizing over the chorus. Realizing congregants were praying in the nave, Letra dropped his voice to a whisper. We followed, and I could hear the congregants' monotone prayers reverberate through the church. This quiet, a cappella lament for Chaguinhas, sung over evening prayer in the church where Chaguinhas is said to have prayed before his execution, struck me as a solemn testament to Liberdade's Black past.[25]

IN AN INTERVIEW IN 2018, Letra told me he learned about Chaguinhas a few years earlier, while working with a performance troupe that put on shows on stilts "in homage of spaces of Black memory" in São Paulo. "I was disquieted [*fiquei inquietado*] by this story," he told me.[26] In a recorded panel discussion, he later explained, "I was upset at first, you know? Revolted, because how can we not know this [story]? How is it that we don't have any memorial related to it?" Born and raised in São Paulo, Letra's family had once lived in the city center before they were displaced to the periphery by works of urban development, like so many other Black residents. For him, the story of Chaguinhas represented the double injustice of Chaguinhas's execution and the erasure of Blackness in the city center.[27]

"There are various coincidences, right?" Letra told me. "Here in this region . . . you had samba schools. You had Paulistano da Glória," he said. "The first headquarters of the Frente Negra Brasileira [Brazilian Black Front] was here as well." The region was also home to *Menelick* (1915–16), an early and important Black newspaper. When Letra learned of the Cemetery of the Afflicted and realized that "there's no historical record of the removal of these bones," he said, "the first line of the chorus occurred to me: I'm buried under Glory Street. It's ironic, right? Because I'm buried, but I'm in glory. I'll always be remembered. And it seemed like an important and potent irony to me, because Black history has been erased for a long time in the city of São Paulo."[28]

"I wrote a song in honor of Chaguinhas, but it never mentions his name," explained Aloysio Letra. "And it speaks of Liberdade as a mark of Black history, contrary to what people think, right?" In "Rua da Glória," the unnamed Chaguinhas is a metonym for the erasure of Black history by what Letra called "the project of whitening [*branqueamento*] in the city of São Paulo." As part of this project, he said, "you have public works to 'improve' the city . . . works like Francisco Prestes Maia's Plan of Avenues"—which resulted in the "expulsion of the Black population, slaughter, genocide." And, he added, "the resignification of places." Sipping a fresh juice as he looked out onto Liberdade Square, Letra said, "It's not by chance that there was Japanese migration to this place." Like Carla, he saw the city's promotion of the neighborhood's Japanese identity was a way of obscuring its Black past, especially the death and suffering inflicted by the gallows.[29]

About a week before Letra and I first met, the question of Liberdade's Japanese identity became more pressing. On July 25, 2018, the governor of São Paulo approved a request to append "Japão" (Japan) to the names of Liberdade Square and Metrô Station. The change was the result of a campaign by the Cultural Assistance Association of Liberdade (ACAL) to commemorate 110 years of Japanese immigration to Brazil. In exchange, ACAL promised to invest R$200,000 (about US$53,000 at the time) to "revitalize" the Liberdade Square by cleaning and repairing sidewalk tiles, painting lamp posts, and updating some landscaping. ACAL would also install a three-meter-tall granite monument in the square, inaugurated in a ceremony presided over by the Japanese ambassador to Brazil and attended by Princess Mako of the Japanese imperial family. Speaking at the monument's unveiling, Hirofumi Ikesaki, the president of ACAL and a Japanese businessman, made his intentions plain. "I always wanted something that marked the neighborhood as Japanese," he said. "And today . . . we achieved the installation of this historic monument, which will stay here eternally."[30]

When city and state authorities approved the name change, blowback was swift. A day after the governor's announcement, a young lawyer of Japanese descent condemned it in a viral Facebook post. "Long before the arrival of Japanese immigrants," he wrote, Liberdade Square "was called Field of the Gallows, as it was the scene of the execution of fugitive Black slaves and those condemned to death," he wrote. "As a matter of fact, it was because of a Black man [Chaguinhas] that the plaza and the neighborhood were named 'Liberdade.'" It was an "undeniably Black neighborhood . . . [but] with the arrival of immigrants and state policies to whiten downtown São Paulo, a process of gentrification began that pushed the poor and Black population to the outskirts of the city." And now, he argued, Hirofumi Ikesaki, "a Japanese businessman in the cosmetics industry," has "used an (unnecessary) homage to *nikkeis* to reinforce a historic politics of anti-Blackness."[31]

Linking the story of Chaguinhas to Liberdade's neighborhood, the lawyer's post establishes the neighborhood as originally Black. In this common telling, the neighborhood's name is a testament to the spontaneous pleas of the people, who are said to have cried, "Liberdade!" ("Liberty!") when the rope broke. But other etiologies abound. Some scholars have suggested that Liberdade was named as such to erase the memory of the gallows, and others have proposed the name was an allusion to the freedom that the enslaved would gain only in death. The origin story sanctioned by the city is more mundane. In 1831, the city councilman Cândido Gonçalves Gomide originally proposed to rename Largo Curso Jurídico (now Largo São Francisco) to Liberdade Square to commemorate Don Pedro I's abdication of the throne. Rejecting this proposal, the city council gave the name to a fountain that stood in the square. Later, Liberdade Fountain was moved to the Field of the Gallows, the place where Chaguinhas was hanged. The fountain was an important landmark and water source, and in 1858, the city council officially renamed the plaza to Liberdade Square (Praça da Liberdade) "in respect of popular custom." By the 1870s, the surrounding neighborhood took on the name.[32]

The correspondences and disjunctures among these origin stories are instructive. As the historian Patrícia Oliveira notes, the city's bland, sanctioned history of Liberdade's naming affirms the role of the liberal political elite in memorializing Brazilian independence.[33] But "the political liveliness of street names and other toponyms is not reducible to official naming processes and procedures alone."[34] Liberdade's alternative etiologies, like the story of Chaguinhas, point to Brazil's faithless promise of freedom and independence. Liberdade was not a place of unconditional liberty; it was the place where paupers were buried in a simple grave, where Chaguinhas and myriad others were unjustly put to death, and now, where a businessman's wish to "eternally" mark a neighborhood as Japanese threatened to further obscure its other histories.

The Color of Chaguinhas

I first learned about "Rua da Glória" from Renata. One afternoon, I was at the Chapel of the Afflicted when Renata asked if I had read anything saying Chaguinhas was Black. I told her I hadn't found anything definitive. The known primary sources are scant, and the question of his race rarely came up in the secondary literature. My early notes indicate that I assumed, or at least heard, that Chaguinhas was Black, but I hadn't given the issue much attention. As far as I could tell, there had not been much debate about Chaguinhas's race among devotees. But now, Renata said, everyone was saying he was Black. And she suggested Aloysio Letra had something to do with it.[35]

Until after UNAMCA's founding, the only image of Chaguinhas I had seen in the chapel was an oil painting commissioned by a devotee in 2008 in thanks for a favor received (fig. 5.1). Journalists have reproduced the image in their coverage of the chapel, and Renata printed up stickers of it in December 2017, when more people started visiting the chapel after a celebrity recommended the devotion to Chaguinhas on a late-night talk show.[36] Then, in 2019, another employee began using the image on packages of candles to encourage sales.[37] Between these endorsements and its prominent location behind the administrator's desk, the oil painting became the most well-known representation of an elusive historical figure.

"Have you been to the Chapel of the Afflicted?" Márcia Costa asked me. A designer and illustrator who described herself as *negra de pele clara* (a light-skinned Black woman), Costa is the author of a graphic novel about ethnicity and identity in Liberdade, and we met to talk about her book. "There's a painting of [Chaguinhas] there, which, in my opinion, looks like Michael Jackson," she said, laughing. "Like, I did a double take." It was true. Between Chaguinhas's physiognomy and military jacket, devotees often joked about the likeness. Recalling her own struggle in portraying Chaguinhas—when Costa visited the chapel for research, she found that Black devotees said Chaguinhas was Black, and white ones that he was white—Costa suggested the artist who created the portrait hit a similar impasse. She suggested that the artist, whether or not he was aware of it, had designed Chaguinhas in the likeness of Michael Jackson, who personified a kind of racial ambiguity.[38]

If Costa had some reservations about the image, Aloysio Letra was unambiguous about his disapproval. "The image that's in the church is one I don't recognize as Chaguinhas," Letra told me. "It's an image that, just like other things in the Catholic Church, softens and whitens the Black population. He has a Christianized face, Christianized hair, Christianized non-moustache [*não-bigode*]. It's a Christianized image." He said the image reflected a Catholic emphasis on racial reconciliation. "You must have noticed a difference in how widespread images of St. Elesbaan and St. Benedict are," he said. Letra said that St. Benedict ("the African" or "the Moor")—often depicted holding a light-skinned, blond-haired child Christ—is common in Brazilian churches

FIGURE 5.1 *Ex-voto* for Chaguinhas. Since 2018, several new images of a distinctly darker-skinned Chaguinhas have been circulating at the chapel. Even so, as of 2023, this image remains on prominent display. Photograph by author.

because "he's a conciliatory saint, a Black cook." But St. Elesbaan, "not so much," he said. "Because St. Elesbaan is related to the African kingdom of Aksum. He's a warrior." In Brazil, St. Elesbaan (Santo Elesbão) often appears as a dark-skinned Black king standing on a white man, the neighboring king of Dunaan, to whose head he is holding a spear. The church feared such images, Letra said, because they could "motivate Black people to understand the condition they're in." So, too, could an image of a dark-skinned Chaguinhas.[39]

The documentary record offers almost no indication of the color of Chaguinhas's skin. None of the few known primary sources state Chaguinhas's race or offer a physical description of him, and the secondary sources are uneven. One of the earliest known secondary sources, an 1879 article in the *Almanach Litterario Paulista*, describes Chaguinhas as young, "of nice appearance," and "pallid" as he ascended the gallows.[40] While not definitive, the historian Hendrik Kray argues that the press at the time often reserved such positive descriptions of physical appearance for white people.[41] Other secondary accounts affirm he was white or Black or, more commonly, make no mention of his race. Contemporary activists, however, point to a 2004 article by the acclaimed historian Nicolau Sevcenko (1952–2014), which affirms that Chaguinhas and his coconspirator, Cotindiba, were Black. While Sevcenko's piece suggests an intimate understanding of Liberdade's history, it does not cite sources that support his claim.[42]

Knowing the limits of the documentary record, Letra said, "I believe in the oral history. Several older Black people told me this story, and they heard it from their elders. That is, there's an oral tradition that continues until today that says he was a Black man." He had heard that Chaguinhas was a bohemian who lived in the Bom Retiro neighborhood. "The accounts I heard was that he was a Black man, corpulent, very strong. And that's why the cord broke," he said. But more telling, Letra suggested, was Chaguinhas's fate. "What happened to him has a lot to do with what São Paulo always does with Black men. They're made examples of," he said. "Those who are going to revolt forcefully are generally Black men, and they're put to the gallows, put in these spaces and such." While most of the rebel soldiers condemned to death were executed in Santos, Letra noted, Chaguinhas and Cotindiba were brought to São Paulo for the sake of spectacle, hanged at the same place where fugitive enslaved Black people were put to death. "White men don't go through this," he said. "So my hypothesis is that Chaguinhas was, in fact, a Black man."[43]

In the historical record, what we know of Chaguinhas "amounts to 'little more than a register of [his] encounter with power.'"[44] Bound by the archive, historians have struggled to yield the vivid details of Chaguinhas's life.⁴⁵ But like Saidiya Hartman's Venus, a Black girl who briefly appears in the historical record as a captive on a British slave ship, Chaguinhas has taken on new life through acts of "critical fabulation." Painters and illustrators render his likeness; *sambistas* act as mediums for his voice; and devotees knock on his door in the Chapel of the Afflicted, summoning his spirit. As Letra suggested, if Chaguinhas resonates as Black, it is because he was subjected to the spectacular instruments of terror that constituted Blackness in the country that received the largest number of enslaved Africans of any in the Americas and was last to abolish it. Rather than aim to verify these fabulations against the putative reliability of the archive—rather than reproduce, even in a minor way, the broader "preoccupation with the corroboration or verification of authentic pasts" that once defined scholarship on Black Atlantic religion—my point here is to call attention toward the "frameworks of collective memory" that support these popular accounts.⁴⁶ Despite Renata's suspicions, Letra was not singlehandedly responsible for asserting Chaguinhas's Blackness. He could not have been. Rather, his samba—like Márcia Costa's decision to portray Chaguinhas as "like me, Black"—is only legible in light of, and contributes to a growing awareness of, Liberdade's Black past and the history of spectacular violence against enslaved Africans and their descendants (fig. 5.2).

Remembering Liberdade

The call to remember is most urgent in the face of forgetting, omission, or erasure. That is why memory work often depends on what the sociologist Geneviève Zubrzycki calls the "creation of absence." By calling attention to *historical-temporal absence*—that is, an awareness of the "traumatic passage of one state (presence) to another (absence)"—mnemonic activists like Letra make a felt sense of loss (or *phenomenological absence*) possible. In "Rua da Glória," the Black, suffering body of Chaguinhas points to the endurance of Black presence as well as the pain of Black subjection and erasure. Communicating the felt immediacy of phenomenological absence, Zubrzycki argues, is "necessary (albeit not sufficient) to any attempt to recover what was lost." In lyric and melody, in the drawn-out wail of the first syllables of its refrain, "Rua da Glória" compels the listener to experience absence as loss, pleading for us to not "fall in the old trap" of forgetting.⁴⁷

I listened to Letra's samba dozens of times, but the cortege was the first time I heard it performed live. As I looked around the room, I saw that even Renata was singing along, whispering the lyrics with the rest of the group.

FIGURE 5.2 New image of Chaguinhas. Since its publication in August 2021, this image has been increasingly common and now appears on prayer cards, *ex-votos*, and candles sold by the Chapel of the Afflicted. Courtesy of @artecliche.

As we began the last verse, Letra walked over to Luciana, a Black woman in her seventies who was one of UNAMCA's founding members. Taking her hand, he led her into the circle and sang:

Sou chaga no esquecimento
Ferida que teima a sangrar
Ninguém silencia o lamento
A vela não vai se apagar
Não caia na velha armadilha
Cantar melodia pra cor da cidade
Se lembre pagaram com sangue para ter Liberdade

[I'm a sore in the forgetting
A wound that stubbornly bleeds
Nobody silences the lament
The candle won't go out
Don't fall into the old trap
Sing songs for the color of the city
Remember they paid in blood for liberty/Liberdade]

Transitioning into the song's final refrain, Letra took the left hand of Luciana and kissed it. Luciana was dressed in green and gold regalia in her role as Rainha do Congo (Queen of the Congo), a tradition most associated with the Black Catholic brotherhoods of Luciana's home state, Minas Gerais. Repeating the last line of the song, "But look, I'm still here," Letra got on his knees and bowed before the queen, touching his head to the floor. As his head was down, the queen held her right hand above his head, blessing him. Letra got up, slowly singing the final line one more time, and nodded to let us know the song was over. We quietly applauded, and Letra gave a standing bow to the queen.

After the applause died down, Carla asked for the floor. Standing before us wearing a red-and-white UNAMCA T-shirt reading, "We'll save the chapel!" she gave an impassioned, extemporaneous seven-and-a-half-minute speech that located the movement within a broader fight to repair Black history through asserting a connection with the ancestors.

> This movement isn't only about the restoration of a church, the Chapel of the Afflicted . . . but the restoration of the history of a people. Of the Indigenous people who lost their lives with the arrival of the colonizers, as well as what was made by the African population here in

this city. We remember that 1700 was the high-water mark of slavery in this country! We remember that São Paulo was one of the most horrible cities with respect to torture and maltreatment! And, principally, we remember those who were buried there in Liberdade, where there was a cemetery for burying Black people, the enslaved, the homeless, and the poor of this city.

It's not only to restore the chapel but to restore each of us who represent three hundred fifty years of slavery in this country. This year, we're commemorating one hundred thirty years of unfinished abolition. Seventy years of the universal declaration of human rights. Thirty years of a constitution that has not lived up to its goal . . . and forty years of the Black movement, inaugurated on the steps of the Municipal Theater. . . . Understand that this is not just about restoring the church but restoring our ancestrality.

All the work that was done to build that church. And when we were ambushed by the new name of Liberdade Station, "Japão-Liberdade"— that's an offense to all who perished in that place. Because liberty [*liberdade*] is what our ancestors fought to have. And all of us are still fighting for citizenship, because we were mutilated and continue to be mutilated by prejudice, discrimination, and an absence of values by which we understand the Other as an extension of ourselves.

To restore this church is to restore our history, the history of each of us. How many of us, independently of our religious vocation, received graces in that church? Because it's the church of the souls. And the souls are beings of light, and they've given us graces, regardless of whether those who pray to them are homophobic or belong to other religions.

Bringing her speech to a close, Carla continued, "Nothing happens by chance. It isn't by chance that it's raining. Normally, we'd have taken to the streets. But in this moment, it's necessary for us to take a look at ourselves." She implored us to "unite, to seek other objectives, other forms, other strategies to achieve the restoration of this church," and proposed we pressure politicians up for reelection. Our work, she concluded, speaks to our shared humanity, to "each one of us—of those who have passed, and of those who remain," she said. "That's all I have to say. *Beijo* [kiss]."

The group burst into applause. As it quieted down, I looked out the window and saw the rain had stopped. Outside, the photographer from Rio had met with a group of devotees who'd just arrived, and they decided to march together.

FIGURE 5.3 The cortege for Chaguinhas, September 2018. Photograph by author.

Within a few minutes, everyone realized it had stopped raining, and in a confused hurry, we got ready to walk. Renata passed out the candles we had spent the day preparing by wrapping the base of each with a paper guard, attached by a rubber band, so the wax wouldn't drip onto mourners' hands. Soon, it started raining again, so we decided to skip our plans to pause at different significant sites. Instead, we slowly walked straight from Our Lady of the Good Death to the Chapel of the Afflicted, trying to keep our candles lit (fig. 5.3). Letra sang, first his samba about Chaguinhas, then other songs I didn't recognize. As we turned the corner into the Alley of the Afflicted, I looked ahead and saw the chapel's doors open, the bright fluorescent light pouring out into the night's chilly rain.

By one count, seventy-eight people marched that night. Each of us entered the chapel's small candle room, leaving our candles in supplication of Chaguinhas before we went inside to knock on the large wooden door. After resting on one of the pews for a few minutes, I got up and walked outside and stood under the chapel's tattered awning. Aloysio Letra was there, smoking a cigarette. Hoping to address the earlier incident, I tried beginning with small talk.

"Difficult night," I said.

"No one said it would easy," he replied.

I had trouble telling what he was thinking and stayed quiet for the time, texting him the next day to recognize my privilege in being able to travel to Brazil and to apologize for not confronting the photographer during the cortege.

The day after the cortege, I returned to the chapel at around noon. When I arrived, Renata was gossiping with the photographer about last night's crisis, laying blame on different people for it. In the end, Renata told me, the rain was really a gift from God. I was confused and asked why. "Look, Michael," she said, "everyone was taking pictures, and the *movimento negro* came with a film crew. What would the archdiocese think if they saw people from Candomblé marching? What would they think of the drums and loudspeakers? What would they think about people giving speeches about the renaming of Liberdade square?

"Whatever message Aloysio hoped to give was silenced by the rain," she said.⁴⁸

OVER THE NEXT FEW MONTHS, Renata would be proven wrong. Soon after "Japão" was added to the name of Liberdade Station and Square, journalists began covering the blowback and turning attention to the neighborhood's Black history. In a *Carta Capital* article titled, "What does Liberdade mean for the memory of Black people in São Paulo?" Abilio Ferreira asserted the Chapel of the Afflicted's importance as a site of Black memory. "It represents a counterpoint to this process of the name change [of Liberdade Station], because it's where the cemetery of the slaves and the poor were hanged, the criminals who were considered outside the law in that moment," he said. Drawing a parallel between the commercial interests behind the name change and those responsible for the construction in the adjacent lot, Ferreira sharply criticized "this process of development [that is] running over historical patrimony."⁴⁹

A few months after the cortege, G1 and *Folha de São Paulo* reported that archaeologists working at the construction site next to the chapel revealed the remains of nine people buried at the Cemetery of the Afflicted. The remains were in poor condition, having decomposed and been crushed by the weight of the building overhead. Archaeologists' initial analysis was unable to determine cause of death or the dead's race or ethnicity, but they determined that at least two of the bodies belonged to women. They also discovered "a necklace with [blue] glass beads, which indicates [the dead belonged to a] religion of African origin."⁵⁰ Noting that most skeletons were buried with few to no belongings, the project's lead archaeologists affirmed, "at the very least, the discovery proves that the first cemetery in São Paulo was destined for socially marginalized populations," including enslaved Black people.[51]

The discovery set in motion a series of events that would culminate in the legal establishment of the Memorial of the Afflicted. According to Ferreira, after the cortege, the Forum for São Paulo without Racism—a group "made up of entities from the original *movimento negro* in the 1970s," which was created at the suggestion of the Parliamentary Front for the Promotion of Racial Equality in the São Paulo city council—had become increasingly interested in the movement to save the chapel.[52] They solicited City Council member Paulo Batista dos Reis to convoke a public hearing about the future of the archaeological site. At the hearing, a number of participants—including Ferreira and various members of UNAMCA—agreed that a museum or memorial should be created at the site, and later that day, on December 17, 2018, Councilmember Reis submitted a bill to that effect.[53] Over the next year, the movement for the chapel and memorial grew, as did interest in Liberdade's Black history. Then, on January 28, 2020, São Paulo mayor Bruno Covas signed Law 17.310, legally establishing the Memorial of the Afflicted in the lot next to the chapel.[54]

Respiration and Repair

"If museums and memorials materialize a kind of reparation," asks Christina Sharpe, "how do we memorialize an event that is still ongoing?" Even for events that dwell safely in the past—the death of a monarch, say, or of a president—memorialization can be a fraught process. Memorials aim to fix meaning; by positioning "visitors to have a particular experience or set of experiences about an event that is seen to be past," even the least controversial memorials are liable to contending interests in the present.[55] More troubling yet, what the anthropologist John Collins has called the "heritage machine" has a way of turning people into patrimony. As Collins argues with respect to Salvador da Bahia's Pelourinho, a historic district and site of slavery in the city center, "heritage" is a legal mechanism that enables the commodification or displacement of living people in service of tourism, redevelopment, and other forms of capital accumulation.[56]

In an October 2020 panel discussion about the Memorial of the Afflicted, Gabriela de Matos, a Black architect who was working with the movement, anticipated the concerns raised by scholars like Christina Sharpe and Salamishah Tillet. "We can't define an aesthetic or form" just yet, she said, since the city would announce a request for proposals. But, she said, "I think that we have to start with a democratic process . . . that engages all the actors involved in the history of this place." Most of all, de Matos urged resisting the impulse to use the memorial to "tell a single story." "That is what led to the erasure of Black presence here in Liberdade, what has obscured the story of Chaguinhas [and] these places that are important for the history of the Black population," she said. "The idea is not to superimpose, as has always been done . . . [but] to bring other narratives to this place."[57]

Filming in the Alley of the Afflicted, de Matos gestured back toward the chapel, noting how it is "imprisoned here, suffocated" by the surrounding built landscape. "We can no longer permit this confinement. This confinement of the chapel—it reflects the confinement of the Black body in the city," she said. "We're dealing with a suffocated history, and the suffocated architecture illustrates this." Ferreira agreed, likening the chapel's plight to the historical moment. "This suffocation that Gabriela mentioned—it curiously reminds us of that event with global repercussions: the killing of George Floyd through suffocation. It also calls to mind the pandemic in which we're living, which especially affects our breathing, our lungs."

The memorial, said de Matos, "brings the possibility of opening, of breath for the Black population." Long and narrow, the site extends from the presently dead-end Alley of the Afflicted to a parallel commercial street. Organizers said they hoped to let the site connect the two streets, keeping it open to pedestrian transit. "The lot, without this townhouse [that developers demolished], turns into an access. It turns this space into an L, which connects Galvão Bueno Street to Estudantes Street" by way of the Alley of the Afflicted, said Ferreira. Left open, "it would become a boulevard, a place for *convivência* [conviviality or sociability]," he said. Seeking to avoid imposing another hegemonic narrative on the urban landscape, organizers imagined the memorial as a space for Black art, culture, and everyday life. If realized, the memorial could be an ongoing site of care and mnemonic repair—that is, what Sharpe calls "wake work," or "a theory and praxis of being Black in diaspora."[58]

By 2020, the disputes among participants in the movement around the Chapel of the Afflicted had largely faded. While there were more disagreements around racial representation during public demonstrations, UNAMCA's leaders would come to explicitly embrace antiracism and the promotion of Black and Indigenous memory and identity as integral to their work and would stress the importance of the memorial to remediating "systematic erasure of non-white cultural patrimony in the City of São Paulo" in public statements.[59] Some of this shift reflects an exodus of conservatives after the cortege, as well as prominent progressive members taking more active leadership roles. But it also speaks to Black activists' success in changing the conversation around the chapel. Today, leaving race out of discussions around the chapel and memorial would be unthinkable.[60]

Throughout this book, I have talked about the devotion to souls as a kind of memory work, one that leverages a religious language and practice around suffering to sustain the memory of racialized historical trauma in São Paulo. Like all work, remembrance is a human practice and, as such, is susceptible to waxing and waning, as well as to political change. Buildings and memorials, in all their substance and solidity, may serve as anchors for urban memory, but they do nothing in themselves. While scholars sometimes treat memory as a mysterious, autonomous force that pools in the abandoned crevices of the urban landscape, it depends on people for sustenance.

Early on in the day of the cortege, I asked the photographer from Rio de Janeiro whether she had been to the Church of the Hanged and what she thought about the neighborhood's history. She said it was outside of her interest. I asked what her interest was. "Faith," she said. Faith at the chapel. Like Marina, the devotee of the thirteen souls I introduced in chapter 3, the photographer emphasized the chapel's intimate, peaceful ambience in a way that was distinctly apolitical. For the photographer, suffering formed the basis of a sympathetic relationship between the living and the dead. But her take on the chapel and the faith there was divorced from historical context and instead aimed toward individual ends. It mattered that the chapel was old but only insofar as its age conjured modernist nostalgia for the tradition and tranquility of an imagined São Paulo of yore.

But for the activists I have discussed here, the chapel evoked the collective memory of the historical traumas inflicted by colonialism, slavery, and the project of "whitening." While Letra thought the chapel important, for him, it was always a means to an end. People "need to understand that the Black population is going to fight for historical reparation whether or not there's a building," he told me. What he wanted, he said, was a "politics of reparations, a long-term politics" that looked past immediate political crises.[61] That was why figures like Chaguinhas and sites like the chapel mattered. By calling attention to the racial violence and erasure endemic to Brazilian modernity, they act as "site[s] of mourning from which Black freedom and Black futurities may be imagined."[62] In reminding Brazil of slavery and its afterlives, these sites are resources by which artists and activists seek to reconfigure the country's civic myths, complicating trite narratives of liberal progress to exorcise the ghosts of slavery and imagine a liberatory future.

Postscript
The Afflictions of Memory

In April 2023, the city of São Paulo announced the winning design for the Memorial of the Afflicted. It should have felt like a victory. After five years of protest, advocacy, and public outreach, the Movement of the Afflicted was flourishing. The memorial was becoming a reality, and the archdiocese was about to approve UNAMCA's restoration plans for the Chapel of the Afflicted. Through public outreach and partnerships with schools and prominent nonprofits, the movement had encouraged public conversations about Black—and, increasingly, Afro-Indigenous—sites of memory in Liberdade and broader São Paulo. The city installed a statue of the samba matriarch Madrinha Eunice in Liberdade Square. There was a growing movement to add "África" to the name of Liberdade Square and metro station.[1] And during that year's Carnaval, dozens of movement activists marched with Moocidade Unidade da Mooca, a samba school from a historically Italian neighborhood in the city's Eastern Zone, in a procession that celebrated Chaguinhas as the "Black Saint of Liberdade." It was a time of hope and possibility.

But when the winning design was announced, the movement was stunned. The design called for demolishing the chapel's administrative area and candle room and replacing the latter with an *oratório* (prayer room) for Chaguinhas. The memorial had no provisions for a kitchen or bathrooms, which the movement had requested to accommodate events in the chapel and the Alley of the Afflicted. The architects' proposal likewise made no mention of Indigenous memory, which had become increasingly important within the movement and in progressive Brazilian activism more broadly. Worst of all, the winning proposal called for using cemetery soil—that is, sacred ground—to construct rammed-earth walls, which would feature an ossuary for displaying the human remains excavated at the site.

"Why is our memorial, a memorial for us, being made with cemetery earth?" asked Elton, a Black man in his forties. "What evil have we done to this country to deserve this?" A few days after the announcement, about a dozen members of the movement met to strategize. UNAMCA had already published an Instagram post outlining their objections to the design, and now it was time to talk and discuss next steps. Elton said he couldn't sleep after the results were announced. When the archaeologists responsible for the excavations at the future memorial site removed the bones for analysis, Elton urged them to change their protocol. If these had been dinosaur bones, he argued, no one would think of moving them. The people buried at the Cemetery of the Afflicted deserved the same respect, he insisted. And now that they had been taken from the site, they deserved reburial. As he spoke, others came to tears, caught between sadness and outrage.[2]

Some argued that the process was broken from the start. After cutting funding for the memorial, the city published a call for proposals with such a short timeline—less than one month—that only three firms submitted designs. And while the municipal secretary of culture spoke of inclusion and community engagement, the city only appointed two community members—one from UNAMCA and another from Instituto Tebas, a group founded by Abilio Ferreira to valorize "memory and Black and Indigenous cultural patrimony"—to serve on the selection committee. On a committee of seven, their presence was ceremonial.

So what now? The question, as one activist put it, was whether to work within the existing process or *jogar merda no ventilador* (throw shit in the fan). While it was not clear what that would look like, some thought it might be an opportunity to "show the strength of the movement." But the lawyers advising the movement said it would be risky. Better to work within the process, they suggested. Even though the call for proposals only allowed for "minimal alterations" to the selected design, the winning architectural firm signaled they were open to changes. After seeing UNAMCA's social media post, they solicited a meeting with representatives from the movement and the municipal secretary of culture to try to chart a path forward.

We met on a Wednesday afternoon in late May at the Chapel of the Afflicted. Eliz Alves, a white woman in her sixties who took a leadership position in UNAMCA a few years earlier, opened the meeting. "It's nice to have you here. For many of you, I think it's probably the first time you're visiting the chapel," she began. "And we asked to have the meeting here precisely so you could feel the energy of this place." Her point was that too many powerful figures, from the architects to the secretary of culture, had no sense of that energy. "Something that shocked us was the lack of knowledge of our history, the failure to research our history," she said. "We really felt this. And from the beginning, we felt disrespected." The Movement of the Afflicted had come up with the idea for a memorial and spent years fighting for it. But apart from a few brief visits, no one from the winning firm spent any time with the community, and it showed.[3]

After outlining UNAMCA's objections to the proposed design, Alves passed around a scanned reproduction of a burial record for Francizca Índia ("Francisca Indian"), who was laid to rest in the Cemetery of the Afflicted on September 28, 1790, at the age of twelve. "So we know that Indigenous presence is here, and it was something we felt was missing [in the proposal]," she said. "These were things that we discussed, that we spoke about, and I was disappointed that they were not addressed. But I don't think it's too late, because nothing has been built, and that there's time for us to change what needs to be changed."

Then the architects took the floor. One of them, a middle-aged white man and one of the project's lead architects, struck a conciliatory tone. He looked nervous. He explained that he had come to listen and that his firm thought of the memorial as a collective work (*construção coletiva*). The proposed design was merely a starting point for opening a dialogue with the community, he said. With trembling hands, he apologized to the movement, assuring the audience that none of our requests were incompatible with the "essence" of the design.

Soon the conversation turned to the architects' proposed use of cemetery soil. Though they had since abandoned that idea, they explained their reasoning behind it. "We thought it would be a gesture of symbolism and respect . . . and a way to rescue memory," one of the architects said. In their thinking, it was a way to keep the cemetery soil in place (which might otherwise be removed as they laid the foundation for the memorial), as well as a *resgate* (rescue) of *taipa de pilão*, or the rammed earth construction that was typical of colonial São Paulo.

Sofia, one of the project's coauthors and a white woman of Italian descent, spoke up. She had worked on restorations throughout the city, and she questioned whether the soil in the lot could be considered cemetery earth after all. "There was already an excavation there; there's already a structure there, built, of a [building] foundation, right? And we don't even know if the earth that exists there will be sufficient for the construction of this wall . . . that we thought, conceptually, would be built in the development of the project, right?" she said. "So, this earth no longer has the characteristics that maybe, conceptually—"

"That's your opinion," said Roberto. Roberto was the founder of New Pathways, a Black activist group that had been involved in the Movement of the Afflicted since early on.

"No, I'm just saying," Sofia began, before stopping herself. "You don't need to be aggressive."

"I'm not being aggressive," said Roberto. "But you're saying something that's *your opinion*. It's not ours."

"I'm saying the earth was already excavated," Sofia said. "I'm saying that there's already a structure there, right? So this earth that we propose to use, in a sacred manner, as we already described here—it doesn't exist anymore."

"Every cemetery is sacred," said Roberto. "It's sacred land. It's sacred land. And it's not only for us *macumbeiros*," he said, using reappropriated pejorative slang for practitioners of Afro-Brazilian religions. "It's for all religions. Cemeteries are sacred. And *anything* that is put in this place is sacred, because the land is sacred. Right? So it's not even minimally possible to say, 'It was already excavated, so it's not a cemetery,'" he said.

"That's not what I was saying," Sofia said.

"And you know what I think is lacking? The call for proposals [*o edital*] is cold. It's very cold. And you haven't followed the conversations that we've had since 2018 when the bones were discovered. If you'd participated, if you'd perceived this, I'm certain we wouldn't be discussing this. When it comes to the earth, there's no compromise. There's no compromise," said Roberto.

For the next hour, we talked through the architects' proposed changes to the design. In response to the movement's requests, they showed spaces for bathrooms and changing rooms, two areas for lighting candles (one open air and the other more enclosed), and modifications to the structure that would leave more open space around the chapel. There was still friction; at one point, Sofia resisted a suggestion by Bia Purí, an Indigenous woman, that the memorial have a designated space commemorating Indigenous people. It's not the "Memorial of the Black Afflicted" or "Indigenous Afflicted," she said. All people "deserve respect, to be contemplated here," she insisted. Luís, a young activist standing near Sofia, winced and shook his head. But still, it seemed like an agreement might be possible.

The meeting's uneasy peace began to falter. The municipal secretary of culture took the floor, chiding UNAMCA for posting its objections to the winning design on social media rather than contacting her directly. We need to "accelerate the process" or risk losing the money, she said. In response, Luís warned her, "You have to remember that museums and memorials in Brazil, as in the rest of the world, are spatial systems of raciality [*são espaços de dispositivo de racialidade*], as Sueli Carneiro [a prominent Brazilian thinker and Black activist] says. So if we don't think about this collectively, we'll transform this museum here—even if it's as aesthetically beautiful as possible—into a museum that reproduces racism," he said.

Luís then turned to Sofia. "Ms. Delucca said that [the architects] had the 'utmost respect for the memorial.' They didn't. They didn't at any moment. And they didn't study the region, because if they had, they would not have proposed to demolish the administrative area and the candle room. I'm sorry. For the people who are here, it was sad. It was sad. It was sad to see this."

"These attacks are really remarkable," said Sofia.

"They're not attacks!" several responded.

"They are attacks," said Sofia. "They are."

The secretary of culture left, and the conversation turned to Sofia. An anthropologist and longtime movement activist explained that just as she felt disrespected, so did he—after all, the architects made no effort to reach out to the researchers and activists who had been studying the chapel and Liberdade for years.

"For the love of God, what is your problem with me?" asked Sofia.

"*Opa!* [Woah!]" someone said.

Bia Purí tried explaining to Sofia that while we were trying to have a productive discussion, she sat there in the pews with her arms crossed, rolling her eyes and sighing. "*No satê prika koya rayon kaxate* [When Indigenous people speak, who isn't Indigenous must listen]," she began to say.

"Speak Portuguese!" said Sofia. "What is the official language of Brazil?"

"What?!" yelled Bia, shocked.

Something broke. Everyone started speaking at once, some with raised voices. Alves called our attention, reminding us that we were in a sacred space. "Let's soften our tone, lower our vibration, lower our voice," she said. "Look, Sofia . . . This is a process that must be decolonial. Our language can't be the same as it was two years ago, let alone ten. You cannot call people *índio* [Indian] today," which Sofia had done repeatedly. "It's offensive. It's things like that . . . We have to evolve in this sense. That's why there's all this resentment. Because in your language just now, you showed yourself to be a person . . . of the extreme, sick right," said Alves. "This comes from a lack of conviviality" with social movements, she said.

Sofia tried to explain herself, saying that her "grandfather arrived here poor from Italy. Poor!" But it was over. There was no more chance at reconciliation. When we debriefed a few days later, someone pointed out that Sofia listed the Memorial of the Afflicted as a *prêmio*, or prize, on her architectural firm's website. It was too much. "Is this the memory we want to leave for future generations?" someone asked. While some prominent members thought we should continue to work with the architects, they were far outnumbered. A few weeks later, the Movement of the Afflicted issued a statement formally rejecting the winning design and calling on the city to relaunch the design competition.

Problems of Memory

In this book, I have argued that the devotion to souls is a practice of mnemonic repair. In generating sympathy between the living and the dead, the cult of the souls offers one way of tending to the scars wrought by São Paulo's modernization. Moved by their affection for the forgotten dead, devotees move across the city, as well as between religious theologies, identities, and institutional spaces. And for some, the act of petitioning the dead connects their personal afflictions to the memory of social violence. This is not to say that the practice is always an act of resistance. But it is to say that by remembering forgetting, the devotion has enabled the political work of a memorialization in a city Ferreira once described as having a "vocation for destroying memory."[4]

But memory is an elusive concept. Some scholars warn that the term suffers from "semantic overload," "losing precise meaning in proportion to its growing historical power."[5] As the art historian Mark Crinson argues, "The problem with memory in contemporary usage is that it has become not so much a term of analysis as a mark of approval." It has become closely associated with identity and conjures "the authentic, personal, subaltern, auratic and humanised, as opposed to such matters as the mass media and globalization, which are deemed to be agents of amnesia." In the urban context, then, memory would seem to stand for the practice of everyday life beyond the reach of architects, politicians, and urban planners. But as Crinson notes, memory is also "strategically mobilized by those professions."[6] For the architects above, "rescuing memory" meant using vernacular architecture characteristic of colonial São Paulo. For the municipal secretary of culture, it was a way to appear to champion diversity and inclusion while advancing the mayoral administration's conservative agenda.

But I am wary of critically deconstructing memory to the point of oblivion. Ever since the post–World War II "memorialization phenomenon," which grew out of a transnational effort to reckon with the violence of the Holocaust, memory has been a way for marginalized groups to claim space. During a panel discussion at a three-day conference on Afro-Indigenous memory organized by Instituto Tebas, Mário Medeiros, a Black Brazilian sociologist, made this clear. "The idea of the site of memory is a debate about narratives, about the right to have your narrative [told] in the scope of the nation," he said. Brazilian national memory has always been white and male, he said, "and this needs to be disputed. Because memory is power. It is a dispute for power."[7]

However we might define the term, memory has never been lacking at the Chapel of the Afflicted. Ever since its construction in the late eighteenth century, it has been a place for commemorating the socially dead. And as São Paulo changed, even the city's cultural elites celebrated it as an oasis of tradition amid the amnesiac sands of modernity. Memory at the chapel has always been as mobile and fluid as its devotees. Pregnant with absence, it is a place that makes space for presence and possibility—a place where devotees come to pray to the suffering dead, remembering the forgetting that stems from neglect.

But the Chapel of the Afflicted is not a memorial. As a Catholic church, it inevitably imposes certain meanings and channels behavior toward certain ends. That is one reason why activists thought the Memorial of the Afflicted so important. It would convey meanings that the chapel could not. And if activists get their way, it will also feature a space to light candles. While I have argued that the chapel and other sites for the devotion to souls are vectors for religious transit, they also constrain movement by discouraging Afro-Brazilian ritual practices. At the first meeting between the activists and architects, one Candomblé practitioner explained it was imperative that the memorial have a candle area. When he visited the chapel, he said, he only lit white candles "out of respect." A candle area at the memorial would give practitioners of Afro-Brazilian religions not only a place to light colored candles at a site of ancestral presence but a place to worship publicly.

Memorialization inevitably involves compromise and disappointment. That is why the movement activists were so concerned with getting it right. So much of the scholarly work on memorials focuses on the buildings themselves, on what they mean and what they do, on the ways they act upon visitors. But as with the 2018 cortege for Chaguinhas, activists now were as concerned with the process as they were with the result. Theirs was a prefigurative politics, in which "no practice is 'just' a tactic but always has significance in its own right." How they built the memorial mattered. After all, the process itself would one day too become part of the memory of that place.

The Future of the Memorial

As I write this, the future of the memorial is uncertain. It seems likely that something will be built eventually. But at a second meeting between the winning architectural firm and the Movement of the Afflicted, it soon became clear that there was no path forward. At the start of the meeting, Marcio Tenente—the firm's founder and a white man of Italian descent—opened by recognizing that at our fateful initial meeting, the architects "became reactive" at the movement's criticisms. He acknowledged the persistence of structural racism in Brazil, as well as the importance of Indigenous memory to the memorial. And he announced that he had restructured the memorial team, which now included a "specialist in diversity."[8]

It was not enough. After Tenente spoke, someone asked whether Sofia Delucca had signed the architects' letter of apology. She had not. And while Delucca had been "distanced" from the project, she could not be removed completely, since she was one of the coauthors of the winning proposal. Members were frustrated that Tenente neglected to call out her racism and to recognize his own. After the meeting, a few people suggested he may have refrained from doing so because in Brazil, racism is a crime. And they thought that Tenente was not willing to accuse Delucca of a criminal act.

At one point, Tenente returned to the question of building rammed-earth walls. "Construction with wood and earth refers to our ancestrality [*remete ancestralidade*]," he said. "How beautiful!" yelled Aloysio Letra sarcastically. This was language the architects had used before and showed how far they were off the mark. For them, the memorial conjured memory through the use of the vernacular architecture of colonial São Paulo. For the movement, however, rammed-earth walls were irrelevant. They wanted a didactic space as well as a devotional one, where they could hold events and burn colored candles for *orixás* without risking the ire of church employees.

After Tenente finished, Letra went to the podium "*Oprê!* Good evening, *tudo bom* [all good]? I'm Aloysio Letra. I'm from Guaianases, the land of the Guianases," he began, referring to one of the Indigenous peoples of São Paulo. "I'm the child of cultural and social movements from the São Paulo periphery. I'm the child of a family in which three Black men were murdered. I have a relationship to this space not because I have a connection to the Catholic religion but because we were here, and we still are," he said. "We know the political context we're in," said Letra, explaining that the city officials and large companies were co-opting "racial issues and gender issues to take advantage and promote a project of right-wing extremism in the city of São Paulo." Everyone working under the secretary of culture "that says they're an antiracist activist and a feminist is a white man and academic—all of them, without exception," he said. We're not going to let people co-opt our issues, use pretty phrases, do media training, and get diversity and inclusion consultants, he said.

"Today it's not Roberto, who's the violent Black man," Letra continued. "Today it's me. And I'm violent, indeed. Understand? I have no problem with being the violent one today." At the first meeting, Sofia "said her grandparents came here and went hungry," he said. "We go hungry today, and you don't care. You don't even name it. It's nothing to you," he concluded. The room burst into applause.

A few more people spoke, and then Wanderley took the podium. A historian, teacher, and UNAMCA activist, Wanderley was a fiercely intelligent, softspoken Black man—a quiet person who, when he spoke, commanded attention.

> I would like us to reflect a bit about what it's like when we confront something that's too large. Like the first time you see the ocean, you know? The ocean is so large it's hard to understand it at first glance. When something is large, you need to live with it, because you can't understand it right away. These days, we're accustomed to short videos that last a few seconds; we go from one to another. These days, things are accelerated in such a manner that we can't see this dimension of things that are truly immense, that are larger than us.
>
> Try to imagine a time in which things weren't so accelerated. And this was a time in which people did grand things, made things like *pamonha* [a dish prepared from milled corn]. How much time do you need to make pamonha? Pamonha isn't *pastel* [a quick fried treat available at street markets]. Pamonha is a thing that demands a day and demands a group of people. To make *vatapá, caruru, acarajé* [all dishes from the Brazilian northeast]—these things take a day, and they take a community. These things are demanding. So try to imagine, in the time of things that demand community, what four hundred years of slavery means. For this country here. This history of slavery [which included Black and Indigenous people alike] . . . this entire period of slavery that lasted nearly four hundred years is like the ocean, like *kalunga* [a Bantu word for the sea of the dead], like making *acarajé*. It demands a lot of time.
>
> So the question that remains is . . . What is the secretary of culture's reason for not being here today? Because perhaps this *kalunga*, this ocean that is known as the Memorial of the Afflicted, is too large. It's not *pastel*. It's like making *pastel* when someone is asking

for *acarajé*. It takes many steps, and you need a whole community to make it. . . .

And this is the problem you face: you can't get rid of [Sofia] as a coauthor. . . . [And if we allow her to remain on the project], what lesson are we going to leave for the future when the history books are written? Which will be how many years from now—five or ten years? Someone will write about how the Memorial of the Afflicted was created. And what's going to be written? That in yet another racist process, people who were not ethnically linked to these two peoples [Indigenous and Black] built a memorial for them.

This is like burning the ocean. This is treating *acarajé* like fast food. And this is your big problem . . . because you're caught between two things: the secretary of culture isn't positioning herself, because she well knows that not even she has the ability to build a memorial that is bigger than the secretary of culture. This is a memorial for nearly four hundred years of slavery in a city that doesn't call itself slaveocratic, that tries to push an elite history [that the city was] created by *bandeirantes* and developed by immigrants. This secretary is not capable. It's too much. The ocean is too big for her. . . . You're between these two people [Sofia and the secretary of culture], and you're getting torn apart.

And the question is, Can we see the ocean? This *kalunga*? Can your firm resolve all these problems? Can you say, "Look, we're here collaborating with the Movement of the Afflicted to build the memorial, but the memorial is theirs." Can you manage all this? You are confronting something large in a time of small things.

Once again, the room exploded with applause. Ferreira, who was moderating the event, gave Tenente a chance to respond. "I don't even have anything to say," he said. "I don't know if someone wants to give a response, but . . ." He trailed off.

After a few more people spoke, Alves of UNAMCA concluded the meeting. "From my perspective, there's no way we can move forward," she said. "And that's all, everyone. I thank you all, and may God bless you." When she finished, an older Black man and movement activist raised his right hand and began to sing. "I'm buried under Glory Street," he began. Recognizing Letra's samba about Chaguinhas, the other activists joined in.

Estou enterrado na Rua da Glória
Lembre de mim se passar por aqui

Sou fato oculto da tua história
Mas veja ainda estou aqui

[I'm buried under Glory Street
Remember me if you pass through here
I'm a hidden fact of your history
But see, I'm still here]

Letra walked to the center of the chapel, where he led us in the rest of the samba. After the final chorus, he called out, "Long live Tereza de Benguela! Long live Black women!" This was a recognition of the fact that the International Day of Black Latin American and Caribbean Women was on July 25, just a few days later. "And that's it," he said. "*Axé!*" yelled a few people in response, as we all applauded.

I gathered my things and walked over to Luís, the young activist who had confronted the municipal secretary of culture and Sofia Delucca at our first meeting. I asked what he thought of the meeting. "Traumatizing," he said. I may have laughed, not sure if he was half joking. He wasn't. He was still gravely concerned that were the process to proceed, the memorial would reproduce racism. "It's impossible to decolonize this project," he said earlier that night. So long as Sofia's name remained attached to it, he thought, the project was doomed. Now, Luís told me, he was looking into the possibility of registering the memorial as a federal patrimonial site, which would make it less susceptible to city politics.

After we spoke, I walked out of the chapel's side entrance. To my left, a plywood wall blocked off the future memorial site. It had become a mural. One poster depicted a Black woman grasping a dark globe from below, blue beads wrapped around her hands. Her long nails extended upwards, sprouting the neighborhood's characteristic lanterns. Under it, graffiti read phrases like BLACK AND INDIGENOUS MEMORY and HERE WERE BURIED MANY BLACK PEOPLE. Down below, ghostlike black stencil art against the black painted plywood depicted skulls piled against two crosses.

Just past the wall were corporate offices for Ikesaki, the cosmetics company whose owner bankrolled the campaign to add "Japan" to Liberdade Square and metro station. Just a week earlier at that same spot, I asked an employee who was on break if he or any of his colleagues ever had any paranormal experiences working there. "I'm going to tell you something that, I swear to God, I've never seen anything like it before," he said. One day he was working with his colleague in the building's basement (which reaches down into the old cemetery). Out of nowhere, a chair across from them moved some six inches. "I don't know how to explain it, but it happened," he said.

That night, after the meeting, Tenente and his daughter were there, standing in silence and looking across the alley. I wondered what they were thinking. Were they paralyzed with indecision? Were they feeling guilty or confused? Or now, standing there in that dark alley, were they beginning to see the ocean, the *kalunga* that stretched before them?

Notes

Introduction

1. The narrative I present here draws from a from a variety of new sources, several of which can be found in AHM, fl. Edifício Joelma. See especially an eight-page special insert, "A anatomia de um incendio," *Folha de São Paulo*, February 3, 1974. See also "20 anos de Joelma," *Folha de São Paulo*, January 30, 1994; Cláudio de Souza and Andrezza Arnone, "Inferno no Joelma, trinta anos depois," *Diário de São Paulo*, February 1, 2004. See also National Fire Protection Association, *Incendio*.

2. AHM, fl. Edifício Joelma, Daniela Chiaretti and Obinson Borges Costa, "Curto-circuito deu origem ao incêndio," *Folha de São Paulo*, January 30, 1994.

3. National Fire Protection Association, *Incendio*.

4. News reports vary on the number of dead, but as of March 1, 1974, the official count was 187 (*Folha de São Paulo*, March 1, 1974). Some reports list the dead as low as 184 (*Folha de São Paulo*, September 15, 2001) to as high as 189 (*Diário de São Paulo*, February 1, 2004). On the Joelma tragedy relative to others in São Paulo, see Parron, *São Paulo*, 64. Note that the death toll of the 2007 TAM accident at Congonhas Airport was higher, at 199.

5. AHM, fl. Edifício Joelma, José Neumanne Pinto, "Um fogo queima a cidade inteira," *Folha de São Paulo*, February 3, 1974, special insert, 2–3.

6. The river is most likely named after Anhangá, an Indigenous spirit known as a guardian of forests, who Jesuit missionaries identified with the devil. Some, however, have claimed the waters were thought "evil" by Indigenous people because they were unpotable. For an example of a standard interpretation, see "Parque Anhangabaú," Dicionário de Ruas, accessed May 16, 2024, https://dicionarioderuas.prefeitura.sp.gov.br/historia-da-rua/parque-ou-vale-do-anhangabau.

7. Taunay, *História da Cidade*, 109.

8. See, for example, David Plassa, "Edifício Joelma: terreno amaldiçoado?," *R7*, February 1, 2014, https://noticias.r7.com/hora-7/fotos/edificio-joelma-terreno-amaldicoado-16062018. Note that São Paulo was a small enough city that it probably never had more than one set of stockades, which were located at what is now Largo 7 de Setembro. Likewise, as Thiago de Souza of *O que te assombra?* (What haunts you?) has pointed out, the "Indian burial ground" trope seems to be a North American import, likely via films such as *Poltergeist*, *The Shining*, and *Pet Sematary*. Thiago de Souza, personal communication, February 19, 2023.

9. Pinto, "Um fogo queima," 2.

10. National Fire Protection Association, *Incendio*.

11. Pinto, "Um fogo queima," 2.

12. Lévi-Strauss, *Tristes Tropiques*, 101.

13. Weinstein, *Color of Modernity*, 267; Williams, *Brazil*, 192.

14. National Fire Prevention Association, *Incendio*.

15. Caldeira, *City of Walls*, 224. As Caldeira notes, this pattern began to be disrupted in the 1980s when favelas, or neighborhoods defined by autoconstruction and limited public services, began appearing adjacent to wealthy, more central neighborhoods; see chapter 6, "São Paulo: Three Patterns of Segregation." Even so, São Paulo's peripheral neighborhoods tend to be both poorer and Blacker; see Alves, *Anti-Black City*, 49–53. On racial segregation as a "structuring element" in postabolition São Paulo and the continued expulsion of Afro-Brazilians from the city center, see Rolnik, *A Cidade*, 28–29, 75.

16. Pinto, "Um fogo queima," 2.

17. "As sete covas dos homens anonimos," *Folha de São Paulo*, Feburary 6, 1974, 9.

18. "A cidade enterra os sete desconhecidos," *Folha de São Paulo*, February 7, 1974, 8.

19. "Um a um, os corpos desceram às sepelturas," *Folha de São Paulo*, February 7, 1974, 8.

20. "São os ultimos corpos do Joelma," *Folha de São Paulo*, March 1, 1974, 11. On February 5, 1974, *Folha de São Paulo* reported that there were twenty unidentified victims. Two days later, on February 7, they reported that this number decreased to fifteen. As of February 11, 1974, there were only six bodies remaining, details regarding which can be found in that day's edition of *Folha de São Paulo*.

21. Ladd, *Ghosts of Berlin*, 1.

22. "Incêndio do Joelma matou 187 em São Paulo," *O Estado de São Paulo*, February 1, 2014.

23. *O Fluminense*, Classifieds, December 28, 1973, 12.

24. A peculiar grimoire with Iberian roots, *The Book of St. Cyprian* is an unstable text. In Brazil, it has become something of a generic title for various occult manuals, some of which bear little resemblance to others. Nowadays, the prayer to the thirteen souls is common in these manuals, though the earliest copy I could find with the prayer was an edition by Editora Eco from the 1980s. For more on the Book of St. Cyprian, see Davies, *Grimoires*; José Leitão, *Book of St. Cyprian*.

25. Leers, *Catolicismo popular*, 94; see also Pereira, *Devoções marginais*, 55.

26. In Chiclayo, Peru, there is a vibrant devotion to the thirteen souls at the small *Capilla de Ánimas* (Chapel of the Souls). News reports of dubious historical rigor say the devotion began around 1924, when people began bringing skulls—which may have surfaced at a nearby cemetery after torrential flooding—to the chapel. In one version of the legend, the chapel burned sometime between 1948 and 1953, destroying all but thirteen of the skulls, thus giving rise to the contemporary devotion. In another rendition, flooding in 1908 washed away most of the remains buried at a cemetery. The faithful rescued thirteen skulls and put them at the base of the large cross in the area. Whatever the case, the similarities to the São Paulo devotion are clear: the remains of thirteen unidentified dead were joined together, deemed the thirteen souls, and turned into an object of devotion. See "La enigmática historia de las 'trece ánimas benditas' de Chiclayo," *Radio Programas del Perú*, September 10, 2011, http://www.rpp.com.pe/2011-09-10-la-enigmatica-historia-de-las-trece-animas-benditas-de-chiclayo-noticia_402607.html, last accessed September 4, 2015 (site no longer available); "Las Trece ánimas benditas, siempre en el corazón de los chiclayanos," *El Digital*,

December 8, 2012, http://eldigital.pe/publicacion/2012/12/08/catciu/las-trece-nimas-benditas-siempre-en-el-corazn-de-los-chiclayanos#.VUt1hNOrRE5, last accessed September 4, 2015 (site no longer available). Though the thirteen souls are little known among North American Catholics, there is some discussion of them on Catholic (and Hoodoo/conjure) websites and forums. On the prayer's use in Venezuela, see Pollak-Eltz, *La religiosidad popular*, 45–46. For Guatemala, see Figueroa, *Fieles defuntos*, 9. For Costa Rica, see Jiménez, *Devociones*, 204.

27. Orsi, *History and Presence*, 108.
28. "Leia," in discussion with author, July 15, 2019.
29. Paul C. Johnson defines Candomblé as a "Brazilian redaction of West African traditions recreated in the radically new context of a nineteenth-century Catholic slave colony," that is, Brazil. Johnson, *Secrets, Gossip, and Gods*, 41.
30. Many thanks to the historian Jeffrey Lesser for introducing me (and dozens of other young scholars) to Liberdade and the Church of the Hanged, as well as for pointing out the signage in the church's candle room.
31. McAlister, "Madonna of 115th Street," 135–36.
32. Gordon, *Ghostly Matters*, xvi.
33. Laqueur, *Work of the Dead*, 419.
34. "Names on the 9/11 Memorial," 9/11 Memorial and Museum, accessed May 16, 2024, https://www.911memorial.org/visit/memorial/names-911-memorial.
35. "Missa campal lembra os onze anos da tragédia do Jolema," *Folha de São Paulo*, February 4, 1985, Geral 12.
36. Eng and Kanzanjian, "Preface," ix.
37. Ho, *Graves of Tarim*, 4.
38. AMH, fl. Igreja Santa Cruz dos Enforcados, "A Igreja dos Enforcados," *Diario de São Paulo*, December 17, 1967.
39. AMASP, fl. Santa Cruz dos Enforcados, "Um pouco da antigo São Paulo nas igrejas de N. S. da Aquiropita e N. S. dos Enforcados," *Notícias Populares*, August 19, 1974.
40. Certeau, *Practice of Everyday Life*, 115–31.
41. Tweed, *Crossing and Dwelling*, 54, 69–73; Riesebrodt, *Promise of Salvation*, 91.
42. As I discuss in chapter 4, my concept of mnemonic repair is adapted from Salamishah Tillet's notion of "mnemonic restitution." See Tillet, *Sites of Slavery*.
43. On "lost futures," see Fisher, *Ghosts of My Life*, 6–16.
44. Hobart and Kneese, "Radical Care," 4.
45. "Marquinhos," in discussion with author, September 8, 2014.
46. I conducted all interviews and fieldwork with the approval of institutional review boards at my various institutional homes during this project: University of Texas at Austin, Oberlin College, Amherst College, and Occidental College.

Chapter One

1. "Luzia," in discussion with author, July 14, 2014.
2. "Luzia," in discussion with author, July 14, 2014.
3. "Cleuza," in discussion with author, May 12, 2014.
4. "Marília," in discussion with author, May 19, 2014.

5. Schmitt, *Ghosts in the Middle Ages*, 177. See also LeGoff, *Birth of Purgatory*, 37, 299; Campos, *As irmandades de São Miguel*, 98.
6. Michel Vovelle in Cuchet, "Revival of the Cult," 85.
7. Carroll, *Veiled Threats*, 117.
8. Brown, *Ransom of the Soul*, 17, 38.
9. Schmitt, *Ghosts in the Middle Ages*, 17.
10. Brown, *Ransom of the Soul*, 21.
11. For more on All Souls' Day, see Mershman, "All Souls' Day"; Amoruso, "All Souls' Day."
12. LeGoff, *Birth of Purgatory*, 4–6.
13. LeGoff, 5, 12, 293–94; Campos, *As irmandades de São Miguel*, 75. *The Catholic Encyclopedia* dates the first purgatorial society, or confraternity dedicated to saving purgatorial souls, to 1547; Hilgers, "Purgatorial Societies." In Italy, confraternities focused on the release of souls from purgatory became increasingly common in the late sixteenth century; Ehlert, "S. Maria Del Pianto."
14. The literature on Catholic lay brotherhoods in Brazil is extensive, and scholars have long asserted they were central to social life. See, for example, Freyre, "Some Aspects"; Cardozo, "Lay Brotherhoods"; Reis, *Death Is a Festival*.
15. Reis, *Death Is a Festival*, 41–44.
16. Soares, *People of Faith*, 4, 126–27, 138–39.
17. Reis, *Death Is a Festival*, 249.
18. Kiddy, *Blacks of the Rosary*, 98.
19. Campos, *As irmandades de São Miguel*, 96; Boschi, *Os Leigos*, 191.
20. D'Araújo, "Morte, memória," 152–53.
21. Campos, "São Miguel," 151. On *alminhas*, see Campos, *As irmandades de São Miguel*, 67, 73.
22. Vide, *Constituições primeiras*, 303 (Titulo LIX, no. 864), 305 (Titulo LX, no. 869); emphasis added.
23. Ewbank, *Life in Brazil*, vi–viii. For the botanist and traveler Saint-Hilaire's discussion of the devotion, see *Viagem pelas Províncias*, 200, 294.
24. Ewbank, *Life in Brazil*, 66. For more information on the Igreja da Nossa Senhora da Glória, see Mauricio, *Templos históricos do Rio de Janeiro*, 191.
25. Ewbank, *Life in Brazil*, 273.
26. Ewbank, *Life in Brazil*, viii, 285–86.
27. For an analysis of requests for masses in the early nineteenth century, see Reis, *Death Is a Festival*, 189–204.
28. Campos, *As irmandades de São Miguel*, 97.
29. LeGoff argues that petitioning purgatorial souls' intercession became common practice as early as the fourteenth century. LeGoff, *Birth of Purgatory*, 37, 249, 357. Michael Vovelle dates it to the fifteenth. Vovelle, *Ideologies and Mentalities*, 23. On the other hand, scholars like Michael Carroll and Philipe Ariès date *widespread* purgatorial devotion and intercession to the seventeenth century. Carroll, *Veiled Threats*, 119–23; Ariès, *Hour of Our Death*, 462. Guillaume Cuchet suggests that in France, it was a nineteenth-century innovation. Cuchet, "Les morts utiles," 90. With respect to Portugal, Campos convincingly argues seeking souls' intercession became part of popular

practice in the fifteenth century, citing the altar of the souls in the Church of the Convent of Santa Clara in Porto. Campos, *As irmandades de São Miguel*, 63, 68.

30. Campos, *As irmandades de São Miguel*, 36–37.

31. Campos, *As irmandades de São Miguel*, 36–37.

32. "Vanessa," in discussion with author, July 21, 2014.

33. "Marcella," in discussion with author, May 26, 2014.

34. Campos, *As irmandades de São Miguel*, 39. Similarly, as Robert Orsi notes, for Catholics in the midcentury United States, "pain and physical distress of all sorts . . . [was understood] as an individual's main opportunity for spiritual growth." Orsi, *Between Heaven and Earth*, 21.

35. Diana Walsh Pasulka argues that after Vatican II, purgatory was reconceptualized from a place to a process. Pasulka, *Heaven Can Wait*, 23.

36. Though priests rarely mentioned purgatory at the Liberdade churches, those at the Sanctuary of the Souls in the Armênia neighborhood referenced it more frequently. The sanctuary is run by the Missionaries of the Sacred Heart, an organization with a historical interest in purgatory. Victor Jouet, an early missionary, founded the Association for the Souls in Purgatory in Rome, as well as the Museum of Purgatory, which is located in the Chiesa del Sacro Cuore del Suffragio in Rome, which houses ostensible material evidence of the purgatorial souls' actions on earth. Jouet also published the periodical *Le Purgatoire* between 1910 and 1912, as well as a number of devotional books and pamphlets. For a detailed discussion of Jouet, see Pasulka, *Heaven Can Wait*, 128–34.

37. A 2007 Datafolha study claims 37 percent of Brazilians believe in reincarnation, while a 2011 international Ipsos/Reuters poll claims 12 percent believe, with Brazil being second only to Hungary. Patricia Reany, "Belief in a Supreme Being Strong Worldwide: Reuters/Ipsos Poll," Reuters, April 25, 2011, http://www.reuters.com/article/us-beliefs-poll-idUSTRE73O24K20110425; "97% dizem acreditar totalmente na existência de deus; 75% acreditam no diabo," Datafolha, May 5, 2007, http://datafolha.folha.uol.com.br/opiniaopublica/2007/05/1223861-97-dizem-acreditar-totalmente-na-existencia-de-deus-75-"acreditam-no-diabo.shtml.

38. Keane, "Religious Language," 63.

39. "Vanessa," in discussion with author, July 21, 2014.

40. "Maria Cristina," in discussion with author, August 4, 2014.

41. Ochoa, *Society of the Dead*, 14–16. Robert Orsi makes a similar observation about purgatorial souls in relation to the ambient dead; see Orsi, *History and Presence*, 195.

42. Certeau, *Practice of Everyday Life*, 105.

43. Nehamas, *On Friendship*, 113.

44. Freyre, *Masters and the Slaves*, xxxiii.

45. Bruneau, *Church in Brazil*, 14; Bruneau, *Brazilian Catholic Church*, 14–15; Schwaller, *History*, 35, 99–100; Kiddy, *Blacks of the Rosary*, 28. Note that there was no great shift in church-state relations after Brazilian independence (1822), at least until the so-called Religious Question of 1874. The church remained the established faith under the 1824 constitution, and the Padroado continued to apply. Bruneau, *Church in Brazil*, 22.

46. Souza, *Devil and the Land*, 108.

47. Schmitt, *Ghosts*, 11.

48. Souza, *Devil and the Land*, 145.

49. Coral, *Orações Umbandistas*, 4. A nearly identical version of this prayer appears in M. de Andrade, *Música de feitiçaria*, 116.

50. For seventeenth- and eighteenth-century references to *almas penadas*, in which *penar* (to struggle or endure) typically is a way of describing the souls' suffering in purgatory, see Zambrana, *Despertador Christiano Santoral*, 480; Mauricio, *Via Crucis*, 180; *Sermones de las almas del purgatorio*, 47, 189-93.

51. Bruneau, *Church in Brazil*, 24.

52. Bruneau, *Church in Brazil*, 24. On Victor Jouet, see Pasulka, *Heaven Can Wait*, 128-29; Christian, *Visionaries*, 340-41.

53. Ewbank, *Life in Brazil*, 67.

54. Vasconcellos, *Tradições Populares*, 79.

55. Carrol, *Veiled Threats*, 146-47.

56. Vasconcellos, *Tradições Populares*, 35, 301, 303.

57. In her study of the devotion, Maria Angela Vilhena bluntly states that "the candle is not a symbol"; see Vilhena, *Salvação Solidária*, 95.

58. LeGoff, *Purgatory*, 293.

59. Ariès, *Hour of Our Death*, 462-63.

60. Schwaller, *History*, 161, 189-90; Bruneau, *Brazilian Church*, 28. On Pius IX, ultramontism, and the Jesuits, see McGreevy, *American Jesuits*, 16-17.

61. On the early history of Kardecism, see Hess, *Spirits and Scientists*, 59-80.

62. Cuchet, "Revival of the Cult," 82-83. David Hess relates how in 1861, the bishop of Barcelona ordered an auto-da-fé that resulted in the burning of over 300 Kardecist books. His death nine months later only increased Kardec's popularity, as the repentant bishop's spirit appeared to Kardecist mediums. Hess, 67.

63. Thurston, "Communicating with the Dead," 134-44. The text of the ban is printed in the *Analecta Ecclesiastica*, 6:187.

64. Kiddy, *Blacks of the Rosary*, 142; Bruneau, *Church in Brazil*, 17-18. The issue of ultramontism came to a head in the Religious Question of 1874, which was a high-profile altercation between the church and state over the issue of Freemasonry. Bruneau, *Brazilian Catholic Church*, 27-29.

65. Kloppenburg, *O espiritismo no Brasil*, 12, 15.

66. "A actualidade," *O Apostolo* (Rio de Janeiro), April 19, 1868, 122; see also "Missão da cidade de Campos," November 22, 1868, 373. On *O Apostolo*'s ultramontism, see Vieira, *O protestantismo*, 53.

67. Bruneau, *Brazilian Catholic Church*, 34.

68. *Pastoral collectiva dos bispos da provincia ecclesiastica meridional do Brasil*, Capitulo VII, no. 91; *Pastoral collectiva dos senhores arcebispos e bispos das provincias ecclesiasticas de S. Sebastião do Rio de Janeiro, Mariana, S. Paulo, Cuyabá, e Porto Alegre*, Capitulo VII, no. 277; *Nova edição da pastoral colectiva de 1915*, Capitulo XII, no. 1194.

69. Lima, *Breve história*, 157.

70. *Nova edição da pastoral colectiva de 1915*, Capitulo I, no. 65.

71. *Pastoral colectiva de 1915*, Titulo III, Capitulo XVI, nos. 884, 885; see also 834, 889 for general recommendations that priests promote suffrages for the dead.

72. Cuchet, "Revival of the Cult," 83. Also note that Ann Taves's analysis of Catholic devotions in the nineteenth-century United States suggests that devotions to the souls in purgatory became more frequent in the second half of that century (i.e., when Spiritualism was flourishing). Taves, *Household of Faith*, 40, 149.

73. *Pastoral colectiva de 1915*, Capitulo I, no. 63; this recommendation is also in *Pastoral colectiva de 1911*, Capitulo I, no. 41.

74. AMASP, fl. Associações, "Associação pelas almas do Purgatorio, Paroquia de Nossa Senhora de Boa Morte, Arquidiocese de São Paulo." On Catholic revitalization during the Vargas era, see Mainwaring, *Catholic Church and Politics*, 27.

75. S. R. Andrade, "Frei Boaventura Kloppenburg," 140. Kalverkamp and Kloppenburg, *Ação Pastoral Perante*, 17–18.

76. Kalverkamp and Kloppenburg, *Ação Pastoral Perante*, 24, 94; emphasis added. See also Kloppenburg, "A Comunhão Eclesial," 334–35.

77. Azevedo, *O catolicismo no Brasil*, 38.

78. Borges, "Healing and Mischief," 186–87.

79. "História do Santuário," Santuário das Almas, accessed July 17, 2023, http://www.santuariodasalmas.com.br/historia/.

80. This idiosyncrasy is noted in the two extant books on the devotion to souls in Brazil; see Augras, *A segunda-feira*, 34–35; Vilhena, *Salvação Solidária*, 29.

Chapter Two

1. Field notes, February 17, 2014.

2. In 2014–15, devotees commonly referred to the church as "the place where slaves were hanged." By my 2018 visits, more devotees and activists began saying *negros escravizados*, or "enslaved Black people."

3. There are few primary sources related to Chaguinhas's hanging, and historians have long debated the details of the event. The version I relate here, which is the most common, is adapted from R. de Menezes, *Histórias da História*, 163–69. Menezes's account is paraphrased in "Santa Cruz das Enforcados," a short, unpublished history of the chapel composed by Wanderley dos Santos, the former archivist at the Metropolitan Archive of the Archdiocese of São Paulo, which employees of the Church of the Hanged sometimes kept on hand for visitors. Neither Menezes nor the other twentieth-century histories that recount the hanging cite archival sources, and since at least the turn of the twentieth century, the details of Chaguinhas's life and execution have been subject to debate. For a well-known early debate, see entries by Antonio de Toledo Piza and Estevão Rezende in the *Revista do Instituto Histórico e Geográfico de São Paulo*, vol. 5 (1899–1900). While framed as a scholarly debate over sources and methods, Toledo Piza and Rezende were principally focused on questions around the political factions involved in Brazilian independence from Portugal in 1822, a year after Chaguinhas's hanging. For a summary of their exchange, see M. B. N. da Silva, *História de São Paulo Colonial*, esp. 284–85.

4. According to the historian Nicolau Sevcenko, Chico Gago and Chaguinhas were Black men. Sevcenko, "A cidade metastasis," 20. While Sevcenko does not cite any sources to this end, his claim seems plausible. Writing over fifty years earlier, the histo-

rian Paulo Cursino de Moura describes Chico Gago as a *"criação da casa de um antigo marchante"* (i.e., "a servant to a merchant"). Moura, *São Paulo de outrora*, 120. Then as now, domestic service work was typically performed by Afro-Brazilians. For more on *criado* as a category of worker, see Santos, *Nem tudo era italiano*, 154–55.

5. Piza, "O Supplicio de Chaguinhas," 46. On the reconstructions of the chapel, see Wanderley dos Santos, "Santa Cruz dos Enforcados," 10–13, in AMASP, fl. "Igreja Santa Cruz dos Enforcados." It is unclear when the devotion to Chaguinhas and the hanged started. Some suggest the faithful erected a cross within months of the hanging; for an example in fiction, see Sant'Anna, *Santa Cruz dos Enforcados*. Others suggest the cross was erected only after the gallows was dismantled, which different sources say happened in the early 1850s or 1870s; see R. de Menezes, *Histórias de História*, 168; and dos Santos, 9. To the best of my knowledge, the earliest visual depiction of the early devotion is an illustration by Pedro Alexandrino from 1921—well after the church was constructed and gallows dismantled—that shows the Holy Cross of the Hanged and table for candles at the side of the hill where the gallows once stood; see A. A. Freitas, *Tradições e Reminiscencias Paulistanas*, 21. On the construction of the new, expanded Church of the Hanged between 1925 and 1927, see "Chronica Religiosa," *Correio Paulistano*, April 10, 1925, 4; "Novo Templo," *Correio Paulistano*, May 1, 1925, 7; "Chronica Religiosa," *Correio Paulistano*, May 4, 1927, 8.

6. Kowarick and Bonduki in Williams, *Brazil*, 192.

7. Though owned and operated by the archdiocese, the cemetery was referred to as "public" even in early ecclesiastical correspondence, in the sense of being "common" or "of the people." A publication by the city of São Paulo claims the Cemetery of the Afflicted was the first effectively public cemetery in the country. Cidade de São Paulo, *100 anos*, 7–8.

8. AMASP, fl. "Capela Nossa Senhora dos Aflitos," Wanderley dos Santos, "Nossa Senhora dos Aflitos," 1.

9. Willis, "Potter's Field," 539.

10. AMASP, fl. "Capela Nossa Senhora dos Aflitos," Wanderley dos Santos, "Nossa Senhora dos Aflitos," 1. For more on the history of the Cemetery of the Afflicted, see Amaral, "O Cemitério dos Aflitos"; Guimarães, *Liberdade*, 127–29.

11. "Carla," in discussion with author, December 15, 2014.

12. "'Pai do Bairro Oriental', Randolpho Marques Lobato, idealizou o projeto em 3 minutos," *Jornal Nippak*, September 11–12, 2010, 4.

13. Guimarães, *Liberdade*, 92.

14. As Ana Paulina Lee notes, "a common misconception in Brazil is that Asians writ large, and that they live in Liberdade." Lee, *Mandarin Brazil*, xxi.

15. The Meiji Empire annexed and colonized Ryukyu/Okinawa in 1879. Today, there are separate annual Japan and Okinawa festivals. Lee, xvii–xxii, xix.

16. López-Calvo, *Japanese Brazilian Saudades*, 79. On early mentions of Liberdade as a *bairro japonês* or *bairro oriental*, see, e.g., Miagyui, "Eles Não Conseguiram Morrer," *Realidade*, June 1968, 115; "Rota Turistica," *Cidade de Santos*, September 19, 1969, 15.

17. Japanese immigrant migration to the São Paulo capital picked up around the mid-1930s. Even so, by 1941, over 80 percent of Japanese immigrants in São Paulo lived

outside of the capital city. Nishida, *Diaspora and Identity*, 55. On displacements, see Britt, "Re/Mapping São Paulo's Geographies."

18. Britt.

19. While the government did not collect precise statistics on neighborhood racial demographics (partly because race largely disappeared as a statistical category in the First Republic), historians have been able to estimate neighborhoods' racial composition from various sources, such as distributions of live births. Between 1925 and 1929, 9.2 percent of all newborn Afro-Brazilians (i.e., *pardos* and *pretos*) in the city were born in Liberdade—second only to the contiguous neighborhood of Bixiga/Bela Vista, where 41.4 percent of Afro-Brazilian births that year were registered; see K. Butler, *Freedoms Given, Freedoms Won*, 25, 75–76.

20. On *Progresso*'s pioneering use of *negro*, see K. Butler, *Freedoms Given, Freedoms Won*, 57–58. For maps depicting changing patterns of residential segregation over time, see appendixes in Ronlik, *A Cidade*.

21. K. Butler, *Freedoms Given, Freedoms Won*, 57–58, 115–28.

22. In *The Color of Modernity*, Barbara Weinstein argues that Paulista regional identity was a racialized category that privileged "whiteness as a source of regional exceptionalism." Put another way, in trying to explain their region's ostensibly exceptional capacity for industry and progress, Paulista elites emphasized their whiteness, such as through celebrating European-looking *bandeirantes*—haughty explorers and slave hunters credited with colonizing the Paulista plateau—as historical progenitors. Though *bandeirantes* were typically mixed race, images of distinctly European-looking pioneers dot the city, reassuring Paulistanos of the worthiness of their city's spectacular rise. These racialized images of modernity and progress, she argues, "have deeply informed discriminatory policies and practices" and have helped cement "the widely assumed association between whiteness and civilization, between whiteness and modernization, between whiteness and productivity." Weinstein, *Color of Modernity*, 6, 14.

23. Rolnik, *A Cidade*, 28; Toledo, *Prestes Maia*, 9–10.

24. "Sinopse do Censo Demografico 2010," accessed May 16, 2024, https://censo2010.ibge.gov.br/sinopse/index.php?dados=6.

25. I borrow this definition of regional elites from Barbara Weinstein; see Weinstein, *Color of Modernity*, 29.

26. Andrews, *Blacks and Whites*, 33, 47–48, 56–60.

27. This paragraph draws from the abundant literature on *branqueamento*, or "whitening" the population through immigration. See especially Telles, *Race in Another America*, 28–29; Weinstein, *Color of Modernity*, 6; Skidmore, *Black into White*, 23–24, 64–65.

28. Already by 1893, foreign-born residents made up 55 percent of the city population. Rolnik, *A Cidade*, 19.

29. Stepan, *Hour of Eugenics*, 38.

30. For a comprehensive discussion of immigration and employment patterns, see Andrews, *Blacks and Whites*. On managerial preferences during early industrialization, see esp. 66–75.

31. K. Butler, *Freedoms Given, Freedoms Won*, 73–77; Rolnik, *A Cidade*, 75–78.

32. Whereas Kim Butler and Raquel Rolnik estimate São Paulo's Afro-Brazilian population at about 16.5 percent in 1890, Santos estimates it at over 18 percent; see Butler, "Up from Slavery," 182; Rolnik, *A Cidade*; Santos, *Nem tudo era italiano*, 39.

33. Lesser, *Negotiating National Identity*, 4.

34. Lesser, *Negotiating National Identity*, 88.

35. Lesser, *Negotiating National Identity*, 83. See also Lee, *Mandarin Brazil*, 14, 40.

36. Rolnik, *A Cidade*, 28–35.

37. Santos, *Nem tudo era italiano*, 118.

38. Caldeira, *City of Walls*, 216–17; Rolnik, *A Cidade*, 67–69.

39. Olegario de Mouro, vice president of the short-lived São Paulo Eugenics Society (1918–19), insisted that "to sanitize is to eugenicize" and that "sanitation-eugenics is order and progress"; see Stepan, *Hour of Eugenics*, 90.

40. Stepan, *Hour of Eugenics*, 23, 43.

41. Borges, "Puffy, Slothful, Ugly," 249.

42. Leu, *Defiant Geographies*, 30–31.

43. Camargo, "Viver e morrer," 152.

44. Leu, *Defiant Geographies*, 64.

45. Nora, "Between Memory and History," 24. Since 2018, devotees, activists, and scholars have increasingly used this term (in Portuguese, *lugares de memória*) to refer to places like the Chapel of the Afflicted; see, e.g., Sorce, "Bairro da Liberdade concentrava espaços de tortura e morte contra os negros na escravidão," *Carta Capital*, January 3, 2018, https://www.cartacapital.com.br/educacao/liberdade-concentrava-forca-o-pelourinho-cadeia-e-o-cemiterio-dos-negros-na-escravidao.

46. Piexoto-Mehrtens, *Urban Space*, 29–33; Quintão, *Irmandades Negras*, 63; Rolnik, *A Cidade*, 67.

47. Prestes Maia, *Estudo de um Plano*. On decentrist urbanism, see Jacobs, *Death and Life*, "Introduction."

48. Caldeira, *City of Walls*, 218–19. For a map of racial distribution by neighborhood in contemporary São Paulo, see Alves, *Anti-Black City*, 52.

49. Britt, "Spatial Projects of Forgetting," 27.

50. Britt, "Spatial Projects of Forgetting," 26.

51. Britt, "Spatial Projects of Forgetting," 24.

52. Britt, "Spatial Projects of Forgetting," 13, 25.

53. Britt, "Spatial Projects of Forgetting," 14.

54. "Beatriz," in discussion with author, July 7, 2014.

55. Mark Fisher describes haunting as a "failed mourning." Fisher, *Ghosts of My Life*, 22.

56. Gordon, *Ghostly Matters*, xvi.

57. Gillam, "Latent Blackness," 2.

58. Skidmore, *Black into White*, 43.

59. Britt, "Spatial Projects of Forgetting," 2.

60. While the word *pelourinho* (pillory) invokes the memory of slavery, the square's colorful restoration as a "historic city center" obscures both the violence wrought at the place and displaced residents in an effort at urban renewal. For insightful discussions of the locale, see Collins, *Revolt of the Saints*; Smith, *Afro-Paradise*, 50–63.

61. Connerton, *How Modernity Forgets*, 5, 53.
62. Roach, *Cities of the Dead*, 6.
63. Trouillot, "Otherwise Modern," 222.
64. Garcia, "São Paulo nos trilhos." I thank Abilio Ferreira for pointing out this reference.
65. Latour, *We Have Never Been*, 69.
66. Freud, *Uncanny*, 148.
67. "O tempo se esqueceu a velha igreja dos aflitos," *Correio Paulistano*, October 21, 1943, 2. Similarly, over four decades later, another journalist described the chapel as a "veritable oasis" and a "message lost in the modern city that sprouted and grew around it." AHM, fl. Capela dos Aflitos, Zaluar, "Memória," *Diário Popular*, September 7, 1977.
68. Vidler, *Architectural Uncanny*, x.
69. Gordon in Trigg, *Memory of Place*, 286.
70. Jameson, "Marx's Purloined Letter."
71. Fisher, *Ghosts of My Life*, 18.
72. Fisher, *Ghosts of My Life*, 18.
73. Field notes, July 18, 2023.
74. "Incêndio do Joelma matou 187 em São Paulo," *O Estado de São Paulo*, February 1, 2014, https://www.estadao.com.br/sao-paulo/incendio-do-joelma-matou-187-em-sao-paulo-imp-/; Rosa Maria Jaques and João Tocchetto de Oliveira, "CAÇA FANTASMAS BRASIL—Inteligência Ltda. Podcast #716," Inteligência Ltda., streamed live on January 13, 2023, YouTube video, 2:59:04, https://www.youtube.com/watch?v=zBlgcBNur6k.
75. Alves, *Anti-Black City*, 2–4.
76. Obert, "Architectural Unanny," 99.
77. Certeau, *Practice of Everyday Life*.
78. "Emilia," in discussion with author, May 5, 2014.
79. "Claudia," in discussion with author, May 26, 2014.
80. Kishimoto, "Nem tudo era japonês: Insurgências negro-indígenas no bairro da Liberdade."
81. Morrison, "Rootedness," 343–44.
82. "Carla," in discussion with author, December 15, 2014.
83. Matory, *Black Atlantic Religion*, 200.
84. Nora, "Between Memory and History," 8–9.
85. Johnson, "Migrating Bodies, Circulating Signs," 306.
86. Ricœur, *Memory, History, Forgetting*, 4; emphasis added.

Chapter Three

1. "Maria," in discussion with author, October 20, 2014.
2. Field notes, July 1, 2014.
3. Field notes, November 10, 2014.
4. The most prominent and likely numerically largest Santo Daime denomination, for instance, is formally known as ICEFLU (the Church of the Worship of the Eclectic

Flowing Light). On eclecticism as a dominant intellectual trend during the Brazilian Empire before 1965, see Skidmore, *Black into White*, 4.

5. Field notes, October 13, 2014.

6. Rodrigo would repeat this formulation, often explicitly talking about syncretism in terms of racial mixture. Field notes, February 17, March 6, April 14, and August 4, 2014.

7. Selka, "New Religious Movements," 3.

8. Birman, "Modos periféricos de crença," 13. See also Augras, *Salvação Solidária*; Augras, *A segunda-feira*.

9. O'Neill, "Beyond Broken," 1098.

10. Johnson, "Migrating Bodies, Circulating Signs," 302.

11. Stewart and Shaw, "Introduction: Problematizing Syncretism."

12. While hybridity is often cause for celebration in contemporary academic usage, it is unavoidably biological and, in the already fraught discussion of religious (and particularly Afro-) syncretism, conjures up the sort of racial connotations I am trying to avoid. *Creolization*, a term largely attributable to Sidney Mintz and Richard Price, was an attempt to move away from the problems of syncretism and survivals by emphasizing African American creativity; see Matory, *Black Atlantic Religion*, 281. But this term also has problems. As Stephan Palmié notes, the term was originally used to reference things of Old World origin born and raised in the New World and "has served as an immediately significant predicate of selfhood and social practice for close to half a millennium" and thus inevitably has entangled ideas about racial identity and purity. Palmié, "Creolization and Its Discontents," 435; see also Stewart, "Creolization, Hybridity, Syncretism, Mixture"; Stewart, "Syncretism and Its Synonyms." For a helpful critique of syncretism and application of hybridity to Umbanda, see Engler, "Umbanda and Hybridity."

13. Apter, "Herskovits's Heritage," 238. See also Palmié, "Against Syncretism."

14. Souza, *Devil and the Land*, 46. I do not mean to point out Souza's use of "syncretism" as a criticism of this excellent and rigorous work. Rather, I only mean to suggest that a reputable historian's casual usage of the term suggests how deeply it is connected with ideas about blood and race.

15. "Carla," in discussion with author, December 15, 2014.

16. "Iwi," in discussion with author, November 10, 2014.

17. "Iwi," in discussion with author, November 10, 2014.

18. IBGE (Instituto Brasileiro de Geografia e Estatística), "Censo demográfico 2010." 2010. According to a 2020 report by Datafolha, the percentage of evangelicals had grown to 31 percent of the population, or more than 66 million people. Catholic affiliation, by contrast, declined to just 50 percent. Balloussier, "Cara típica do evangélico brasileiro é feminina e negra, aponta Datafolha," *Folha de São Paulo*, January 13, 2020.

19. Gez et al., "From Converts to Itinerants," 142. See also Almeida and Montero, "Trânsito religioso no Brasil"; Frigerio, "Analyzing Conversion in Latin America"; Bartz, Bobsin, and von Sinner, "Mobilidade religiosa no Brasil"; Bitun, "Nomadismo religioso."

20. In this sense, work on religious transit mirrors sociological studies of "religious mobility" in the North Atlantic. See, for example, Sandomirsky and Wilson, "Processes of Disaffiliation"; Hadaway, Kirk, and Marler, "All in the Family"; Breen and Hayes, "Religious Mobility"; Sherkat, "Tracking the Restructuring."

21. Almeida and Montero, "Trânsito religioso no Brasil." The phrase *trânsito religioso* first came into use in the early 1990s as a way to grapple with the changes wrought on the Brazilian religious field by the "aggressive missionary style and strong religious competition" of the Pentecostal churches. The concept is intimately connected to but marks a progression from concepts like religious syncretism, "popular ecumenism," or bricolage, which many scholars take as having characterized the Brazilian status quo from at least the turn of the twentieth century—or from the colonial period, according to some scholars—until the 1960s. Drawing on North American sociologists like Peter Berger, Roger Finke, and Rodney Starke, Brazilian scholars came to see Pentecostalism as a harbinger, if not the vehicle, of the religious configuration of modern societies, in which multiple, distinct religions compete for followers in a religious marketplace. In this model, identity comes to the fore, and the possibility of multiple religious identities is severely limited; see Bennedetti, "Propostas teóricas para entender"; Machado and Mariz, "Sincretismo e trânsito religoso"; Rolim, "O propósito do trânsito religioso."

22. Almeida and Montero, "Trânsito religioso no Brasil," 93.

23. A 2004 survey by Centro de Estatísticas Religiosas e Investigações Sociais, which is linked with the National Conference of Brazilian Bishops, asked similar questions and found that the majority (58.9%) of respondents who switched affiliation moved to "evangelical Protestantism." This survey did not, unfortunately, distinguish between the mediumship religions and grouped them all into the category "other religions"; Fernandes, *Mudança de religião no Brasil*.

24. Almeida and Montero, "Trânsito religioso no Brasil," 103.

25. Other studies, though not specifically about religious transit, make this distinction. See, for example, a 2014 Pew study, which found that 30 percent of Brazilians—33 percent of self-identified Catholics and 16 percent of Protestants—reported "medium" to "high" levels of engagement with Afro-Brazilian or Indigenous religions. Pew Research Center, "Religion in Latin America." Note that there are some problems with this figure, however, in that the survey advances normative religious boundaries qualifying practices such as "offering flowers or food to spirits" and "participating in spiritual cleansing ceremonies" as "indigenous beliefs and practices."

26. Almeida, "Religião na metrópole Paulista," 19.

27. I do not mean to suggest that the notion of religious transit is only or even especially appropriate to religion in Brazil. To the contrary, I want to suggest it might also apply to a place like the contemporary United States, where religion is hardly rigid. In her textbook on US religious history, Catherine Albanese highlights religious "combination"—a term she opted for after moving away from "syncretism"—as a major theme in American religion. Albanese, *America*, xxii. Work by Emily Sigalow reframes syncretism in actor-oriented terms. Sigalow, "Towards a Sociological Framework." And Courtney Bender, in her study of Cambridge "metaphysicals," argues that "spirituality is produced in multiple social institutions, including many that

we regularly do not consider religious." Bender, *New Metaphysicals*, 182. A 2009 Pew study found that about one-quarter of all Americans visit religious places of different faiths. This movement is somewhat restricted, however. For example, while three in ten Protestants who regularly attend religious services said they visited places of multiple faiths, the vast majority of those visited different Protestant denominations. Pew Research Center, "Many Americans Mix."

28. Rabelo, "Moving Between Religions," 848.
29. Certeau, *Practice of Everyday Life*, 115.
30. "Maria," in discussion with author, October 20, 2014.
31. "Maria," in discussion with author, July 28, 2014.
32. Ahmed, "Happy Objects," 32.
33. O'Neill, "Beyond Broken," 1103.
34. Abreu, "FedEx Saints," 324.
35. "Cecília," in discussion with author, August 7, 2014.
36. "Cecília," in discussion with author, August 7, 2014. For a detailed history of disobsession in Brazilian spiritism, see Hess, *Spirits and Scientists*, esp. 81–98.
37. Hess notes that while the Brazilian Spiritist Federation (Federação Espírita Brasileira, or FEB) is the "leading national federalizing body" in Brazil, FEESP is "probably the largest [federation] in Brazil, and much larger than the FEB itself." Hess, *Spirits and Scientists*, 28.
38. Field notes, February 27, 2014.
39. "Cecília," in discussion with author, May 19 and August 7, 2014.
40. Field notes, August 5, 2022.
41. "Cecília," in discussion with author, May 19, 2014.
42. Field notes, February 27, 2014.
43. "Dúvidas mais frequentes," FEESP, accessed July 7, 2016, http://www.febnet.org.br/blog/geral/o-espiritismo/duvidas-mais-frequentes/.
44. Amoruso, "Transcendental Mission."
45. I borrow the phrase "boundary work" from Hess, who adapted it from Thomas Gieryn. Hess, *Spirits and Scientists*, 6.
46. "Cecília," in discussion with author, May 19 and August 7, 2014.
47. "Maria," in discussion with author, October 20, 2014.
48. "Cecília," in discussion with author, May 19, 2014.
49. As John Eade and Michael Sallnow argue, "One can no longer take for granted a universal definition of the phenomenon of 'pilgrimage.'" Taken together, the work they present in their edited volume *Contesting the Sacred* aims to move past older functionalist, Turnerian, and Eliadian approaches toward an understanding of pilgrimage as a "realm of competing discourses." To be sure, places like the Chapel of the Afflicted are venues for contesting not just the meaning of the sacred but the boundaries between different notions of sacrality and the sacred/secular itself. At the same time, the devotion lacks the common qualities of Catholic pilgrimage: the journey is not a test of physical fortitude, there are no planned routes, and penitential work en route is not a feature of the devotion. But most of all, the fact that devotees did not describe this practice as a pilgrimage (but did describe others, like the journey to the Shrine of Our Lady of Aparecida, as such) makes me reluctant to give the category much analytical weight.

50. "História do Santuário," Santuário das Almas, accessed July 24, 2023, https://santuariodasalmas.com.br/historia-do-santuario/.

51. "Cecília," in discussion with author, May 19, 2014.

52. Scheper-Hughes, *Death without Weeping*, 434. See also Ishi, "Searching for Home," 89.

53. Scheper-Hughes, *Death without Weeping*, 437.

54. I am using "gardens of memory" more poetically than precisely. *Garden-cemetery* is a technical term for the type of parklike cemeteries that became common in England and the United States at the end of the nineteenth century.

55. Scheper-Hughes, *Death without Weeping*, 437.

56. The *Oxford English Dictionary* traces "emotion" back to the classical Latin *ēmōt-*, the past participial stem of *ēmovēre*, meaning "to remove, expel, banish from the mind, to shift, displace." *Oxford English Dictionary*, s.v. "emotion (n.)," December 2023, https://doi.org/10.1093/OED/2262908073.

57. For more on the history of saudade, including its promotion as a distinctly Portuguese emotion by the Saudosista poets in the early twentieth century, see Amoruso, "Saudade."

58. "Bruno," in discussion with author, August 4, 2014.

59. "Jair," in discussion with author, January 22, 2018.

60. "Carla," in discussion with author, December 15, 2014.

61. Orsi, *Between Heaven and Earth*, 13

62. "Beatriz," in discussion with author, July 7, 2014. Many scholars have noted that this understanding of the dead is widespread in Brazil. Carlos Brandão, for example, writes that the dead "are especially empowered to help the living . . . but are at the same time especially dependent upon the living for their own salvation." Brandão, *Os deuses do povo*, 187. A group of Catholic clerics likewise wrote, regarding the religiosity of "simple people," that "death, the souls, and the other world . . . assumed great importance in the eyes of the people, because popular religiosity is characterized by a profound respect for the souls of the other world." Hauck et al., *História da igreja*, 148.

63. "Beatriz," in discussion with author, July 7, 2014.

64. P. R. de Oliveira, "Pequenos Santos," 80.

65. "Carla," in discussion with author, December 15, 2014.

66. "Beatriz," in discussion with author, July 7, 2014.

67. J. Smith, *To Take Place*, 25.

68. Leal, "Making of Saudade," 274.

69. J. Smith, *To Take Place*, 25.

70. "De cachimbos às imagens religiosas," Museu da Pessoa, accessed March 21, 2016, https://www.museudapessoa.net/pt/conteudo/historia/de-cachimbos-as-imagens-religiosas-43668.

71. Orsi, *History and Presence*, 2.

72. Ortiz, *A morte branca*.

73. "Dr. Efrem," in discussion with author, August 19, 2014.

74. David Scott in Palmié, *Cooking of History*, 46.

Chapter Four

1. "Bruna," in discussion with author, October 27, 2014.
2. "Olinda," in discussion with author, October 27, 2014. Olinda was eager to tell her story and repeatedly suggested I write a book about her life. It was only much later that I realized she narrated her significant life events at ages that were multiples of seven. "I'm a twin, born at seven months," "I'd go missing for twenty-one days," "I have roots from twenty-one days of birth until seven years," and so on. We can read Olinda's numerological attentiveness as what Elizabeth Pérez, drawing from Bakhtin, calls a *speech genre*—in this case, a style of spiritual biographical narrative common among practitioners of Black Atlantic traditions.
3. See Capone, *Searching for Africa*, esp. ch. 3.
4. Capone, *Searching For Africa*; see esp. ch. 4, in which Capone describes the separation of ritual spaces for the dead in the Candomblé *terreiros* of priests and priestesses who had similar trajectories to Olinda.
5. Hobart and Kneese, "Radical Care," 2.
6. Mattern, "Maintenance and Care."
7. Orsi, *Between Heaven and Earth*, 2.
8. "Maria," in discussion with author, May 5, 2014.
9. "Thiago," in discussion with author, December 1, 2014.
10. Field notes, June 22, 2015.
11. *Benzedeiras* are typically thought of as Catholic, though they operate outside the authority of the church and make use of prayers, rituals, herbs, and amulets that suggest a more "combinative" approach to religious healing that draws from esoteric and folk currents as much as Catholic ritual. Though there are male *benzedeiros*, they are typically women and often Black. For a collection of interviews with and prayers used by *benzedeiras*, see Sant'Ana and Seggiaro, *Benzedeiras and Benzeduras*.
12. Field notes and discussion with "José," June 22, 2015.
13. For an overview of research on empathy, including the term's varied and sometimes contradictory denotations, see Batson, "These Things Called Empathy."
14. Jahoda, "Theodor Lipps,'" 151–54; Batson, "These Things called Empathy."
15. Cox, *Body and Soul*, 5, 26–29. Note that Brazilian social thought was deeply influenced by the positivist philosophy of Auguste Comte, who drew deeply from Hume's and Smith's arguments about sympathy and the emotional basis of social cohesion; see Pickering, *Auguste Comte*, 158, 310.
16. Schaeffer, *Religious Affects*, 146.
17. "José" in discussion with author, June 22, 2015.
18. Luhrmann, Nusbaum, and Thisted, "Absorption Hypothesis"; Pérez, "Staging Transformation." Similarly, Kristina Wirtz has argued that there is an "aesthetics of sensibility" when it comes to spirits and other dead; see Wirtz, "Spirituality, Agency," 102.
19. Ochoa, *Society of the Dead*, 21.
20. On habitus, I look to Marcel Mauss as much as Pierre Bourdieu. See Mauss, "Bodily Techniques," 100; Bourdieu, *Distinction*, 101–2.
21. Cox, *Body and Soul*, 27.

22. Elaine Freitas suggests that violence is critical to the efficacy of precarious saints like Natal's João Baracho, a criminal accused of murder. Similar to the purgatorial souls, or *exús*, in Umbanda, these figures help the living as a way of paying penance for past sins. Freitas, "Violencia e Sagrado." See also Johnson, "Moods and Modes," 29, for a discussion of Freitas in relation to Escrava Anastácia.

23. "José," in discussion with author, June 22, 2015.

24. "Sandra," in discussion with author, July 7, 2014.

25. With respect to Chinese religion, Shahar and Weller suggest that the Chinese heavens are envisioned in bureaucratic terms because "in the eyes of Chinese commoners state bureaucrats wield power so overwhelming that bureaucratic terms offer a clear way to understand power, even divine power." The "bureaucratic heavens" can serve the interests of a bureaucratic state, but it is just as true that state bureaucracy (such as the Han administrative structure) could be "based on a pre-existing religious model." See Shahar and Weller, "Introduction," 6–8.

26. "Junia," in discussion with author, July 21, 2014.

27. Mahoney, "Intercession."

28. "958. Communion with the dead," *Catechism of the Catholic Church*, 2nd ed., part 1, sec. 2, ch. 3, art. 9, para. 5. On debates over the place of the dead in the world of the living, see Schmitt, *Ghosts in the Middle Ages*, 19–22, 71, 75.

29. "José," in discussion with author, June 22, 2015.

30. While less developed than Catherine Albanese's notion of "metaphysical religion," I find Sidney Ahlstrom's concept of "harmonial religion" especially evocative for describing a religious current common to Brazil and the United States alike. In addition to devotees' explicit references to energy, vibrations, *sintonia* (syntony or harmony), and mesmeric "fluids," harmonial language resonates with contemporary affect theory. See Ahlstrom, "Harmonial Religion."

31. "Maria," in discussion with author, July 28, 2014.

32. "Tereza," in discussion with author, July 7, 2014.

33. Though *pedido* is typically translated as "petition" or "request," neither translation captures its full range of connotations in Brazilian Portuguese. Derived from *pedir* (to ask), it is one of the most commonly used words in Portuguese (as well as in Spanish). In quotidian commercial contexts like a store or restaurant, *pedido* means something like "order" or "request." But it can mean to make a wish. For example, in an episode of *A Viagem*, a popular spiritist-themed telenovela, a couple sees a falling star. Turning to his wife, the husband whispers, "*Faça seu pedido*" (Make your wish).

34. R. de. C. Menezes, "Saber pedir."

35. Field notes, September 15, 2014.

36. "Rafa," in discussion with author, May 19, 2014.

37. Field notes, May 5, 2014.

38. Field notes, February 23, 2015.

39. The cult of the souls' ostensibly instrumental quality has prompted some scholars to characterize it as "magical." Demoted from religion to magic, the devotion becomes a free-floating, transposable "technique" aimed at "pure efficacy," lacking religion's systematic coherence. It is no coincidence that talk of magic tends to surface in discussions of syncretism. Magic, it would seem, offers a way to talk about

marginalized practices or even popular practices that are not aligned with a particular orthodoxy. But like syncretism, it can only do so by positing a point of essential stability against which to measure change, cultural "survivals," and other varieties of spiritual deviance. See Augras, *A segunda-feira*, 13–14; Pierucci, *A Magia*, 83–85. For two potent critiques of magic as an analytical category, see Styers, *Making Magic*; and Palmié, *Wizards and Scientists*.

40. Leon, *La Llorona's Children*, 67. See also Graber, *Debt*, 90; Singh, *Divine Currency*.
41. Žižek, "Return of the Living"; Gordon, *Ghostly Matters*, xvi; emphasis added.
42. Alves, *Anti-Black City*, 2. See also Willis, "Potter's Field," 539.
43. "Beatriz," in discussion with author, July 7, 2014.
44. While activists on the Left had long emphasized self-care as critical to enduring the fight for social justice, Davis affirmed, "Self-care and healing and attention to the body and the spiritual dimension—all of this is now a part of radical social justice struggles. That wasn't the case before." Hobart and Kneese, "Radical Care," 1.
45. Mattern, "Maintenance and Care."
46. Hobart and Kneese, "Radical Care," 2.
47. *Oxford English Dictionary*, s.v., "care (v.)," June 2024, https://doi.org/10.1093/OED/9286555014; Murphy, "Unsettling Care," 721. Michelle Murphy cautions against "equating care with positive feelings" and "argues for the importance of grappling with the non-innocent histories in which the politics of care already circulates, particularly in transnational couplings of feminism and health." Care work is typically poorly renumerated, and the burden of doing such work typically falls on people who are socially and economically marginalize—namely, women of color. See also Russell and Vinsel, "After Innovation," 13.
48. Butler, "Violence, Mourning, Politics," 14.
49. Mattern, "Maintenance and Care."
50. De la Bellasca, "Matters of Care," 85.
51. Jackson, "Rethinking Repair," 222.
52. As Jackson notes, conceptualized in broad terms by the Defense Advanced Research Projects Agency (DARPA) in the 1960s, the internet "grew by breaking, bumping up against the limits of existing protocols and practices and working around them," which is to say, everyday acts of maintenance and repair organized around solving problems. Some of the internet's most distinctive applications—email, the World Wide Web—emerged from this recursive process of breaking, tinkering, maintenance, and repair. Jackson, "Rethinking Repair," 228.
53. Jackson, "Rethinking Repair," 226–229.
54. Rabelo, "Moving between Religions," 852.
55. Pérez, *Religion in the Kitchen*, 40–41.
56. As Thomas Nail notes, the English word *assemblage* is the common but somewhat misleading translation of Deleuze and Guattari's concept of *agencement*. Whereas *agencement* means configuration or arrangement of heterogenous elements, the English (and French) word *assemblage* refers to the "bringing or coming together" of multiple things into unities. Nail, "What Is an Assemblage?"
57. Wilhelm, "Heroic Act of Charity."

58. The distinction between charity and solidarity is a common one, with the former linked to "neoliberal discourses of moral obligation and individual character" and the latter as more befitting of social movements. See Hobart and Kneese, "Radical Care," 10; Spade, "Solidarity Not Charity."

59. On the ancestors as a guide for future action, see Morrison, "Ancestor as Foundation"; Tillet, *Sites of Slavery*.

60. Schaefer, *Religious Affects*, 11; Newell, "Affectiveness of Symbols," 2.

Chapter Five

1. Unless otherwise specified, my discussion on the cortege is based on my field notes from September 20, 2018.

2. While the Archdiocese of São Paulo advanced plans to renovate the Chapel of the Afflicted in 2011, this never happened. On the proposed renovation, see Vanessa Correa, "Igrejinha de 1770 terá seu 1° restauro completo na Liberdade," *Folha de São Paulo*, October 25, 2011, https://m.folha.uol.com.br/cotidiano/2011/10/996205-igrejinha-de-1779-tera-1-restauro-completo-na-liberdade-em-sp.shtml.

3. The Chapel of the Afflicted is protected both by CONDEPHAAT (see Process no. 20125/76 and Resolução SC S/N/78, October 23, 1978), the state-level patrimonial organization, and CONPRESP (Resolution no. 05/91), the city-level one. Likewise, as activists would later realize, that 2016 CONPRESP resolution (Resolution no. 20/2016) recognizing the potential archaeological significance of Liberdade for "Black culture and . . . oriental groups" required that construction be approved by the CONPRESP and the city's Department of Historical Patrimony (DPH). Activists were able to halt the construction adjacent to the chapel in part because it proceeded without any such approval. See Ferreira, "Memorial dos Aflitos."

4. Abilio Ferreira, in discussion with author, July 22, 2019.

5. Rios, "O protesto negro," 61–74. Note that 2018 also marked the fortieth anniversary of the founding of the Unified Black Movement (Movimento Negro Unificado, or MNU), one of the country's most important and influential Black activist groups.

6. Rios, "O protesto negro," 68. On fugitivity, see the work of Fred Moten, especially *The Universal Machine*.

7. C. Smith, *Afro-Paradise*, 20.

8. C. Smith, *Afro-Paradise*, 11.

9. Tillet, *Sites of Slavery*, 136.

10. Aloysio Letra, in discussion with author, August 3, 2018.

11. According to the 2010 census, 54.5 percent of Guainases residents identify as *negro*, *preto*, or *pardo*, making it the subprefecture with the fourth-highest concentration of Black residents in the city of São Paulo. Tatiana Santiago, "Parelheiros tem 7,8 vezes mais negros que Pinheiros, diz levantamento," *G1*, September 16, 2023, http://g1.globo.com/sao-paulo/noticia/2015/09/parelheiros-tem-78-vezes-mais-negros-que-pinheiros-diz-levantamento.html.

12. Field notes, September 7, 2018.

13. "Tarcísio," in discussion with author, July 16, 2019.

14. Tilly, *Social Movements*, 3.
15. Abilio Ferreira, in discussion with author, July 22, 2019.
16. Field notes, September 21, 2020.
17. Field notes, September 13, 2020.
18. Escola Sem Partido, "Perguntas Frequentes," accessed January 12, 2020, https://escolasempartido.org/perguntas-e-respostas.html. Note that while groups like MBL (Movimento Brasil Livre, or Free Brazil Movement) began to articulate a coherent policy platform around June 2013, the historian Benjamin Cowan persuasively argues that its basic platform—centered on reactionary opposition to communism, ecumenism, secularization, egalitarianism, and the perceived loss of moral order—has roots in the highly organized (and state-supported) religious conservatism of late authoritarian Brazil; see Cowan, *Moral Majorities*.
19. Jonathan Watts, "Dilma Rousseff proposes referendum on political reform," *The Guardian*, June 25, 2013, https://www.theguardian.com/world/2013/jun/25/brazil-president-dilma-rousseff-reform.
20. Vargas, "Black Disidentification," 5.
21. See Caldeira, *City of Walls*, esp. ch. 1, "Talk of Crime and Ordering the World."
22. Vargas, "Black Disidentification," 10–11.
23. Vargas, "Black Disidentification," 8.
24. Field notes, September 18, 2018.
25. Field notes, September 20, 2018.
26. Aloysio Letra, in discussion with author, August 3, 2018.
27. Abilio Ferreira, Alexandre Kishimoto, and Paulo Pereira, "ConVIDA!—O Memorial dos Aflitos Com Alexandre K., Aloysio L., Abílio F., Gabriela M. e Eliz A.(SP)," SescBrasil, October 15, 2020, YouTube video, 1:04:26, https://www.youtube.com/watch?v=F44PSdUMXxU.
28. Aloysio Letra, in discussion with author, August 3, 2018; Ferreira, Kishimoto, and Pereira, "ConVIDA!"
29. Aloysio Letra, in discussion with author, August 3, 2018.
30. Lívia Machado, "Praça e estação Liberdade do Metrô de SP ganham 'Japão' no nome," *G1*, August 1, 2018, https://g1.globo.com/sp/sao-paulo/noticia/2018/08/01/praca-e-estacao-liberdade-do-metro-de-sp-ganham-japao-no-nome-e-alteracao-gera-criticas-nas-redes-sociais.ghtml; Adriana Farias, "Empresario Ikesaki investe 200 000 reais e revitaliza Praça da Liberdade," *Veja São Paulo*, July 19, 2018, https://vejasp.abril.com.br/cidades/empresario-ikesaki-investe-200-000-reais-e-revitaliza-praca-da-liberdade/ (site no longer available); Aldo Shiguti, "Embaixador do Japão prestigia inauguração de monumento na 'Praça da Liberdade-Japão,'" *Jornal Nippak*, September 1, 2018, https://www.jnippak.com.br/2018/embaixador-do-japao-prestigia-inauguracao-de-monumento-na-praca-da-liberdade-japao/.
31. "A Praça da Liberdade mudou de nome," Facebook, July 26, 2016. For an extract and discussion of the post (which is no longer available), see Machado, "Praça e estação Liberdade."
32. "Praça da Liberdade África-Japão," Diconário de Ruas, accessed May 16, 2024, https://dicionarioderuas.prefeitura.sp.gov.br/historia-da-rua/praca-da-liberdade-africa-japao. For an early reference to the *bairro da Liberdade*, see Firminho A.

Rodrigues dos Passos, "Firmino A. Rodrigues dos Passos e a professora da rua da Liberdade," *O Estadão de São Paulo*, November 10, 1878, 2. For further discussion of Liberdade's renaming, see Britt, "Spatial Projects of Forgetting," 6–7.

33. Patricia Oliveira quoted in Marcelle Souza, "Grupos trazem à frente narrativas negras apagadas das cidades brasileiras," *ECOA*, July 10, 2020, https://www.uol.com.br/ecoa/reportagens-especiais/grupos-trazem-a-frente-narrativas-negras-apagadas-das-cidades-brasileiras.

34. Rose-Redwood, Alderman, and Azaryahu, "Urban Streetscape," 3.

35. Field notes, July 23, 2018, and June 19, 2020.

36. *The Noite com Danilo Gentili*, aired December 21, 2017, on SBT.

37. Field notes, July 23, 2018, and July 8, 2019.

38. "Márcia Costa," in discussion with author, July 18, 2019.

39. Aloysio Letra, in discussion with author, August 3, 2018.

40. Lisboa, "Movimento Popular em Santos a 29 de Junho de 1821," *Almanach Literrario Paulista*, 201.

41. Kraay, "Bystander Interventions."

42. Sevcenko's article was written for a nonspecialist audience and is based on secondary research. As far as I have been able to tell, none of the secondary sources he cites offer details about Chaguinhas's race. On secondary sources that describe Chaguinhas as white, see, e.g., Sant'Anna, *Santa Cruz dos Enforcados*, 224; Terezinha Rocha, "O Dia das Almas," 76. As far as I know, no contemporary has succeeded in locating Chaguinhas's baptismal records, and since the name Francisco José das Chagas was relatively common, it could be difficult to positively identify his records without more detail about his life, like his birth year or parents' names. Chaguinhas's burial record should be easier to find, but it either never existed or has long gone missing, as scholars have regularly mentioned the absence. There is some documentation related to Chaguinhas's execution, such as receipts for the cord used to hang him and the candles used to light his cells. But neither these records nor the few military documents that mention Francisco José das Chagas by name say anything about his physical appearance. Patricia Cristina Rodrigues de Oliveira offers a detailed discussion of the primary and secondary source that mentions Chaguinhas's appearance. P. C. R. de Oliveira, "Tortura e morte," 107–22.

We can make a few inferences about Chaguinhas based on what we know about the late colonial military. He was probably poor, given his low rank and his participation in a rebellion over unpaid wages. It seems unlikely that he would have been enslaved at his time of service; masters rarely enlisted those they enslaved outside of wartime, and an enslaved man may have had less incentive to rebel over wages. Furthermore, the unit to which he belonged, Primeiro Batalhão de Caçadores, was probably part of the *primeira linha*, or regular army. Men raced as *preto*—a classification that, at the time, was reserved for African or enslaved people—were technically prohibited from serving in the regular army and were instead supposed to be relegated to segregated militias. This rule, however, was rarely enforced. *Pardo* is a more complicated category. While typically translated as "brown" or "mixed race," in the early nineteenth century, the word "sometimes referred to all free-born nonwhites." Kraay, *Race, State*, 22. Barring a detailed physical description of Chaguinhas's physiognomy, the historical record may tell us little about how Chaguinhas understood his own racial identity or how he would be perceived by others if he were alive today.

43. Aloysio Letra, in discussion with author, August 3, 2018.
44. Hartman, "Venus in Two Acts," 2.
45. Hartman, "Venus in Two Acts," 9.
46. Scott, "That Event, This Memory," 278; Halbwachs, *On Collective Memory*.
47. Zubrzycki, "Politics of Jewish Absence," 251, 275.
48. Field notes, September 21, 2018.
49. Giovanna Constanti, "O que a Liberdade significa para a memória dos negros em São Paulo," *Carta Capital*, September 2, 2018, https://www.cartacapital.com.br/sociedade/o-que-a-liberdade-significa-para-a-memoria-dos-negros-em-sao-paulo/.
50. Archaeologists have similarly found blue beads at plantations and other slavery-related dig sites in North America. Orser, "Archaeology," 40.
51. Vivian Reis, "Arqueólogos encontram ossadas da época da escravidão em terreno no Centro de São Paulo," *G1*, December 6, 2018, https://g1.globo.com/sp/sao-paulo/noticia/2018/12/06/arqueologos-encontram-ossadas-da-epoca-da-escravidao-em-terreno-no-centro-de-sao-paulo.ghtml; Rafaella Bonilla, "Sítio arqueológico na Liberdade pode virar memorial da cultura negra," *Veja São Paulo*, January 3, 2020, https://vejasp.abril.com.br/cidades/sitio-arqueologico-liberdade/; meeting minutes, Comissão de Constituição, Justiça e Legislação Participativa, December 7, 2017, http://documentacao.saopaulo.sp.leg.br/iah/fulltext/audiencias/AP17399-2018JUST.pdf. See also A Lasca, "Relatório final."
52. Field notes, September 16, 2020. On the Forum for São Paulo without Racism, see Suplicy, "Fórum São Paulo Sem Racismo foi lançado na Câmara," Suplicy, March 22, 2017, https://www.eduardosuplicy.com.br/site/forum-sao-paulo-sem-racismo-e-lancado-na-camara/.
53. Jota Abreu, "Audiência debate futuro do sítio arqueológico onde foram encontradas ossadas de escravos do séc. XVIII," *A Lasca Arqueologia*, January 14, 2020, https://alascaconsultoriablog.wordpress.com/2020/01/14/audiencia-debate-futuro-do-sitio-arqueologico-onde-foram-encontradas-ossadas-de-escravos-do-sec-xviii/.
54. "LEI Nº 17.310 DE 28 DE JANEIRO DE 2019," January 28, 2019, https://legislacao.prefeitura.sp.gov.br/leis/lei-17310-de-28-de-janeiro-de-2019.
55. Sharpe, *In the Wake*, 20, 8. The geographer Brian Ladd makes a similar point, noting memorials can reduce historical complexity, obscuring context by offering observers "an emotionally gripping symbol." Ladd, *Ghosts of Berlin*, 167–68.
56. Collins, *Revolt of the Saints*.
57. Ferreira, Kishimoto, and Pereira, "ConVIDA!"
58. Sharpe, *In the Wake*, 18–19.
59. UNAMCA, "Programa de necessidades," September 14, 2020.
60. Growing public awareness of Liberdade's Black history is perhaps most evident in media coverage. Ever since 2018, a series of articles in major news outlets has called attention to activists' work and narrated some of Liberdade's obscured histories. See Constanti, "O que a Liberdade"; Marcelle Souza, "Grupos trazem à frente narrativas negras apagadas das cidades brasileiras," *ECOA*, July 10, 2020, https://www.uol.com.br/ecoa/reportagens-especiais/grupos-trazem-a-frente-narrativas-negras-apagadas

-das-cidades-brasileiras; "Conheça a história negra no centro da cidade de SP," *Folha de São Paulo*, June 2020, https://www1.folha.uol.com.br/webstories/turismo/2020/06/conheca-a-historia-negra-no-centro-da-cidade-de-sp/; Guilherme Soares Dias, "A história dos negros no bairro da Liberdade," *Revista Trip*, November 1, 2019, https://revistatrip.uol.com.br/trip/historia-dos-negros-no-bairro-liberdade-e-o-movimento-de-preservacao-sitio-arqueologico-dos-aflitos. Likewise, the story of Chaguinhas has made its way into other forms of popular culture, beyond the work of artists like Márcia Costa and Aloysio Letra. In 2020, Netflix released *Spectros*, a fictional series about ghosts in Liberdade. The series, whose opening scene is set at the Chapel of the Afflicted, depicts Chaguinhas as distinctly Black. In private communication, the show's executive producer explained that they decided to represent Chaguinhas as Black out of respect for devotees and Liberdade's Black history, "which was never properly told."

61. Aloysio Letra, in conversation with author, July 21, 2019.
62. Leu, "Settlement."

Postscript

1. The name of the square officially changed to Praça Liberdade África-Japão on June 1, 2023. Councilman Paulo Reis (PT), who introduced legislation to create the Memorial of the Afflicted, joined Councilmen Luana Alves (PSOL) in advocating for changing the square's name. There is also talk of changing the name of the metro station, though such a change would have to happen at the level of state rather than city government.
2. Field notes, April 28, 2023.
3. Field notes, May 24, 2023. For an abbreviated video of the encounter, see Movimento dos Aflitos and Instituto Tebas de Educação e Cultura, "No satê prika koya rayon kaxate (Onde os indígenas falam, quem não é indígena escuta)," Instituto Tebas, July 2, 2023, YouTube video, 53:38, https://www.youtube.com/watch?v=zXusSFPi2iY.
4. Abilio Ferreira, in discussion with author, July 22, 2019.
5. Klein and Gillis in Berliner, "Uses and Abuses," 197.
6. Crinson, "Urban Memory," xii.
7. Instituto Tebas de Educação e Cultura, "Dia 14—Mesa 2. Lugares de Memória Negro-Indígena: Um Conceito em Construção (íntegra)," Instituto Tebas, November 7, 2022, YouTube video, 1:41:42, https://www.youtube.com/watch?v=iW8vi6u5zdU.
8. Field notes, July 21, 2023.

Bibliography

Archives

Arquivo Histórico Municipal de São Paulo (AHM)
Arquivo Metropolitano do Arquidiocese de São Paulo (AMASP)
Arquivo Publico do Estado de São Paulo (AESP)

Newspapers and Magazines

Cidade de Santos
Correio Paulistano
Diário de São Paulo
Diário Popular (São Paulo)
ECOA
El Digital
Folha de São Paulo
G1
Guardian
Jornal Nippak
Notícias Populares (São Paulo)
O Apostolo (Rio de Janeiro)
O Cruzeiro
Radio Programas del Perú
Realidade
Reuters
R7

Primary Sources Related to the Movement of the Afflicted

A Lasca. "Relatório final — Programa de gestão arqueológica no terreno localizado à Rua dos Aflitos, 64 — Liberdade."
Ferreira, Abilio. "Memorial dos Aflitos." Unpublished manuscript, March 2020, typescript.
UNAMCA. "Programa de necessidades a ser introduzido no escopo do edital do Memorial dos Aflitos."

Secondary Sources

Abreu, Maria José de. "The FedEx Saints: Patrons of Mobility and Speed in a Neoliberal City." In *Things: Religion and the Question of Materiality*, edited by Birgit Meyer and Dick Houtman, 321–35. New York: Fordham University Press, 2012.
Ahlstrom, Sydney. "Harmonial Religion since the Later Nineteenth Century." In *A Religious History of the American People*, 2nd ed., 1019–36. New Haven, CT: Yale University Press, 2004.
Ahmed, Sarah. "Happy Objects." In *The Affect Theory Reader*, edited by Gregory J. Seigworth and Melissa Gregg, 29–51. Durham, NC: Duke University Press, 2009.
Albanese, Catherine L. *America: Religions and Religion*. 5th ed. Boston: Wadsworth, 2013.
———. *A Republic of Mind and Spirit: A Cultural History of American Metaphysical Religion*. New Haven, CT: Yale University Press, 2007.

"All Souls' Day." In *New Catholic Encyclopedia*, 2nd ed., vol. 7, edited by Thomas Carson and Joan Cerrito, 290–91. Detroit: Gale, 2003.

Almeida, Ronaldo de. "Religião na metrópole Paulista." *Revista Brasileira de Ciências Sociais* 19, no. 56 (2004): 15–27.

Almeida, Ronaldo de, and Paula Montero. "Trânsito religioso no Brasil." *São Paulo Em Perspectiva* 15, no. 3 (July 2001): 92–100.

Alves, Jaime Amparo. *The Anti-Black City: Police Terror and Black Urban Life in Brazil*. Minneapolis: University of Minnesota Press, 2018.

Amaral, Antônio Barreto do. "O Cemitério dos Aflitos—a Capela dos Aflitos." *Revista do Instituto Histórico e Geográfico de São Paulo* 73 (1977): 22–27.

Amoruso, Michael. "All Souls' Day." In *Encyclopedia of Latin American Religions*, edited by Henri Gooren, 1–2. Cham: Springer International Publishing, 2016. https://doi.org/10.1007/978-3-319-08956-0_180-1.

———. "Saudade: The Untranslatable Word for the Presence of Absence." *Aeon: A World of Ideas*, October 8, 2018. https://aeon.co/ideas/saudade-the-untranslateable-word-for-the-presence-of-absence.

———. "A Transcendental Mission: Spiritism and the Revolutionary Politics of Francisco I. Madero, 1900–1911." Master's thesis, University of Texas at Austin, 2013.

Analecta Ecclesiastica: Seu Romana Collectanea de Disciplinis Speculativis et Praticis circa Theologiam, Ius Canonicum, Administrationem in Foro contentioso et gratioso, Sacram Liturgiam, Etc. Rome: [s.n.], 1906.

Andrade, Mário de. *Música de Feitiçaria No Brasil*. 2nd ed. Belo Horizonte, Brazil: Editora Itatiaia Limitada, 1983.

Andrade, Solange Ramos. "Frei Boaventura Kloppenburg e a história da Igreja Católica no Brasil: aspectos de uma biografia." *História Unisinos* 16, no. 1 (January–April 2012): 139–48.

Andrews, George Reid. *Blacks and Whites in São Paulo, Brazil, 1888–1988*. Madison: University of Wisconsin Press, 1991.

Apter, Andrew. "Herskovits's Heritage: Rethinking Syncretism in the African Diaspora." *Diaspora: A Journal of Transnational Studies* 1, no. 3 (1991): 235–60. https://doi.org/10.1353/dsp.1991.0021.

Araujo, Ligia Fernandes. "A escola de samba Lavapés: Um património cultural no Glicério." Master's thesis, University of São Paulo, 2012.

Ariès, Philippe. *The Hour of Our Death*. New York: Oxford University Press, 1991.

Augras, Monique. *A segunda-feira é das almas*. Rio de Janeiro: Pallas Editora, 2012.

Azevedo, Thales de. *O catolicismo no Brasil: um campo para a pesquisa social*. Salvador: EDUFBA, 2002.

Batson, C. Daniel. "These Things Called Empathy: Eight Related but Distinct Phenomena." In *The Social Neuroscience of Empathy*, edited by Jean Decety and William Ickes, 3–15. Cambridge, MA: Boston Review, 2009.

Bellacasa, Maria Puig de la. "Matters of Care in Technoscience: Assembling Neglected Things." *Social Studies of Science* 41, no. 1 (February 1, 2011): 85–106. https://doi.org/10.1177/0306312710380301.

Bender, Courtney. *The New Metaphysicals: Spirituality and the American Religious Imagination*. Chicago: University of Chicago Press, 2010.
Benedetti, Luiz Roberto. "Propostas teóricas para entender o trânsito religioso." *Comunicações Do ISER* 45 (1994): 18–23.
Birman, Patricia. "Modos periféricos de crença." In *Catolicismo: unidade religiosa e pluralismo cultural*, edited by Pierre Sanchis, 167–96. Rio de Janeiro: Edições Loyola, 1992.
Bitun, Ricardo. "Nomadismo Religioso: trânsito religioso em questão." *Horizonte* 9 no. 22 (2011): 493–503.
Borges, Dain. "Healing and Mischief: Witchcraft in Brazilian Law and Practice, 1890–1922." In *Crime and Punishment in Latin America: Law and Society since Late Colonial Times*, edited by Ricardo D. Salvatore, Carlos Aguirre, and Gilbert M. Joseph, 181–210. Durham, NC: Duke University Press, 2001.
———. "'Puffy, Ugly, Slothful and Inert': Degeneration in Brazilian Social Thought, 1880–1940." *Journal of Latin American Studies* 25, no. 2 (1993): 235–56.
Bourdieu, Pierre. *Distinction: A Social Critique of the Judgement of Taste*. Cambridge, MA: Harvard University Press, 1984.
Brandão, Carlos Rodrigues. *Os deuses do povo: um estudo sobre a religião popular*. 2nd ed. São Paulo: Brasiliense, 1980.
Breen, Richard, and Bernadette C. Hayes. "Religious Mobility in the UK." *Journal of the Royal Statistical Society. Series A (Statistics in Society)* 159, no. 3 (1996): 493–504. https://doi.org/10.2307/2983327.
Britt, Andrew G. "Re/Mapping São Paulo's Geographies of African Descent." *Items: Insights from the Social Sciences*, April 25, 2020. https://items.ssrc.org/layered-metropolis/re-mapping-sao-paulos-geographies-of-african-descent/.
———. "Spatial Projects of Forgetting: Razing the Remedies Church and Museum to the Enslaved in São Paulo's 'Black Zone', 1930s–1940s." *Journal of Latin American Studies*, August 11, 2022, 1–32. https://doi.org/10.1017/S0022216X22000669.
Brown, Peter. *The Cult of the Saints: Its Rise and Function in Latin Christianity*. Enlarged ed. Chicago: University of Chicago Press, 2015.
———. *The Ransom of the Soul: Afterlife and Wealth in Early Christianity*. Cambridge, MA: Harvard University Press, 2015.
Bruneau, Thomas. *The Brazilian Catholic Church*. Cambridge: Cambridge University Press, 1974.
———. *The Church in Brazil*. Austin: University of Texas Press, 1982.
Butler, Judith. "Violence, Mourning, Politics." *Studies in Gender and Sexuality* 4, no. 1 (January 3, 2003): 9–37. https://doi.org/10.1080/15240650409349213.
Butler, Kim D. *Freedoms Given, Freedoms Won: Afro-Brazilians in Post-Abolition São Paulo and Salvador*. New Brunswick: Rutgers University Press, 1998.
———. "Up from Slavery: Afro-Brazilian Activism in São Paulo, 1888–1938." *Americas* 49, no. 2 (October 1992): 179–206. https://doi.org/10.2307/1006990.
Caldeira, Teresa. *City of Walls: Crime, Segregation, and Citizenship in São Paulo*. Berkeley: University of California Press, 2000.
Camargo, Luis Soares de. "Viver e morrer em São Paulo: A vida, as doenças e a morte na cidade do século XIX." PhD diss., Pontifícia Universidade Católica São Paulo, 2007.

Campos, Adalgisa Arantes. *As irmandades de São Miguel e as almas do purgatório: culto e iconografia no setecentos mineiro*. Belo Horizonte: C/ Arte, 2013.

———. "São Miguel, as Almas do Purgatório e as balanças: iconografia e veneração na Época Moderna." *Memorandum* 7 (2004): 102–27.

Capone, Stefania. *Searching for Africa in Brazil: Power and Tradition in Candomblé*. Durham, NC: Duke University Press, 2010.

Cardozo, Manoel S. "The Lay Brotherhoods of Colonial Bahia." *Catholic Historical Review* 33, no. 1 (1947): 12–30.

Carroll, Michael. *Veiled Threats: The Logic of Popular Catholicism in Italy*. Baltimore: Johns Hopkins University Press, 1996.

Certeau, Michel de. *The Practice of Everyday Life*. Berkeley: University of California Press, 1984.

Christian, William A. *Visionaries: The Spanish Republic and the Reign of Christ*. Berkeley: University of California Press, 1996.

Cidade de São Paulo. *100 anos de serviço funerário*. São Paulo: Prefeitura do Município de São Paulo, 1977.

Collins, John F. *Revolt of the Saints: Memory and Redemption in the Twilight of Brazilian Racial Democracy*. Durham, NC: Duke University Press, 2015.

Connerton, Paul. *How Modernity Forgets*. Cambridge: Cambridge University Press, 2009.

Constituições Eclesiásticas do Brasil. *Nova edição da pastoral colectiva de 1915*. Canoas: Editora La Salle, 1950.

Coral, Caboclo Cobra. *Orações Umbandistas de todos os tempos*. Rio de Janeiro: Pallas Editora, 1987.

Cowan, Benjamin A. *Moral Majorities across the Americas: Brazil, the United States, and the Creation of the Religious Right*. Chapel Hill: University of North Carolina Press, 2021.

Cox, Robert S. *Body and Soul: A Sympathetic History of American Spiritualism*. Charlottesville: University of Virginia Press, 2003.

Cuchet, Guillaume. "Les morts utiles du purgatoire." *Terrain: Revue d'ethnologie de l'Europe* 62 (March 4, 2014): 82–99.

———. "The Revival of the Cult of Purgatory in France (1850–1914)." *French History* 18, no. 1 (2004): 76–95.

D'Araújo, Ana Cristina Bartolomeu. "Morte, memória e piedade barroca." *Revista de História de Ideais* 2 (1989): 129–74.

Davies, Owen. *Grimoires: A History of Magic Books*. Oxford: Oxford University Press, 2009.

Eade, John, and Michael J. Sallnow. *Contesting the Sacred: The Anthropology of Christian Pilgrimage*. Urbana: University of Illinois Press, 2000.

Ehlert, Rebecca Lisabeth. "S. Maria Del Pianto: Loss, Remembrance and Legacy in Seventeenth Century Naples." Master's thesis, Queen's University, 2008.

Eng, David L., and David Kanzanjian. "Preface." In *Loss: The Politics of Mourning*, edited by David L. Eng and David Kazanjian, ix–x. Berkeley: University of California Press, 2003.

Ewbank, Thomas. *Life in Brazil: Or, a Journal of a Visit to the Land of the Cocoa and the Palm*. New York: Harper & Brothers, 1856.

Fernandes, Silvia Regina Alves. *Mudança de religião no Brasil: desvendando sentidos e motivações*. São Paulo: Palavra & Prece, 2006.

Ferreira, Glayce Marina Alves, and Nelson Simplício da Silva. "Mapas e Memórias: Edição 'Imprensa Negra Paulistana.'" Universidade de São Paulo, 2018.

Figueroa, Celso A. Lara. *Fieles difuntos, santos y ánimas benditas en Guatemala: Una evocación ancestral*. Guatemala City: Librerias Artemis Edinter, 2003.

Fisher, Bernice, and Joan Tronto. "Toward a Feminist Theory of Caring." In *Circles of Care: Work and Identity in Women's Lives*, edited by Emily K. Abel and Margaret K. Nelson, 35–62. Albany: SUNY Press, 1990.

Fisher, Mark. *Ghosts of My Life: Writings on Depression, Hauntology and Lost Futures*. Alresford, UK: Zero Books, 2014.

Freitas, Affonso Antonio. *Tradições e reminiscencias paulistanas*. São Paulo: Monteiro Lobato, 1921.

Freitas, Eliane Tânia Martins de. "Violência e sagrado: o que no criminoso anuncia o santo?" *Ciencias Sociales y Religión* 2, no. 2 (December 1, 2000): 191–203. https://doi.org/10.22456/1982-2650.2166.

Freud, Sigmund. *The Uncanny*. New York: Penguin, 2003.

Freyre, Gilberto. *The Masters and the Slaves*. 2nd English-language ed. New York: Knopf, 1956.

———. "Some Aspects of the Social Development of Portuguese America." In *Concerning Latin American Culture*, edited by Charles C. Griffin, 79–103. New York: Columbia University Press, 1940.

Frigerio, Alejandro. "Analyzing Conversion in Latin America: Theoretical Questions, Methodological Dilemmas, and Comparative Data from Argentina and Brazil." In *Conversion of a Continent: Contemporary Religious Change in Latin America*, edited by Timothy J. Steigenga and Edward L. Cleary, 33–51. New Brunswick: Rutgers University Press, 2010.

Garcia, Rodrigo. "São Paulo nos trilhos." *Revista Apartes*, October 25, 2022. https://www.saopaulo.sp.leg.br/apartes/sao-paulo-nos-trilhos/.

Gez, Yonatan N., Yvan Droz, Edio Soares, and Jeanne Rey. "From Converts to Itinerants: Religious *Butinage* as Dynamic Identity." *Current Anthropology* 58, no. 2 (March 3, 2017): 141–59. https://doi.org/10.1086/690836.

Gillam, Reighan. "Latent Blackness: Afro-Brazilian People, History, and Culture in São Paulo, Brazil." *Journal of Latin American and Caribbean Anthropology* 26, no. 3–4 (December 2021): 451–67. https://doi.org/10.1111/jlca.12584.

Gordon, Avery. *Ghostly Matters: Haunting and the Sociological Imagination*. Minneapolis: University of Minnesota Press, 2008.

Graber, David. *Debt: The First 5,000 Years*. Hoboken: Melville House, 2011.

Guimarães, Laís de Barros Monteiro. *Liberdade*. São Paulo: Prefeitura do Município de São Paulo, 1979.

Hadaway, C. Kirk, and Penny Long Marler. "All in the Family: Religious Mobility in America." *Review of Religious Research* 35, no. 2 (1993): 97–116. https://doi.org/10.2307/3511778.

Halbwachs, Maurice. *On Collective Memory*. Chicago: University of Chicago Press, 1992.

Hartman, Saidiya. "Venus in Two Acts." *Small Axe* 12, no. 2 (2008): 1–14.
Hauck, João Fagundes, Hugo Fragoso, José Oscar Beozzo, Klaus Van der Grijp, and Benno Brod. *História da igreja no Brasil: Ensaio de interpretação a partir do povo: segunda época, a igreja no Brasil no século XIX*. Petrópolis: Vozes, 1980.
Hess, David. *Spirits and Scientists: Ideology, Spiritism, and Brazilian Culture*. University Park: Pennsylvania State University Press, 1991.
Hilgers, Joseph. "Purgatorial Societies." In *The Catholic Encyclopedia*, vol. 12, edited by Charles G. Herbermann, Edward A. Pace, Condé B. Pallen, Thomas J. Shahan, and John J. Wynne, 572–75. New York: Robert Appleton Company, 1909.
Ho, Engseng. *The Graves of Tarim: Genealogy and Mobility across the Indian Ocean*. Berkeley: University of California Press, 2006.
Hobart, Hiʻilei Julia Kawehipuaakahaopulani, and Tamara Kneese. "Radical Care: Survival Strategies for Uncertain Times." *Social Text* 38, no. 1 (March 1, 2020): 1–16. https://doi.org/10.1215/01642472-7971067.
Instituto Brasileiro de Geografia e Estatística. "Censo demográfico 2010: Características gerais da população, religião e pessoas com deficiência." Rio de Janeiro: Instituto Brasileiro de Geografia e Estatística, 2010.
Ishi, Angelo. "Searching for Home, Wealth, Pride, and 'Class': Japanese Brazilians in the 'Land of Yen.'" In *Searching for Home Abroad: Japanese Brazilians and Transnationalism*, edited by Jeffrey Lesser, 75–102. Durham, NC: Duke University Press, 2003.
Jackson, Steven J. "Rethinking Repair." In *Media Technologies: Essays on Communication, Materiality, and Society*, edited by Tarleton Gillespie, Pablo J. Boczkowski, and Kirsten A. Foot, 221–39. Boston: MIT Press, 2014.
Jacobs, Jane. *The Death and Life of Great American Cities*. New York: Knopf Doubleday, 2016.
Jahoda, Gustav. "Theodor Lipps and the Shift from 'Sympathy' to 'Empathy.'" *Journal of the History of the Behavioral Sciences* 41, no. 2 (2005): 151–63. https://doi.org/10.1002/jhbs.20080.
Jiménez, Carlos María Campos. *Devociones populares: Introducción a su estudio en Costa Rica*. San Pedro de Montes de Oca: Revista Senderos, 1984.
Johnson, Paul C. "Migrating Bodies, Circulating Signs: Brazilian Candomblé, the Garifuna of the Caribbean, and the Category of Indigenous Religions." *History of Religions* 41, no. 4 (May 1, 2002): 301–27.
———. "Modes and Moods of 'Slave Anastácia,' Afro-Brazilian Saint." *Journal de la Société des Américanistes* 104, no. 1 (June 15, 2018): 27–73. https://doi.org/10.4000/jsa.15584.
———. *Secrets, Gossip, and Gods: The Transformation of Brazilian Candomblé*. New York: Oxford University Press, 2002.
———, ed. *Spirited Things: The Work of "Possession" in Afro-Atlantic Religions*. Chicago: University of Chicago Press, 2014.
Kalverkamp, Desidério, and Boaventura Kloppenburg. *Ação Pastoral Perante o Espiritismo: Orientação para Sacerdotes*. Rio de Janeiro: Editora Vozes, 1961.
Keane, Webb. "Religious Language." *Annual Review of Anthropology* 26 (1997): 47–71.

Kiddy, Elizabeth W. *Blacks of the Rosary: Memory and History in Minas Gerais, Brazil*. University Park: Pennsylvania State University Press, 2005.

Kishimoto, Alexandre. "Nem tudo era japonês—Insurgências negro-indígenas no bairro da Liberdade," PhD diss., Universidade Federal do ABC, forthcoming.

Kloppenburg, Boaventura. "A Comunhão Eclesial depois da Morte." *Revista Eclesiástica Brasileira* 31, no. 122 (June 1971): 333–46.

———. *O espiritismo no Brasil: orientação para os católicos*. Petrópolis: Editora Vozes, 1960.

Kraay, Hendrik. "Bystander Interventions and Literary Portrayals: White Slaves in Brazil, 1850s–1880s." *Slavery and Abolition* 41, no. 3 (July 2, 2020): 599–622. https://doi.org/10.1080/0144039X.2020.1711565.

———. *Race, State, and Armed Forces in Independence-Era Brazil: Bahia, 1790s–1840s*. Palo Alto, CA: Stanford University Press, 2004.

Ladd, Brian. *The Ghosts of Berlin: Confronting German History in the Urban Landscape*. Chicago: University of Chicago Press, 1998.

Laqueur, Thomas W. *The Work of the Dead: A Cultural History of Mortal Remains*. Princeton, NJ: Princeton University Press, 2018.

Latour, Bruno. *We Have Never Been Modern*. Cambridge: Harvard University Press, 1993.

Leal, João. "The Making of Saudade." In *Roots and Rituals: The Construction of Ethnic Identities*, edited by Ton Dekker, John Helsloot, and Carla Wijers, 267–87. Amsterdam: Het Spinhuis, 2000.

Lee, Ana Paulina. *Mandarin Brazil: Race, Representation, and Memory*. Palo Alto, CA: Stanford University Press, 2018.

Leers, Bernadino. *Catolicismo popular e mundo rural: um ensaio pastoral*. Petrópolis: Editora Vozes, 1977.

LeGoff, Jacques. *The Birth of Purgatory*. Chicago: University of Chicago Press, 1984.

Leitão, José. *The Book of St. Cyprian: The Sorcerer's Treasure*. Keighly: Hadean Press, 2014.

León, Luis D. *La Llorona's Children: Religion, Life, and Death in the U.S.-Mexican Borderlands*. Berkeley: University of California Press, 2004.

Lesser, Jeffrey. *Negotiating National Identity: Immigrants, Minorities, and the Struggle for Ethnicity in Brazil*. Durham, NC: Duke University Press, 1999.

Leu, Lorraine. *Defiant Geographies: Race and Urban Space in 1920s Rio de Janeiro*. Pittsburgh: University of Pittsburgh Press, 2020.

———. "Settlement: Rosana Paulino and Black Women's Insubordinate Geohistories." *Afterall Journal* 55/56 (Summer/Autumn 2023). https://doi.org/10.1086/729131.

Lévi-Strauss, Claude. *Tristes Tropiques*. Translated by John Russell. New York: Criterion Books, 1961.

Lima, Maurílio César de. *Breve história da igreja no brasil*. Rio de Janeiro: Editora Restauro, 2001.

Lisboa, José Maria. *Almanach Litterario Paulista de São Paulo para 1880*. São Paulo: Typografia da Provincia, 1879.

López-Calvo, Ignacio. *Japanese Brazilian Saudades: Diasporic Identities and Cultural Production*. Louisville: University of Colorado Press, 2019.

Luhrmann, Tanya M., Howard Nusbaum, and Ronald Thisted. "The Absorption Hypothesis: Learning to Hear God in Evangelical Christianity." *American Anthropologist* 112, no. 1 (March 1, 2010): 66–78.

Machado, Maria das Dores Campos, and Cecília Mariz. "Sincretismo e trânsito religoso: Comparando carismáticos e pentecostais," *Comunicações Do ISER* 45 (1994): 24–34.

Mahoney, P. J. "Intercession." In *New Catholic Encyclopedia*, 2nd ed., vol. 7, edited by Thomas Carson and Joan Cerrito, 519–20. Detroit: Gale, 2003.

Mainwaring, Scott Patterson. *The Catholic Church and Politics in Brazil, 1916–1982*. Palo Alto, CA: Stanford University, 1983.

Matory, J. Lorand. *Black Atlantic Religion: Tradition, Transnationalism, and Matriarchy in the Afro-Brazilian Candomblé*. Princeton, NJ: Princeton University Press, 2005.

Mattern, Shannon. "Maintenance and Care." *Places Journal*, November 20, 2018. https://placesjournal.org/article/maintenance-and-care/.

Mauricio, Leonardo de Porto. *Via Crucis: explanado y ilustrado con los breves y declaraciones de los sumos pontifices Clemente XII y Benedicto XIV y de la sagrada congregacion de indulgencies, y con la resolucion de todos las dudas suscitadas para impeder tan santa e devota devocion*. Madrid: Imprensa de la Viuda de Manuel Fernandez, 1758.

Mauss, Marcel. "Bodily Techniques." In *Sociology and Psychology: Essays by Marcel Mauss*, 97–123. London: Routledge, 1979.

McAlister, Elizabeth. "The Madonna of 115th Street Revisited: Vodou and Haitian Catholicism in the Age of Transnationalism." In *Gatherings in Diaspora: Religious Communities and the New Immigration*, edited by R. Stephen Warner and Judith G. Wittner, 133–60. Philadelphia: Temple University Press, 1998.

McGreevy, John T. *American Jesuits and the World: How an Embattled Religious Order Made Modern Catholicism Global*. Princeton, NJ: Princeton University Press, 2016.

Menezes, Raimundo de. *Histórias de História de São Paulo*. São Paulo: Edições Melhoramentos, 1954.

Menezes, Renata de Castro. "Saber pedir: A etiqueta do pedido aos santos." *Religião e Sociedade* 24, no. 1 (2004): 46–64.

Millington, Nate. "Critical Spatial Practices of Repair." *Society and Space*, August 26, 2019. https://www.societyandspace.org/articles/critical-spatial-practices-of-repair.

Morrison, Toni. "Rootedness: The Ancestor as Foundation." In *Black Women Writers (1950–1980): A Critical Evaluation*, edited by Mari Evans, 339–45. New York: Anchor, 1984.

Moten, Fred. *The Universal Machine*. Durham, NC: Duke University Press, 2018.

Moura, Paulo Cursino de. *São Paulo de Outrora: Evocações Da Metrópole*. Belo Horizonte: Editora Itatiaia, 1980.

Museu da Cidade de São Paulo. "Memórias Soterradas." February 8, 2024. https://www.museudacidade.prefeitura.sp.gov.br/memorias-soterradas/.

Nail, Thomas. "What Is an Assemblage?" *SubStance* 46, no. 1 (March 7, 2017): 21–37.

National Fire Protection Association. *Incendio*. Quincy, MA: National Fire Protection Association, 1974.

Nehamas, Alexander. *On Friendship*. New York: Basic Books, 2016.

Newell, Sasha. "The Affectiveness of Symbols: Materiality, Magicality, and the Limits of the Antisemiotic Turn." *Current Anthropology* 59, no. 1 (December 27, 2017): 1–22. https://doi.org/10.1086/696071.

Nishida, Mieko. *Diaspora and Identity: Japanese Brazilians in Brazil and Japan*. Honolulu: University of Hawai'i Press, 2017.

Nora, Pierre. "Between Memory and History: Les Lieux de Mémoire." *Representations* 26 (1989): 7–24.

Obert, Julia C. "The Architectural Uncanny." *Interventions* 18, no. 1 (January 2, 2016): 86–106. https://doi.org/10.1080/1369801X.2014.998256.

Ochoa, Todd Ramón. *Society of the Dead: Quita Manaquita and Palo Praise in Cuba*. Berkeley: University of California Press, 2010.

Oliveira, Patricia Cristina Rodrigues de. "Tortura e morte na Liberdade: Forca e pelourinho como lugares de memória e consciência da escravidão em São Paulo." Master's thesis, Universidade Federal do ABC, August 2020.

Oliveira, Pedro Ribeiro de. "'Pequenos Santos': Uma Devoção Familiar." *PLURA, Revista de Estudos de Religião* 2, no. 1 (2011): 80–100.

O'Neill, Kevin Lewis. "Beyond Broken: Affective Spaces and the Study of American Religion." *Journal of the American Academy of Religion* 81, no. 4 (December 1, 2013): 1093–116.

Orser, Charles E. "The Archaeology of African-American Slave Religion in the Antebellum South." *Cambridge Archaeological Journal* 4, no. 1 (April 1994): 33–45. https://doi.org/10.1017/S0959774300000950.

Orsi, Robert A. *Between Heaven and Earth: The Religious Worlds People Make and the Scholars Who Study Them*. Princeton, NJ: Princeton University Press, 2005.

———. *History and Presence*. Cambridge: Belknap Press of Harvard University Press, 2016.

Ortiz, Renato. *A morte branca do feiticeiro negro*. Petrópolis: Editora Vozes, 1978.

Palmié, Stephan. "Against Syncretism." In *Counterworks: Managing the Diversity of Knowledge*, edited by Richard Fardon, 74–103. London: Routledge, 1995.

———. *The Cooking of History: How Not to Study Afro-Cuban Religion*. Chicago: University of Chicago Press, 2013.

———. "Creolization and Its Discontents." *Annual Review of Anthropology* 35 (January 1, 2006): 433–56.

Parron, Milton. *São Paulo, a trajetória de uma cidade: história, imagens e sons*. São Paulo: Editora Nobel, 2003.

Pastoral collectiva dos bispos da provincia ecclesiastica meridional do Brasil. Rio de Janeiro: Typografia Leuzinger, 1904.

Pastoral collectiva dos senhores arcebispos e bispos das provincias ecclesiasticas de S. Sebastião do Rio de Janeiro, Mariana, S. Paulo, Cuyabá, e Porto Alegre. Rio de Janeiro: Typografia Leuzinger, 1911.

Peixoto-Mehrtens, C. *Urban Space and National Identity in Early Twentieth Century São Paulo, Brazil: Crafting Modernity*. New York: Palgrave Macmillan, 2010.

Pereira, José Carlos. *Devoções marginais: interfaces do imaginário religioso*. Porto Alegre: Editora Zouk, 2005.

Pérez, Elizabeth. *Religion in the Kitchen: Cooking, Talking, and the Making of Black Atlantic Traditions*. New York: New York University Press, 2016.

———. "Staging Transformation: Spiritist Liturgies as Theatres of Conversion in Afro-Cuban Religious Practice." *Culture and Religion* 13, no. 3 (September 1, 2012): 361–89. https://doi.org/10.1080/14755610.2012.708230.

Pew Research Center. "Many Americans Mix Multiple Faiths." December 9, 2009. https://www.pewresearch.org/religion/2009/12/09/many-americans-mix-multiple-faiths/.

———. "Religion in Latin America: Widespread Change in a Historically Catholic Region." November 13, 2014. https://www.pewresearch.org/religion/2014/11/13/religion-in-latin-america/.

Pickering, Mary. *Auguste Comte: An Intellectual Biography*. Vol. 1. New York: Cambridge University Press, 2006.

Pierucci, Antônio Flávio. *A Magia*. São Paulo: PubliFolha, 2001.

Piza, Antonio de Toledo. "A Bernarda de Francisco Ignacio." *Revista do Instituto Histórico e Geográfico de São Paulo* 5 (1899–1900): 95–125, 131–44.

———. "Martim Francisco e A Bernarda." *Revista do Instituto Histórico e Geográfico de São Paulo* 5 (1899–1900): 48–78.

———. "O Supplicio de Chaguinhas." *Revista do Instituto Histórico e Geográfico de São Paulo* 5 (1899–1900): 3–47.

Pollak-Eltz, Angelina. *La religiosidad popular en Venezuela*. Caracas: San Pablo, 1994.

Quintão, Antonia Aparecida. *Irmandades negras: Outro espaço de luta e resistência (São Paulo: 1870–1890)*. São Paulo: FAPESP, 2002.

Rabelo, Miriam. "Moving between Religions in Brazil: Space and the Analysis of Religious Trajectories." *Current Anthropology* 56, no. 6 (2015): 848–64.

Reis, João José. *Death Is a Festival: Funeral Rites and Rebellion in Nineteenth-Century Brazil*. Chapel Hill: University of North Carolina Press, 2003.

Rezende, Estavão. "A Bernarda de Francisco Ignacio." *Revista do Instituto Histórico e Geográfico de São Paulo* 5 (1899–1900): 79–94, 126–30.

Ricœur, Paul. *Memory, History, Forgetting*. Chicago: University of Chicago Press, 2004.

Riesebrodt, Martin. *The Promise of Salvation: A Theory of Religion*. Chicago: University of Chicago Press, 2010.

Roach, Joseph R. *Cities of the Dead: Circum-Atlantic Performance*. New York: Columbia University Press, 1996.

Rolim, Francisco. "O propósito do trânsito religioso." *Comunicações do ISER* 45 (1994): 12–17.

Rolnik, Raquel. *A cidade e a lei: legislação, política urbana e territórios na cidade de São Paulo*. São Paulo: Studio Nobel, 1997.

Rose-Redwood, Reuben, Derek Alderman, and Maoz Azaryahu. "The Urban Streetscape as Political Cosmos." In *The Political Life of Urban Streetscapes: Naming, Politics, and Place*, edited by Reuben Rose-Redwood, Derek Alderman, and Maoz Azaryahu, 1–24. London: Routledge, 2017.

Saint-Hilaire, Auguste de. *Viagem pelas Provincías do Rio de Janeiro e Minas Gerais*. Belo Horizonte: Itatiaia, 1975.

Sandomirsky, Sharon, and John Wilson. "Processes of Disaffiliation: Religious Mobility among Men and Women." *Social Forces* 68 (1990): 1211–29.

Sant'Ana, Elma, and Delizabete Seggiaro. *Benzedeiras and benzeduras*. Porto Alegre: Alcance, 2008.

Sant'Anna, Nuto. *Santa Cruz dos Enforcados*. São Paulo: Tipografia Rossolillo, 1937.

Santos, Carlos José Ferreira dos. *Nem tudo era italiano: São Paulo e pobreza, 1890–1915*. São Paulo: Annablume, 2007.

Schaefer, Donovan O. *Religious Affects: Animality, Evolution, and Power*. Durham, NC: Duke University Press, 2015.

Scheper-Hughes, Nancy. *Death without Weeping: The Violence of Everyday Life in Brazil*. Berkeley: University of California Press, 1992.

Schmitt, Jean-Claude. *Ghosts in the Middle Ages: The Living and the Dead in Medieval Society*. Chicago: University of Chicago Press, 1998.

Schwaller, John Frederick. *The History of the Catholic Church in Latin America: From Conquest to Revolution and Beyond*. New York: New York University Press, 2011.

Scott, David. "That Event, This Memory: Notes on the Anthropology of African Diasporas in the New World." *Diaspora: A Journal of Transnational Studies* 1, no. 3 (1991): 261–84. https://doi.org/10.1353/dsp.1991.0023.

Selka, Stephen. "New Religious Movements in Brazil." *Nova Religio* 15, no. 4 (2004): 3–12.

Sermones de las almas del purgatorio: sacados de diversos y graves autores por un sacerdote devoto de las mismas almas. Gerona: Joseph Brò, 1767.

Sevcenko, Nicolau. "A cidade metástasis e o urbanismo inflacionário: incursões na entropia paulista." *Revista USP* 63 (2004): 16–35.

Shahar, Meir, and Robert P. Weller. "Introduction: Gods and Society and China." In *Unruly Gods: Divinity and Society in China*, edited by Meir Shahar and Robert P. Weller, 1–36. Honolulu: University of Hawai'i Press, 1996.

Sharpe, Christina. *In the Wake: On Blackness and Being*. Durham, NC: Duke University Press, 2016.

Sherkat, Darren E. "Tracking the Restructuring of American Religion: Religious Affiliation and Patterns of Religious Mobility, 1973–1998." *Social Forces* 79, no. 4 (2001): 1459–93. https://doi.org/10.1353/sof.2001.0052.

Sigalow, Emily. "Towards a Sociological Framework of Religious Syncretism in the United States." *Journal of the American Academy of Religion* 84, no. 4 (2016): 1029–55. https://doi.org/10.1093/jaarel/lfw033.

Silva, Marcelo Vitale Teodoro da. "Territórios Negros em Trânsito: Penha de França—Sociabilidades e Redes Negras na São Paulo do Pós-Abolição." Master's thesis, Universidade de São Paulo, December 2018.

Silva, Maria Beatriz Nizza da. *História de São Paulo Colonial*. São Paulo: Editora Unesp, 2008.

Singh, Devin. *Divine Currency: The Theological Power of Money in the West*. Palo Alto, CA: Stanford University Press, 2018.

Skidmore, Thomas E. *Black into White: Race and Nationality in Brazilian Thought*. Durham, NC: Duke University Press, 1993.

Smith, Christen A. *Afro-Paradise: Blackness, Violence, and Performance in Brazil*. Urbana: University of Illinois Press, 2016.

Smith, Jonathan Z. *To Take Place: Toward Theory in Ritual*. Chicago: University of Chicago Press, 1987.

Soares, Mariza de Carvalho. *People of Faith: Slavery and African Catholics in Eighteenth-Century Rio de Janeiro*. Durham, NC: Duke University Press, 2011.

Souza, Laura Mello e. *The Devil and the Land of the Holy Cross: Witchcraft, Slavery, and Popular Religion in Colonial Brazil*. Austin: University of Texas Press, 2003.

Spade, Dean. "Solidarity Not Charity: Mutual Aid for Mobilization and Survival." *Social Text* 38, no. 1 (March 1, 2020): 131–51. https://doi.org/10.1215/01642472-7971139.

Stepan, Nancy Leys. *The Hour of Eugenics: Race, Gender, and Nation in Latin America*. Ithaca, NY: Cornell University Press, 1996.

Stewart, Charles. "Creolization, Hybridity, Syncretism, Mixture." *Portuguese Studies* 27, no. 1, (January 1, 2011): 48–55.

———. "Syncretism and Its Synonyms: Reflections on Cultural Mixture." *Diacritics* 29, no. 3 (October 1, 1999): 40–62.

Stewart, Charles, and Rosalind Shaw. "Introduction: Problematizing Syncretism." In *Syncretism/Anti-Syncretism: The Politics of Religious Synthesis*, edited by Charles Stewart and Rosalind Shaw, 1–26. New York: Routledge, 1994.

Styers, Randall. *Making Magic: Religion, Magic, and Science in the Modern World*. New York: Oxford University Press, 2004.

Taunay, Affonso de E. *História da Cidade de São Paulo no Século XVIII (1735–1765)*. Vol. 1. São Paulo: Divisão do Arquivo Histórico, 1949.

Taves, Ann. *The Household of Faith: Roman Catholic Devotions in Mid-Nineteenth-Century America*. Notre Dame, IN: University of Notre Dame Press, 1986.

Thurston, Herbert. "Communicating with the Dead." *The Month: An Illustrated Magazine of Literature, Science and Art*, 129 (January–June 1917): 134–44.

Tillet, Salamishah. *Sites of Slavery: Citizenship and Racial Democracy in the Post–Civil Rights Imagination*. Durham, NC: Duke University Press, 2012.

Tilly, Charles. *Social Movements, 1768–2004*. New York: Routledge, 2019.

Toledo, Benedito Lima de. *Prestes Maia e as origens do urbanismo moderno em São Paulo*. São Paulo: Empresa das Artes Projetos e Edições Artísticas, 1996.

Trigg, Dylan. *The Memory of Place: A Phenomenology of the Uncanny*. Athens: Ohio University Press, 2012.

Trouillot, Michel-Rolph. "The Otherwise Modern: Caribbean Lessons from the Savage Slot." In *Critically Modern: Alternatives, Alterities, Anthropologies*, edited by Bruce M. Knauft, 220–37. Bloomington: Indiana University Press, 2002.

Tweed, Thomas A. *Crossing and Dwelling: A Theory of Religion*. Cambridge, MA: Harvard University Press, 2006.

Vargas, João H. Costa. "Black Disidentification: The 2013 Protests, *Rolezinhos*, and Racial Antagonism in Post-Lula Brazil." *Critical Sociology* 42, no. 4–5 (July 1, 2016): 551–65. https://doi.org/10.1177/0896920514551208.

Vasconcellos, José Leite de. *Tradições Populares de Portugal*. Porto: Livraria Portuense de Clavel, 1882.
Vide, Sebastião Monteiro da. *Constituições primeiras do Arcebispado da Bahia feitas, e ordenadas pelo Illustrissimo, e Reverendissimo Senhor D. Sebastião Monteiro da Vide: propostas, e aceitas em o Synodo Diocesano, que o dito Senhor celebrou em 12 de junho do anno de 1707*. São Paulo: Typographia Antonio Louzada Antunes, 1853.
Vidler, Anthony. *The Architectural Uncanny: Essays in the Modern Unhomely*. Boston: MIT Press, 1992.
Vieira, David Gueiros. *O protestantismo, a maçonaria e a questão religiosa no Brasil*. Brasília: Editora Universidade de Brasília, 1980.
Vilhena, Maria Angela. *Salvação Solidária: O culto das almas à luz da teologia das religiões*. São Paulo: Paulinas Editora, 2013.
Vovelle, Michel. *Ideologies and Mentalities*. Cambridge, MA: Polity, 1990.
Weinstein, Barbara. *The Color of Modernity: São Paulo and the Making of Race and Nation in Brazil*. Durham, NC: Duke University Press, 2015.
Wilhelm, Joseph. "Heroic Act of Charity." In *The Catholic Encyclopedia*, vol. 7, edited by Charles G. Herbermann, Edward A. Pace, Condé B. Pallen, Thomas J. Shahan, and John J. Wynne, 292. New York: Robert Appleton, 1909.
Williams, Richard J. *Brazil*. London: Reaktion, 2009.
Willis, Graham Denyer. "The Potter's Field." *Comparative Studies in Society and History* 60, no. 3 (July 2018): 539–68. https://doi.org/10.1017/S001041751800018X.
Wirtz, Kristina. "Spirituality, Agency, and Materiality in Cuba." In *Spirited Things: The Work of "Possession" in Afro-Atlantic Religions*, edited by Paul C. Johnson, 99–130. Chicago: University of Chicago Press, 2014.
Zambrana, José de Barcia y. *Despertador Christiano Santoral: De varios sermons de santos, de anniversaries de animas, y honras, en orden à exciter en los fieles la devocion de los santos, y la imitacion de sus virtudes*. Barcelona: Rafael Figverò, 1699.
Žižek, Slavoj. "Return of the Living Dead." *IAI News* 82 (October 2019). https://iai.tv/articles/return-of-the-living-dead-slavoj-zizek-auid-1261.
Zubrzycki, Geneviève. "The Politics of Jewish Absence in Contemporary Poland." *Journal of Contemporary History* 52, no. 2 (April 1, 2017): 250–77. https://doi.org/10.1177/0022009416664020.

Index

Italicized page numbers indicate illustrations

Abreu, Maria José de, 76–77
affect: affective ties, 99–101; affective topography of São Paulo, 34, 61, 76; and empathy, 90–91, 99; and memory, 64, 70; production and mobilization of, 132
affirmative action, 109
Afro-Brazilians: cultural and religious traditions of, 9–10, 42, 72, 86, 133; employment of, 54–55; in São Paulo, 56–57, 147n19, 148n32
Ahmed, Sarah, 76
Alley of the Afflicted, 60, 121, 124, 127
All Souls' Day, 26–27
Almanach Litterario Paulista, 116
almas benditas (blessed souls), 31–32, 63, 93
almas penadas (wandering souls), 36–37
alminhas (altars), 28
altruistic reciprocity, 14, 16, 34
Alves, Eliz, 128, 131, 136
Alves, Jaime Amparo, 61, 96
"ambient dead" (*kalunga*), 34, 91, 135
ancestors: connection with, 63, 100, 119–20; familial dead, 83
Anhangabaú River, 2–3, 57, 139n6
The Anti-Black City (Alves), 61
anti-Semitism, 37
"architectural uncanny," 60
Arquivo do Estado de São Paulo (AESP), 18
Arquivo Histórico Municipal de São Paulo (AHM), 18

Arquivo Metropolitano do Arquidiocese de São Paulo (AMASP), 18
Association for the Souls in Purgatory, 41
author's methodology: book's organization, 14–16; fieldwork, 9–10; sources and methods, 16–19
Avenues Plan (Prestes Maia), 57–58
Azevedo, Thales de, 42

Bahia, Salvador da, 39, 99, 123
Baird, Robert D., 72
Barra Funda neighborhood, 55
Bastide, Roger, 98
Batista dos Reis, Paulo, 123
Beleth, Jean, 24
Bell, Catherine, 79
benzedeiras, 154n11
Birman, Patricia, 72
Bixiga neighborhood, 50, 55
Black activism: Night March for Racial Democracy, 103–4; priorities and strategy, 104–110; and racial identity, 107–8; and reparations, 103, 104, 105, 125
The Black Book of Spiritism (Kloppenburg), 41
Black brotherhoods, 27–31, 57
Black press, 50, 101
Black social movements, 18
blessed souls (*almas benditas*), 31–32, 63, 93
Bodanese, Antonio, 13
Bolsa Familia, 109
Bolsonaro, Jair, 104, 106
Book of St. Cyprian, 6, 140n24

Brazil: Brazilian Empire (1822–89), 38; Brazilian race (*raça Brasileira*), 54; epidemics in, 56; Japanese immigration to, 50, 55; New Republic, 2, 54; presidential elections in, 106; sanitation eugenics, 56. *See also* São Paulo, Brazil

Brazilian Black Front (Frente Negra Brasileira), 51

Brazilian Democratic Movement (MDB), 100–101

Brazilian Social Democracy Party (PSDB), 101

Britt, Andrew, 57–58

Brotherhood of Saint Elesbaan and Saint Ephigenia, 30

Brotherhood of Saint Michael and Souls of Caeté, 30

Brotherhood of Saint Michael and Souls of Pitangui, 30

Brotherhood of the Holy Cross of the Souls of the Hanged, 62, 78–79, 88

Brown, Peter, 25–26, 92

Butler, Judith, 97

Butler, Kim, 50

Caldeira, Teresa, 57, 109, 140n15

Campos, Adalgisa Arantes, 31–32

candles: borrowing, 95–96; ritual use of, 79–80; sale of, 84

Candomblé religion, 86–87, 141n29; initiation into, 87; practitioners of, 71, 72, 73, 75, 98; *terreiros*, 73

capitalism and forgetting, 15, 59–60

care: "radical care," 16, 87–88; relational care, 97–98; self-care, 97, 156n44; "Toward a Feminist Theory of Caring," 100

Carneiro, Sueli, 129

Carta Capital (magazine), 122

Casa de Velas Santa Rita (Santa Rita Candle House), 23, 84

Catholic Church: *Catechism of the Catholic Church*, 93; during colonial period, 35; devotion to souls, 40, 42–43; foundation of cult of the souls (*culto das almas*), 25–31; images, 9; intercession, 92–93; lay brotherhoods, 15, 23, 27–31, 142n14; during Portugese colonial period, 24–25; Sacred Congregation of Indulgences, 100; saints, 88–89; against Spiritism, 38–42; theory of ghosts, 37; weakness of organization, 35; and "whitening" of Black people, 114–16

Cemetery of the Afflicted: archaeological site, 122–23; and Chapel of the Afflicted restoration, 127–28; establishment of, 54

Cemitério Vila Alpina, 4, 31, 76, 86; fieldwork, 17

center-periphery models, 3, 57

Certeau, Michel de, 14, 34, 61

Chaguinhas (Francisco José das Chagas), 44–45, 102, 145n3, 159–60n42; Blackness of, 113–17, *115*, *118*; devotion to, 10, 47–48, 146n5; Door of Chaguinhas, 48; Letra's song for, 112

Chapel of Our Lady of the Afflicted, 11, 46, 46–48, 60, 69, 76, 100; Catholic and Umbandista fusion, 71; cortege for Chaguinhas (2018), 102–3, 110–11, 119–22, *121*; fieldwork, 17–18; memorial and restoration, 129–32; memorial design contest, 127–28; restoration movement, 102–4, 119–20

Chiclayo, Peru, 140–41n26

Christianity: Pentecostal churches, 74, 95, 151n21; Protestant churches, 73–74. *See also* Catholic Church

Church of Our Lady of Glory (Rio de Janeiro), 29

Church of Our Lady of Mt. Carmel, 9

Church of Our Lady of the Good Death, 102, 103

Church of Our Lady of the Remedies, 58

Church of Our Lady of the Rosary of Black Men, 57

Church of the Holy Cross of the Souls of the Hanged, 7–10, *8*, 71–72; day of the

souls, 23; fieldwork, 17; ghosts, 58; history of, 44–45; rebuilding of (1929), 42
Cluny Abbey, 26–27
Code of Postures (Codigo de Posturas), 55–56
code switching, 32–34, 70
Collins, John, 123
The Color of Modernity (Weinstein), 147n22
Connerton, Paul, 59
Correio Paulistano (newspaper), 60
Costa, Márcia, 114, 117
Cotindiba, José Joaquim, 44
Covas, Bruno, 123
COVID-19 pandemic, 97
cowry shell divination, 9, 23, 72
Cox, Robert, 90
"creation of absence," 117
"Crime of the Well," 2–3
Crinson, Mark, 132
Cross of the Thirteen Souls, 12
cruz das almas, 43
Cuchet, Guillaume, 39, 40
culto das almas (cult of the souls). *See* cult of the souls (*culto das almas*)
cult of the souls (*culto das almas*), 11, 155–56n39; and ancestors, 63; Catholic antecedents, 25–31; as Catholic anti-spiritist effort, 40, 42–43; maintenance and care, 96–100; and memory, 124–25, 131–32; motivation of devotees, 15, 23–24; political movement, 16; and slavery, 63–64; souls' proximity to the living, 92–96; suffering, 25, 90
Cultural Assistance Association of Liberdade (ACAL), 112
"cultural Marxism," 106, 108
curanderismo (healing), 56

Davis, Angela, 97
"day of the souls," 5, 10–11
de Almeida, Ronaldo, 74–75
debt, 94–96

de la Bellasca, María Puig, 100
Delucca, Sofia, 134, 135, 137
de Matos, Gabriela, 123–24
de Morães, Zelio, 98
Derrida, Jacques, 60
devotion to souls (*devoção às almas*). *See* cult of the souls (*culto das almas*)
Diaz, Porfírio, 79
"disincarnation," 83, 92, 97

eclecticism and syncretism, 70–73, 74, 82
Edifício Andraus fire (1972), 3
Edifício Copan, 61
Edifício Joelma fire (1974), 1–2, 4–5, 61; as haunted site, 5; Prayer to the Thirteen Souls, 5–6; unidentified victims of, 14. *See also* Thirteen Souls
Edifício Martinelli building, 3, 61
Edifício Praça de Bandeirantes building, 4
empathy, 89–90; affective vs. cognitive, 90
erasure, cultural, 13, 45, 51, 64, 103, 111–12, 117, 125. *See also* memory
escolas de samba (samba schools), 50, 111, 127
Escola Sem partido, 108
esoteric stores, 9, 84
Espiritismo (Puerto Rico), 99
eugenics, 2, 56, 148n39. *See also* racial issues
evangelical Christian churches, 74, 91, 97, 150n18
evil eye, 36
Ewbank, Thomas, 29–30, 37
Exu Tranca Ruas Institute, 17

family histories and kinship networks, 32, 34
Ferreira, Abilio, 103, 104, 107, 110, 122, 123, 124, 136
Field of the Gallows (Campo da Forca), 47, 65
First Constitutions of the Archbishopric of Bahia (1707), 28–29
First Vatican Council (1869–70), 39
Fisher, Bernice, 100

Folha de São Paulo (newspaper), 2, 4, 13, 108, 122
forgetting. *See* erasure, cultural; memory
Forum for São Pualo without Racism, 123
Fox, Kate, 38
Fox, Margaret, 38
Freitas, Elaine, 92
Frente Negra Brasileira (Brazilian Black Front), 51, 111
Freud, Sigmund, 60
Freyre, Gilberto, 35
friendship and souls, 30, 34, 82, 93, 99

G1 (periodical), 122
Gago, Chico, 45
garden-cemeteries, 153n54
Ghost (film), 93
ghosts, 58–65; Catholic theory of, 37; Christian theory of, 26; genesis of, 59; ghost hunters, 45; "needy" or "hungry," 96; as objects of experience, 61; as signs, 60–61
Gomes da Resurreicão, Domingas, 36
Gomide, Cândido Gonçalves, 113
Gonçalves, Olegário Pedro, 45
Gordon, Avery, 11, 59, 96
Grupo Fimilar do Espiritismo, 39
Guaianases neighborhood, São Paulo, 105, 134

Haddad, Fernando, 106
Hartman, Saidiya, 117
haunted sites: Edifício Joelma building, 5; haunting, 59; São Paulo sites for devotion to souls, 45. *See also* ghosts
historical-temporal absence, 117
History and Presence (Orsi), 7
Ho, Engseng, 13
Hobart, Hiʻilei Julia Kawehipuaakahaopulani, 87, 97
Holy Cross of the Hanged (Chaguinhas commemoration), 45
Holy House of Mercy (Santa Casa de Misericórdia), 27–28

How Modernity Forgets (Connerton), 59
Hume, David, 97

Ikesaki, Hirofumi, 113, 137
Index of Prohibited Books, 39
intercession, 92–93, 142–43n29
International Day of Black Latin American and Caribbean Women, 137

Jackson, Steven, 98
João V, Dom, 28
Jornal Nippak, 49
Jouet, Victor, 37

kalunga (ambient dead), 34, 91, 135
Kalverkamp, Desidério, 42
Kardec, Allan, 17, 38, 79, 82
Kardecist Spiritism, 15, 17, 25, 38, 42, 69, 75, 79–80. *See also* Spiritist Federation of the State of São Paulo (FEESP)
Keane, Webb, 32
Ketu Candomblé, 86–87, 99
kinship networks and family histories, 34
Kishimoto, Alexandre, 62
Kloppenburg, Boaventura, 41–42
Kneese, Tamara, 87, 97
Kray, Hendrik, 116

Ladd, Brian, 4
Laqueur, Thomas, 11
Latour, Bruno, 60
lay brotherhoods, 15, 23, 27–31, 57, 142n14
Lee, Ana Paulina, 50
Leers, Bernardino, 7
LeGoff, Jacques, 27, 142–43n29
Lesser, Jeffrey, 55
Letra, Aloysio, 103, 105–112, 114, 116–17, 119, 121–22, 134–37
Leu, Lorraine, 56
Lévi-Strauss, Claude, 3
Liberdade district (Japantown): African settlement, 50; Black history, 50–51; Black social clubs, 62; changes to (2018), 16; decoration of, 49–50;

ethnicity and identity in, 114; haunted sites, 45; Japanese identity, 48–49, 49; Japanese identity and Black erasure, 112–13; Japão naming, 122; map with historical markers, 53; and memory work, 117–22; Monday mornings in, 23
Liberdade Foundation, 113
lieux de mémoire (sites of memory), 64–65
Life in Brazil (Ewbank), 37
Lobato, Randolfo Marques de, 49
Luís, Washington, 56
Lula da Silva, Luiz Inácio, 106

Macondes, Rosemeire, 62
Madero, Francisco I., 79
Madrinha Eunice, 127
maroon communities, 51
The Masters and the Slaves (Freyre), 35
Matory, Lorand, 64
Mattern, Shannon, 98
McAlister, Elizabeth, 9
Medeiros, Mário, 131–32
mediumship religions, 10–11, 15. *See also* Kardecist Spiritism
Memorial of the Afflicted: design contest, 127; future of, 133–38
memory: Black and Indigenous, 124–25; "creation of absence," 117; and devotion to souls (*devoção às almas*), 124–25, 132–33; forgetting as structural feature, 59; historical-temporal absence, 117; Liberdade churches as sites of, 103–4; *lieux de mémoire* (sites of memory), 57, 64–65; memory work and Liberdade, 117–22; political aspects, 64–65; rescue, 129
Menelick (newspaper), 111
Menezes, Renata de Castro, 94
Mesquita, Júlio, 59
Mil Misericordias (Thousand Mercies), 47
Missionaries of the Sacred Heart, 37, 42, 80–81
mnemonic repair, 14–15, 34, 62, 101, 104, 117, 124, 131

"modernist nostalgia," 64, 125
Montero, Paula, 74–75
Moocidade Unidade da Mooca, 127
Morrison, Toni, 63
Morro do Castelo neighborhood, 56–57
Movement of the Afflicted, 17, 101, 127, 128, 129, 131–32, 134
movimento negro, 101, 104, 107, 122–23
Movimento Passe Livre, 109
mutual aid, 27, 34, 87–88

Nagô Candomblé, 87
National Conference of Bishops of Brazil (CNBB), 41
"negro" (term), 50–51
neo-Lamarckian genetics, 2, 55, 56
Neumanne Pinto, José, 2, 3
New Pathways (Black activist group), 128
newspapers, 50
New Spiritualist Brotherhood, 88, 89, 100
Niemeyer, Oscar, 61
Night March for Racial Democracy, 103, 107
9/11 Memorial (Manhattan), 11
Nora, Pierre, 57, 64
nostalgia, 19; "modernist nostalgia," 64, 125
Novena of the Afflicted Souls, 90, 94

O Apostolo (Catholic newspaper), 39
Obert, Julia, 61
Ochoa, Todd Ramón, 34, 91
Odilo, Saint, 26
O Estado de São Paulo (newspaper), 4–5, 59
Oliveira, Patrícia, 113
O'Neill, Kevin Lewis, 76
orixás (Yorùbá), 71–72, 82–83, 87, 98
Orsi, Robert, 7, 82–83, 84
Our Lady of Lampadosa, 31

Palmares Civic Center (Centro Cívico Palmares), 51
Pastoral Coletiva (1904), 40
Pastoral Coletiva (1915), 40–41
Pasulka, Diana Walsh, 32

Paulistano da Glória, 111
pedido (petitionary prayer), 91, 94, 155n33
Pedro II, Dom (emperor), 38, 39
Pelourinho district, 123
Penadinho (Little Wanderer character), 36
Penteado, Fernando, 62
Pentecostal churches, 74, 95, 151n21
Pérez, Elizabeth, 91, 99
Pessoa, Epitácio, 56
petition, prayers of, 91, 94
pilgrimage, 13, 80, 152n49
Pius IX (pope), 38, 39
Plan of Avenues, 112
Portugal: death rituals in nineteenth century, 37; devotion to souls, 28
Prado, Antônio, 57, 59
Prayer to the Thirteen Souls, 5–6, 90, 94
Prestes Maia, Francisco, 57–58, 112
pretos velhos (Umbanda spirit entities), 9–10, 88
Progresso (newspaper), 50
promessas (promises), 62, 78, 83, 94–95
Protestant churches, 73–74
public health, 56–57
purgatory, 25–31, 142–43n29, 143n36; purgatorial doctrine, 32, 35–36; treatises on and anti-spiritualism, 40–41
Purí, Bea, 130–31

quitandeiras (street produce vendors), 56

Rabelo, Miriam, 75, 99
racial issues: anti-Black violence, 96; eugenics, 2, 56, 148n39; identity and Black activism, 107–8; racism as crime in Brazil, 134; scientific racism, 2, 54–55; and urban modernization, 56–57; white supremacy, 55
"radical care," 16, 87–88
Radio Taissô, 51
religion: Chinese, 155n25; contrasted with religiosity, 70–71; meaning-making after trauma, 7; "meta-physical religion," 155n30; syncretism, 99–100; syncretism contrasted with eclecticism, 70–73
religious supply stores, 9, 23
religious switching. *See* religious transit (*trânsito religioso*)
religious transit (*trânsito religioso*), 15, 69–70, 73–76, 151–52n27, 151n21, 151n25; and physical culture and objects, 99–100; *saudades* (sadness), 81–85; urban trajectories, 76–81
reparations, 103, 104, 105, 125
"responsive dead," 34, 91
Revue Spirite (periodical), 39
Ricœur, Paul, 65
Rio de Janeiro, Brazil, 29
Rivail, Hippolyte Léon Denizard, 38. *See also* Kardec, Allan
Roach, Joseph, 59
rolezinhos (gatherings), 109
"Rootedness: The Ancestor as Foundation" (Morrison), 63
Royal Patronage (Padroado Real), 35
"Rua da Glória" (Letra), 112, 117, 119, 136–37

Sacred Congregation of Indulgences, 100
Sacro Cuore del Suffragio, 37
Saint-Hilaire, Augustin, 30–31
samba schools (*escolas de samba*), 50, 111, 127
Sanctuary of the Souls, 17, 80–81
Sanitary Code (1890), 56
sanitation and eugenics, 2, 56, 148n39
Santa Casa de Misericórdia (Holy House of Mercy), 27–28
São Paulo, Brazil: affective topography of, 61; Afro-Brazilian population, 59; Armênia neighborhood, 80–81; author's focus on, 14; Avenues Plan (Prestes Maia), 57–58; Black history of, 105; Black "sites of memory," 57; Carmo floodplain, 56; city council, 123; Code of Postures, 55–56; crime and safety, 109; cultural geography

of, 15; fires, 1–4; flooding in, 2; Guaianases neighborhood, 105; haunted places in, 80; haunted tours of, 61; legacy of slavery in, 59, 61, 62, 123–25; mid-nineteenth to mid-twentieth centuries in, 3–4, 54–58; immigration of Europeans, 54–55; Japanese settlements in, 7, 50, 55, 146–47n17; Kardecist centers, 69; maps, 52, 53; memory, erasure of, 45–46, 51, 59–60; neighborhood racial demographics, 147n19; racial history and urban development, 101; regional identity, 147n22; religious transit within, 76–81; sites for devotion to souls, 45–46; Tatuapé neighborhood, 88; topography over time, 64–65; walking tours, 61

saudades (nostalgia/sadness), 19, 81–84

Schaeffer, Donovan, 91

Scheper-Hughes, Nancy, 81

Schmitt, Jean-Claude, 26

séance practices, 38, 39

Seicho-no-Ie (Japanese new religion), 77

Selka, Stephen, 72

"semantic overload," 132

Sevcenko, Nicolau, 116

Seventh Day Adventist church, 82

Sharpe, Christina, 123

Sicard of Cremona, 24

sites of memory (*lieux de mémoire*), 15, 57, 64–65; Liberdade churches, 103–4; *saudades*, 81–82

slavery, 58; and contemporary ghosts, 58; and devotion to souls (*devoção às almas*), 63–64; legacy of, 61, 123–25, 148n60; maroon communities, 51; slave trade, 54; and violence, 24, 60, 117, 148n60

Smith, Adam, 90, 97

Smith, Christen, 103

Smith, J. Z., 84

Soares, Angelina, 13

"social press," 50

social violence: and economics, 96; and ghosts, 59; memory of, 15, 132; sites of, and devotion to souls, 11, 45–46, 70, 73

Society of the Dead (Ochoa), 91

solidarity, 27, 100, 157n58. *See also* lay brotherhoods

souls: afflicted, 31–32; "ambient dead" vs. "responsive dead," 34; blessed, 31–32; contrasted with spirits, 32–34; holy and blessed souls, 31–32; power to aid the living, 92–96; types of, 33; wandering dead, 35–38

Specters of Marx (Derrida), 60

Spectros (Netflix series), 61

spirit communications, 39. *See also* séance practices

Spiritism: Catholic resistance to, 38–42; séance practices, 38. *See also* Kardecist Spiritism

Spiritist Federation of the State of São Paulo (FEESP), 17, 77–78; Department of Orientation and Routing, 78

The Spirits' Book (Kardec), 17

spirits contrasted with souls, 32–34. *See also* souls

Spiritualism, 38

suffering: in Catholic theology, 32; and ghosts, 58; and memory, 117, 125; mutual suffering, 16; sites of, 70, 85; as souls' defining quality, 11, 14, 89–90

Syllabus of Errors (Pius IX), 38, 39

sympathy, 88–91; and empathy, 90

syncretism and eclecticism, 70–73, 150n12

Tatuapé neighborhood, São Paulo, 88

Teles de Menezes, Luís Olímpio, 39

Tenente, Marcio, 134, 136, 138

Teodoro, Joã, 54

Thirteen Souls, 76, 89, 90; Cross of the Thirteen Souls, 12; defining qualities, 11; Prayer to the Thirteen Souls, 5–6. *See also* Edifício Joelma fire (1974)

Tillet, Salamishah, 123
"Toward a Feminist Theory of Caring" (Fisher & Tronto), 100
trauma and religious meaning-making, 7, 34, 125
Tristes Tropiques (Lévi-Strauss), 3
Tronto, Joan, 100
Trouillot, Michel-Rolph, 59

Umbanda religion, 25, 70–71, 75, 98; initiation into, 86; practitioners, 71, 72; prayers, 36; *pretos velhos* (spirit entities), 9–10; *terreiros*, 43
"the uncanny," 60
União dos Amigos da Capela dos Aflitos (UNAMCA), 102–3, 105, 106–7, 114, 124, 136; Chapel of the Afflicted restoration, 127, 128–29
Universal Church of the Kingdom of God, 74

Vai-Vai samba school, 62
Vallone, Giuliana, 108
Vargas, Getúlio, 41, 51
Vargas, João Costa, 108, 109
Vasconcellos, José Leite de, 37
Veiga dos Santos, Arlindo, 51
Vidler, Anthony, 60
violence: police, 109; racialized, 47; and slavery, 24, 60, 117, 148n60. *See also* social violence
Vovelle, Michel, 25

Weinstein, Barbara, 51, 147n22
white supremacy, 55. *See also* racial issues
Workers' Party, 106, 108–9
The Work of the Dead (Laqueur), 11

Xavier, Chico, 75, 82

yard shrines, 62, 88
Yorùba *orixás*, 71–72, 82–83, 87, 98

Žižek, Slavoj, 96
Zubrzycki, Geneviève, 117

www.ingramcontent.com/pod-product-compliance
Lightning Source LLC
Chambersburg PA
CBHW020234250325
24032CB00006B/50